ALL THROUGH THE HOUSE

A GUIDE TO HOME WEATHERIZATION

THOMAS BLANDY

DENIS LAMOUREUX

McGRAW-HILL BOOK COMPANY

New York   St. Louis   San Francisco   Auckland   Bogotá   Düsseldorf
Johannesburg   London   Madrid   Mexico   Montreal   New Delhi   Panama
Paris   São Paulo   Singapore   Sydney   Tokyo   Toronto

To Susan, Charley, and Jim,
who thought we would never finish

To Dallam Blandy, Sr., who
will never see it finished

First McGraw-Hill edition, 1980

1 2 3 4 5 6 7 8 9 0 S M S M 8 3 2 1 0

LIBRARY OF CONGRESS CATALOGING IN
PUBLICATION DATA
Blandy, Thomas.
   All through the house.
   Includes index.
   1. Dwellings—Energy conservation. 2. Dwellings—
Insulation. I. Lamoureux, Denis, joint author.
II. Title.
TJ163.5.D86B55   693.8′34   79-14794
ISBN 0-07-005871-7

Book design by Marsha Picker.

CONTENTS

PREFACE

On a cold Saturday in February 1977, the United Urban Ministry in Troy, New York, held a home energy workshop. Members of the organizing committee realized that getting people to come to workshops isn't the most effective way to educate them about home energy, since the problems to be confronted are at home. Thus was born the Thermal Diagnosis, a house-visit format utilizing a simple proportional system, invented by Denis Lamoureux. Trying out our Diagnosis on the citizens of Troy and Albany, and meanwhile doing a lot of reading, Denis and I gained in knowledge and wisdom. Writing a book was a logical next step, and we were encouraged in this by McGraw-Hill editor Jeremy Robinson.

To the project Denis brought Vermont flavor, a lot of energy, and a clarity and logic that I cannot help but think is French. My roles were to come beagling along finding fatal flaws, to edit and re-edit, to put our ideas across graphically, and to generally put together a book that would have wide appeal. This has been a true collaboration; there are parts of this book which neither of us remembers who wrote, and every writing and researching role has been reversed innumerable times.

Organizer George Garrelts and the staff of the United Urban Ministry lead the list of those we must thank, for they provided the occasion for us to start, and they guided us through a season of diagnosing and grant seeking. We thank also the Central-South Neighborhood Organization and other residents of Troy who sought our services and provided the necessary opportunities to test and develop the Diagnosis. Across the Hudson River, Louise Merritt and the members of Historic Albany did a similar favor. To these we add Denis's solar house clients Joanna and Warren, and John and Mary, with whom the concepts in Chapter 11 were discovered and organized.

Dean Patrick Quinn of the School of Architecture at Rensselaer Polytechnic Institute has been a major help, reviewing our work, providing assistance at crucial points, and making available the services of the school. We thank Mrs. Fitzgerald, Mrs. Bailey, and Mrs. Powers, of the RPI staff, for secretarial and research assistance. Throughout this year of research and writing, many friends of *The Haven* on Third Street relieved our isolation and provided friendly critiques: Leonardo, Hans, Chris, Koni, Robin, Dale, Pearce, Rob, Margarette, Safie, Caren, Lorrie, and Nerys. With Glenn Alcorn and the House of Sigma Chi, the mysteries of thermal and fluid dynamics were explored and discovered.

We thank also the many organizations and businesses that responded to our requests for information: Al Hems of the State Bank of Albany, who reviewed the loans material; Mr. Hemmrich of Rochester (New York) Gas and Electric; Steve Caruso of A-Copy, Albany; Mr. Bordner of the National Solar Heating and Cooling Center; Mat Kelley of the Pennsylvania Governor's Energy Council; and David Norris of the Energy Task Force in New York City.

Putting us up occasionally, and putting up with us, were the Goldwaters of Yonkers, New York, and the Griswolds of Exeter, New Hampshire.

Bringing it all together, we were favored with an in-house librarian and communications specialist—Susan Blandy. Final critical reviews were provided by Judy Barnes, Malcolm Willison, and Tom Oliphant. We thank Bruce Anderson of Harrisville, New Hampshire, for his vote of confidence in our early manuscript. And, finally, thanks to our patient editors, Jeremy Robinson and Ellen LaBarbera.

THOMAS BLANDY AND DENIS LAMOUREUX
Troy, New York

INTRODUCTION

Surely energy conservation is a timely subject for a book, and more so every day. As we write we can no longer depend on oil from Iran, and the Saudis and Mexicans are unhappy with us; Shell and Texaco have decided not to sell their products in the Northeast anymore. An atomic reactor in Pennsylvania threatened to go to pieces, and the confidential word from the Department of Energy is that natural gas will quadruple in price by 1990. Evidently, things aren't going to get any easier.

Nonetheless one is entitled to ask, Why another energy book when there are so many others? An energy book that hopes to motivate people into doing something about the situation must provide three things: information, inspiration, and a working perspective on the first two.

We have tried to present information clearly and concisely in the coverage of insulation, weather stripping, thermostats, and similar energy-conserving techniques. We have attempted to remove some of the usual barriers to action by explaining the procedures for dealing with bankers and contractors and ways to stimulate cooperation among neighbors. We hope to inspire your efforts by exploring some of the more unorthodox (and often old-fashioned) ways to keep warm; we speculate on still others.

We believe the greatest value of this book will be the perspective we create for this information. We found great pleasure in the explanation of how a wall works (Chapter 1), how the human body reacts to heat and cold (Chapter 2), and trying to convey a sense of the history and even the cosmic significance of heating. The Thermal Diagnosis (Chapter 3) puts numbers on heat losses, but its more important function is to allow you to see the proportional aspect of the various heat losses in the building. Sources of largest heat loss are thereby identified and indicate areas of greatest immediate concern. The Map of Household Energy (also in Chapter 3) is a one-page diagram that indicates everything that affects a building thermally. In this diagram related subjects are indicated for each particular focus of concern. The Diagnosis and Map should guide you through the process of improving your own home using the best available materials and techniques.

Weatherization is not usually the sort of activity that inspires enthusiasm. However, there is more than one way to view the situation. On a pragmatic level, your home must be heated, and our first angle is to tap your wallet and prod your investor's instinct by saying that weatherization can be one of the highest returns you can find for your money. Money invested in home improvements can be made to earn three times the return of money left sitting in a bank. At a more profound level, home improvements are a way to gain greater control over your own life. A serious weatherization program is creative; it's not a process of acquiring but of generating something. And it can be very satisfying.

Think for a moment of the enthusiasm that has developed in the past few years for vegetable gardens, both urban and rural. There are now acres and acres of American cities being cultivated. This effort can't be accounted for simply by money saved. Somebody is having fun out there in the sun and soil; somebody is enjoying those tomatoes and squashes; somebody is getting satisfaction out of accomplishing things for and by himself or herself.

It's our feeling that, like gardening, taking better care of a home has been and will continue to be an activity undertaken initially from necessity that becomes a source of satisfaction and pride. There are several similarities between gardening and weatherization. Both require continuing attention and observation year in and year out. There is always some new theory and technique to make it more interesting and productive. In this respect, solar heating and organic gardening are blood brothers.

What about solar? We hardly discuss it as such, but it has been on our minds all the time. We even considered calling the book *Backing into Solar Heating,* for the things we deal with in this book are just what needs to be done before the sun can economically be put to work for you.

1. THE HOUSE AND THE HOME

This book is about changing and improving things around the house, but before we launch into that we would like to take a look at things as they already are. The world is a remarkable place, both the natural and the man-made parts, with fascinating mechanisms and interesting histories. Accordingly, this chapter is devoted less to immediately useful information and more to an appreciation of how our houses shelter us and how other things inside and outside help in that task.

The lowest possible temperature is called absolute zero, and is 460 degrees Fahrenheit (°F) below what we usually call zero. At this temperature all molecules of matter, which are usually in some kind of movement, come to total and absolute rest. An object in space with no source of heat to warm it would approach absolute zero. By contrast the temperature of the northern United States averages about 45° F over the year, which is about 500° absolute. Moreover, the annual temperature *range* for any one place is only about 100° F, while on the surface of the moon temperature can swing about 500° F, both way above and way below what living forms (as we know them) can tolerate. Our earth's atmosphere makes the difference by capturing sunlight for us and holding the temperature of the earth warm enough and steady enough for our survival. This is what we have to start from and it's very good indeed. Earth temperatures vary from the equator to the poles but a cold day of 10° F is nine-tenths of the way from absolute zero to room temperature. *Our buildings provide only the last tenth of our needed shelter.*

Where winters are nasty, this may sound like cold comfort, but it's clear that the earth retains a large part of the energy the sun gives us. This *sun-earth shelter* is a reality and is solar heating. It is our little patch of Creation, and compared to the rest of the universe, it's a good place to be.

THE SUN-EARTH SHELTER

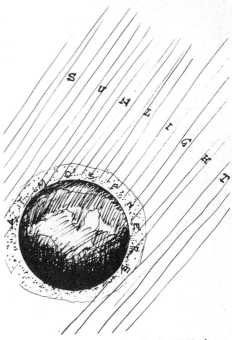

The sun-earth shelter—about 500° above absolute zero

Seen in this perspective, our task of energy conservation is one of closing a rather small gap, that last tenth. Our present troubles result in part from using too much fuel to do it, but there are two other directions to work from. One way to close the gap is to collect more solar energy, which is the approach of most solar houses and what many other people are writing about. The conservation of energy within the building is the other approach, and this is our subject.

CONSERVATION IS PREPARATION FOR SOLAR

A good solar building, in fact, gives attention to both aspects: sun and earth. Successful solar-heated structures all have another thing in common besides a focus on the sun! They retain heat very effectively and should have only one-fourth the heat loss of an ordinary house. That job being done well, it is relatively easy to collect enough sunlight to do the rest. In fact we have seen buildings that do the job of conservation so well that the only collectors required are some south-facing windows—and not very many of them at that.

A HOUSE FULL OF HOLES

Alas, holding on to energy in this way is the weak point of most of our buildings because few of them were constructed with that in mind. Most have thousands of holes and cracks; the ceilings have them, the walls, windows, and doors have them, and the foundation has them. A house is made of hundreds of pieces of material held together with nails, and nothing seems to fit just right. Older buildings, which may have been put together well in the beginning, have developed problems with age. New buildings are often assembled carelessly and have just as many weak points as the older ones, although the quality of windows and doors has definitely improved. Yet, whether a house is a hundred years old or only five, its problems are similar.

There is no one simple way to tighten up a house. Insulation helps and plugging holes makes a difference, but the biggest change comes with an overall approach to careful home management. Many effective ways to reduce heat loss are both economical and technically simple. *The main requirement is to take the trouble to learn about energy processes and become a part of the solution.* Your reward for the fuss and attention will be greater comfort and substantial energy savings. Your *house* will be more efficient and your *home* more comfortable.

HOMEMAKING

The continuing care and attention of the homeowner marks the distinction between *house* and *home*. Home maintenance is the key to energy conservation. Homeowners must renew caulking and weatherstripping, clean the furnace, and repair the various parts of the house if they wish to have an efficient shelter.

The things that give us emotional warmth within the home can also provide physical comfort. Do you remember what your living room was like before you moved in with all your possessions? Probably rather cold and inhuman. As you settled in, all these

. . . rather cold and inhuman

Furnishings make it warmer.

things that are a part of you enriched the room and made it more comfortable. Your rugs, furniture, and fabrics softened the angles of the room and made it more pleasant visually and acoustically. They also make it warmer—*really* warmer.

There ought to be a standard way to measure and describe just how much difference these things make. Insulation gets a technical rating and furnaces are measured for capacity and efficiency; why not curtains and rugs? That would give us some guidance on how to plan and budget for home improvements to obtain the greatest advantages on our tight allowances. We might then decide to buy an attractive rug to insulate the living room floor and thus obtain emotional satisfaction while attacking a thermal problem.

Another example: A large window looks unfinished without something to temper the summer sun and relieve the winter cold; this is the reason for blinds and curtains. They don't come with the house yet are an indispensable part of the home. Each homeowner has a different idea of what a window should look like, and nearly everyone feels the need to add some window treatment to make it a part of the kind of space he or she enjoys. *Done the right way, curtains may contribute more to energy conservation than storm windows.*

A LANGUAGE OF THERMAL VALUES

HOUSE

Before we can describe and compare things like curtains and storm windows, we will have to understand the basic processes that make us comfortable within a house. Not surprisingly, many of us think of a house as an expensive container into which we place our things and ourselves for safekeeping. Those who pay the bills go a step further and see this container as a financial investment, something that needs to be protected so that it doesn't deteriorate and lose value. An observant homeowner can go even further and understand the parts and processes of his or her house and home.

In this sense, a building is alive. Buildings have life spans and fall prey to illness and accidents. If homeowners give their houses an annual checkup and a little preventive maintenance, they may avoid major problems in the future. This kind of medical comparison can be useful for understanding a house and will be the basis of an entire program of improvements later in the book.

Let us now take a close look at our patient, the house, and see how it functions. A house itself tells a remarkable and interesting story, but it also contains a variety of services that tell even more. We need to appreciate the ingenuity of these services, how they work, and how we came to depend on them. Our analysis of the house is divided into two parts: first, the physical enclosure of the house, and then the kit of services that today make this enclosure comfortable.

Enclosure

The walls, roof, and floor of a house combine to form an *envelope,* those elements that are wrapped around the spaces we live in. The extent to which this envelope creates a secure interior space as distinct from the out-of-doors is called the *enclosure.* The *envelope* is an object (an assembly of pieces), while the *enclosure* is an achievement (how well those pieces fit together). An envelope is kind of all or nothing; you either have one or not depending on whether the builder finished putting on the roof or left out a few windows. But an enclosure is never complete, like a granite tomb. We need openings to enter and leave houses, and other openings to admit sunlight, air, and views. These contacts with the outside we call *exposures.* The necessity for both exposure and enclosure determine the ways we construct our houses.

The envelope of the house is made up of walls, roof and floor. Everybody understands what a roof does, and there is general agreement about what constitutes a good and a bad one. In an old house, fixing the roof is the first order of business because without this, all other improvements are beside the point. Foundations also have a simple purpose. Whether the foundation is wood on some stones or an elaborate basement, its basic purpose is to keep the house out of the mud.

The function of the wall is more complex. Our daily interaction with walls is more intense and personal; we can ignore floors and ceilings, but we can't help looking at walls. We fill our walls with ducts, pipes, and wires and poke them full of holes for windows and doors. Because they are not as fundamental as roofs and foundations we tolerate many imperfections in their construction. These imperfections are a primary source of our heating problems. Most walls are okay as envelopes but terrible as enclosures.

The Parts of a Wall

What happens inside a wall? What are its parts and what is each part supposed to do? It's fairly complex. Starting from the

ENVELOPE AND ENCLOSURE

A tent is a structure that performs only the first function of a house. What is the next thing that is added to make it more comfortable? You guessed it— a floor!

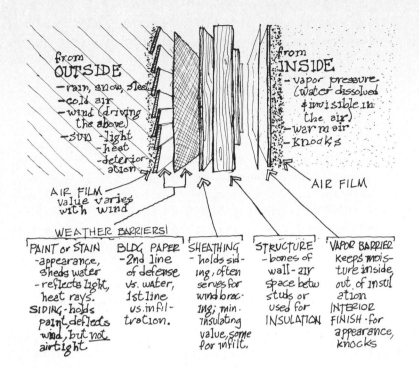

from **OUTSIDE**
- rain, snow, sleet
- cold air
- wind (driving the above)
- sun - light
  - heat
  - deterior- ation

from **INSIDE**
- vapor pressure (water dissolved & invisible in the air)
- warm air
- knocks

AIR FILM
value varies
with wind

AIR FILM

WEATHER BARRIERS!

PAINT or STAIN	BLDG PAPER	SHEATHING	STRUCTURE	VAPOR BARRIER
- appearance, sheds water - reflects light, heat rays. SIDING - holds paint, deflects wind, but not airtight	- 2nd line of defense vs. water, 1st line vs. infiltration.	- holds siding, often serves for wind bracing; min. insulating value, some for infilt.	- bones of wall - air space betw studs or used for INSULATION	keeps moisture inside, out of insulation INTERIOR FINISH - for appearance, knocks

Weather barriers

outside, the first layer is the *weather barrier*. This was traditionally painted wood but today is often of aluminum or vinyl siding. The purpose of this outside layer is to absorb the impact of the elements. Paint is a barrier that attempts to defy the existence of time and appear forever new, which of course doesn't work, so it needs frequently to be redone and returned to a fresh appearance. Aluminum and vinyl siding somewhat more successfully deny the forces of nature. Stained wood and masonry, on the other hand, are intended to age gracefully with time. All weather barriers protect the inner layers of the wall and take a beating over the seasons from rain, snow, and the summer sun. You will notice that trim and siding on the sunny side of the house are apt to be in much worse shape than on the other sides, as the result of exposure to the ultraviolet rays of the sun.

Siding is intended to stop wind and rain, but it is *not*, surprisingly, the place to seal the building tight against air leakage. In fact, siding generally needs to be ventilated to the outside so that moisture coming from within the building can escape. When you see a house with peeling paint, it usually means that moisture has been trapped behind the weather barrier.

The layer behind the siding—*building paper*—is very cheap and very important. This black, asphalt-impregnated paper sheds water that may get through the siding but still allows water vapor from the inside of the wall to get out. It also stops drafts from coming through. Many old buildings do not have building paper, and the wind is often able to come right through various cracks.

Sheathing, the next layer, supports the siding. Usually made of boards or plywood, it resists the forces of wind and is important

WEATHER BARRIER

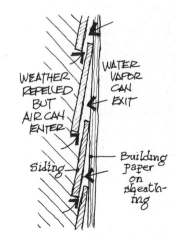

WEATHER REPELLED BUT AIR CAN ENTER

WATER VAPOR CAN EXIT

Siding

Building paper on sheathing

The concept of siding. (The gaps are exaggerated.)

in bracing the structure. Fiberboard is sometimes used instead of wood to save money and add a little insulation, but it gives less structural strength and requires more complex measures for windbracing.

Windbracing is indirectly important to energy conservation. When it is lacking, wind forces rack the building out of shape and little cracks and openings develop in the wall and allow air infiltration. In an existing house there is not much to be done to improve windbracing (short of resheathing the wall with plywood).

The layer of *studs* is actually the first step in the sequence of construction and carries the weight of loads placed on the wall. Studs are usually vertically placed 2 × 4's (actually $1\frac{1}{2}$ × $3\frac{1}{2}$ inches but called "tewbforz" by ancient custom); they are spaced 16 inches apart and joined at top and bottom with horizontal 2 × 4's. The hollow spaces between the studs accommodate ducts, pipes, and wiring. This is also the place for insulation. Diagonal windbracing is sometimes placed here if plywood or diagonal sheathing is not used.

Insulation for a stud wall is any kind of material placed in the cavity to reduce the circulation of air that carries heat from the inside layer to the outside layers of the wall. Wood was once considered a good insulator, but fiberglass and foams are much better. Foamboards are now sometimes added either inside or outside the studs to further reduce heat transfer through the studs themselves.

When a wall has insulation, a *vapor barrier* becomes essential on the *warm* side of the insulation to prevent water vapor within the house from entering the insulation. Any water vapor that penetrates into insulation will condense as it reaches the cold on the outer side of the insulation. A small amount of vapor may safely pass into a wall and out through sheathing, paper, and siding, but heavy vapor transfer condenses, accumulates, and soaks the insulation. This reduces its insulating value and may damage the wall. For new construction, a good vapor barrier is created with plastic sheets; but a few layers of the right kind of paint on an existing wall will help to some degree.

An *inside finish* of plaster on lath or gypsum wallboard (Sheetrock) completes the wall. This finish receives the interior decoration and absorbs knocks and abuse from within the house. A durable interior finish is necessary to protect the more sensitive inner layers of vapor barrier and insulation. The edges of the wall and the penetrations for windows, doors, and services are the weak parts of the interior finish and the most likely places for air and vapor to leak through.

As a container for heat, the wall has two different functions to perform. The first is to seal against the passage of air. The building paper and vapor barrier do most of this. The other function is to slow the passage of heat. The insulation does most of this but all layers have some insulating value. In this sense,

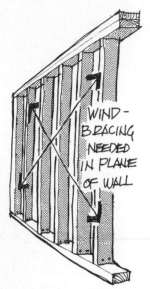

Studs (the bones of the wall)

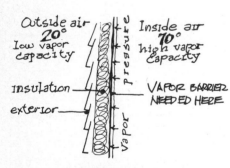

CONCEPT OF VAPOR BARRIERS As water vapor travels through the wall, it encounters progressively colder air. At a certain point it condenses. If this point is ventilated, the moisture will re-evaporate and escape to the outside; if not, the insulation and other surfaces become wet.

there are actually a few more layers to the wall than those we have mentioned. *Air films* next to the surface of materials are a kind of insulation. Heat is slow to transfer from one material across an air space and into another material because still air is a poor conductor. Wind blowing across an exterior wall wipes away most of its air film, but interior walls have air films with enough resistance that a number of them sandwiched together can be significant insulation. The situation for a window is similar: The air films on either side of each layer of glass are much more important than the glass itself in preventing heat loss.

Windows and Doors

While walls create an enclosure, the window allows exposure. We need exposure to sunlight, air, and view for health and well-being, but have to keep these under control. A window is a *filter* that admits varying amounts of each into the room, depending on the season and our daily needs and moods. The varying needs for enclosure and exposure mean that a well-designed house should provide a number of spaces with different qualities of light, air, and view. Southern windows will actually gain heat over the course of the day. With the proper use of curtains or shutters they can become one-way filters for solar heat.

Windows have a long history; they were not always as versatile and marvelous as filters as they are today. In the old days, openings in the wall—called "wind-eyes"—were to see out of and let air in. In cold weather or in battle the choice was either light or

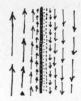

AIR FILMS ON 1 LAYER OF MATERIAL
R-VALUE ABOUT 1

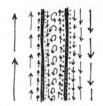

AIR FILMS ON 2 LAYERS WITH AIR SPACE
R-VALUE ABOUT 2

For very thin sheets like glass, the insulating is done by slow-moving air next to the surface. The more layers of material, the more air films.

Windows have complex functions.

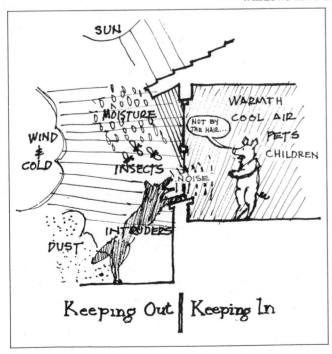

Keeping Out | Keeping In

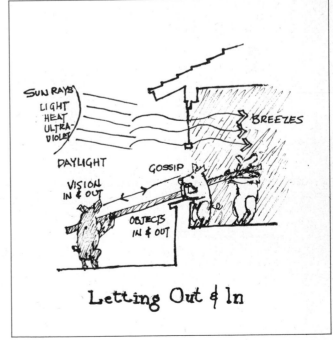

Letting Out & In

protection, because the only window cover was a wooden shutter or a sheet of leather. Eventually panes of glass—called "lights"—became available, but glass was still scarce and rarely used. The story goes that when the English monarchs traveled about the kingdom they took their casements with them and had them installed in each castle as they arrived.

We now take for granted many of the complex functions that a window performs. Large sheets of glass have been available for about seventy years. Modern window woodwork is a precision product with tolerances of about one-fiftieth of an inch, which is about five times as good as was common a generation ago. A good window is now encased in vinyl, to prevent even minor changes in size that come from the expansion and contraction of wood with different summer and winter humidities. Windows now may have elaborate weatherstripping and gaskets to ensure tight closure. The degree of enclosure possible in a modern window permits as little as 2 percent of the air infiltration of an old, loose-fitting window.

The door is a special filter for the greeting and passage of people. It provides an opening that pierces the envelope yet must be a convincing element of the enclosure when closed. Constant air infiltration around a closed door and large blasts of cold air through an open door are sufficient reasons for it to receive additional attention. An effective doorway requires careful detailing if it is to function well and over long periods of time. The annals of architecture are full of doorways in which the functional, decorative, and ceremonial elements are hard to separate.

A ceremonial door

SERVANTS AND SERVICES

The Kit of Services

Nothing in the home has changed more than the things that get used up and the way they are supplied and disposed of. Consider a typical house in the early nineteenth century and what people did to maintain themselves—to get all the things that we have supplied to us inside the house. Most people, except those who had servants to do for them, had to leave the house to get heating fuel or water, to eliminate, or to communicate with the rest of the world. Moreover, these things were supplied at a much lower level than today; candles and, on special occasions, whale-oil lanterns were long the only lights for most people. And of course there was no long-distance rapid communication. These services and their systems were added bit by bit during the nineteenth and twentieth centuries.

It is possible to live in a very old house that looks almost as it would have when it was built, but practically everybody lives with most of these services that, while not exactly invisible, are inconspicuous to most of us. These things make us more independent, in the sense of being able to pursue more interesting matters than chopping wood and scrubbing clothes. Today every-

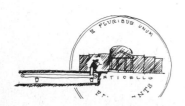

One of the more interesting and advanced features Thomas Jefferson built into Monticello was a bucket conveying system in a tunnel underneath his inside privy.

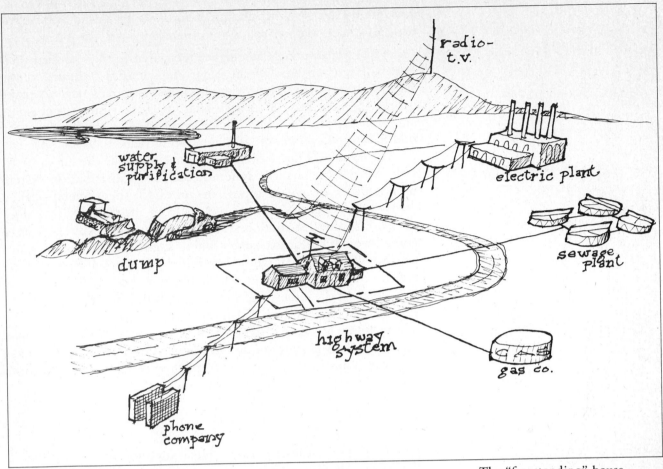

The "freestanding" house

body has the equivalent of a number of servants, not to mention entertainers.

Freedom from household chores has been a good thing for the most part, but we have paid a price in becoming more dependent than ever on the various utility companies that provide us with everything from heat to amusement. By and large most of us are satisfied with this arrangement, and very few of us would do without the convenience and freedom that these services give us. Perhaps, however, we have gone too far in our expectations of what can be done for us. Part of the home energy strategy might be to try to lessen reliance on and dismiss a few unnecessary and overpaid servants. The many people using wood stoves for heat these days instead of a furnace are a good example of this approach.

A less drastic step is to get to know what the servant/services do and how they do it. You can learn to repair and service some of your equipment. To begin, you might learn simple maintenance, like oiling the motors to prolong their trouble-free life. Aside from this, we think you should learn a little something about mechanical equipment in general, just to appreciate it. All those dusty gadgets down there in the basement are really quite remarkable. In the spirit of appreciation we are going to describe how a furnace works, just as we described a wall.

A house that is kept at a higher temperature than its surroundings will give up heat to the environment until both are at the same temperature, unless something else supplies heat to make up for the heat loss. A furnace is a device that burns fuel safely and under controlled conditions. (In the case of electric heat, the fuel is burned elsewhere, at a generating plant.)

The heat generated by burning fuel can heat the air directly, as in a fireplace, but it is generally fed into a distribution system of hot-water or steam pipes, or tubes of sheet metal—called ducts—for hot air. Note that hot air from the burner flame does not go into the distribution system; it goes up the chimney, after going through a heat exchanger where it gives up its heat to water or air, which is what gets distributed. A *heat exchanger* is an arrangement of tubes over which the hot gases from the flame play, heating the tubes, and in turn the water or air within them. The water or air is then distributed to the various rooms of the house, where it goes through other heat exchangers called *radiators* or *convectors* to heat room air. In an air system the hot air mixes with room air directly; cool air from further regions of the room is drawn away to be reheated at the furnace.

The radiators, convectors, or hot-air registers are usually along the outside walls, and most frequently under windows. This is because the colder air of the outside walls drops down and goes across the floor, causing drafts. Heat supplied at the bottom of the outer walls will counteract this movement and cut down drafts. In older houses, one may find hot-air registers on the inside walls. This was a simpler way to do it because all the ductwork could be near the furnace in the middle of the house. It is also a cheaper way to heat, as we will explain later.

The automatic controls keep all this running at the proper rate. In comparison to the controls for rocket navigation or even a small airplane, those of a home heating or air-conditioning system are quite simple, but to someone not accustomed to such things, they seem fairly complicated. The *thermostat* is an automatic switch that keeps track of the room temperature and turns the furnace on and off accordingly. Other automatic controls either help the thermostat or are for safety, such as one that shuts off the fuel supply if the boiler runs dry. These controls work remarkably well year after year.

Problems result from the most unexpected situations. A friend discovered that a noisy motor for a furnace circulator pump was mounted upside down. The lubrication caps had been underneath, out of sight, out of mind, and out of oil for at least six years—as long as he had owned the house. The motor quieted down and worked fine after it was set to rights. The results of near-perfect reliability can be pure hell when things go wrong and we have no familiarity or experience with a simple device.

Many of us turn off the whole scene.

HOME ECONOMICS

Home Economics has been an official program for girls in public schools for over fifty years, and economics of the home reaches back to ancient history as the domain of women. Today the liberation of women and the resulting new roles for men are changing the meaning of the home. A respect for home economics creates an entirely new perspective on the value of house, home, and family.

A home is a business. If you own a house and understand mortgages, interest, insurance, and taxes, you will agree that banks treat homeowners much like any other business. A house is essentially the same as any other commercial space and houses are frequently turned into apartments, offices, and stores—and back again. The main difference between a home and a business is that a home generates little of what is generally recognized as income or profit.

HOME WORK

There was not such a distinction between home and work in the past. With the back-to-the-land movement and other changes, the home workplace is making something of a comeback. Besides the conventionally valued productive work that is returning to the home, there is an even more important movement toward recognizing and giving value to *all* the work being done in the home. In his book *Home Inc.,* Scott Burns points out that the value of unpaid labor within households is nearly equal to all other economic activity in the country. As an example, compare the cost of taking the family out to restaurants for twenty meals to your weekly food budget. Every meal cooked and served in a restaurant costs about five times the cost of the food itself, but the expense of food preparation within the home is usually forgotten and unacknowledged. The same point can be made for nearly every other kind of housework.

Work within the house does have economic value, and learning to do more things for yourself within the home will increase your effective income. You will have in effect earned the money that you would have had to pay someone else to do it.

THE HOME

HOUSE + HOMEOWNER = HOME

A home is the experience of living in a house. A builder forms the house, but the way you live in it creates the home. An old house you have lived in for years means more to you than a house that is newly occupied. The house itself tends to deteriorate as doors and windows warp and wear; a home, on the other hand, tends to improve with the addition of curtains, furnishings, and landscaping. When you undertake energy-saving improvements, the value to the house multiplies because you save on operating costs and add to the market value of the house.

SUGGESTIONS FOR FURTHER READING

Your Engineered House, by Rex Roberts. At last an introduction to all the aspects of a well-designed house by a builder with common sense and more than a few innovative and excellent ideas. An eye-opener.
New York: M. Evans and Co., Inc., 1964. $4.95

The Owner-Built Home, by Ken Kerns. No one has worked harder than Ken to assemble and package useful information for owner-builders. An incredible amount of information in one little book.
Oakhurst, Cal. (93644): Owner-Builder Publications, $7.50

The Architecture of the Well-Tempered Environment, by Reyner Banham. One of the first books to expose the modern division between architectural design and the environmental sciences—a departure from their traditional union. An especially good treatment of historic systems of natural ventilation.
London: The Architectural Press, 1969. $5.95

The Place of Houses, by Charles Moore, Gerald Allen, and Donlyn Lyndon. A number of very fine architects reveal the meaning and reasoning that lie behind the design of good houses.
New York: Holt, Rinehart and Winston, 1974. $17.95

Country Comforts, by Christian Bruyere and Robert Inwood. Shows you how to build a house with a chainsaw, forge your own hardware, and make your own shakes for the roof. Dozens of down-to-earth construction projects that a homesteader plans and builds daily as a natural course of events. Good drawings and pictures; thought-provoking text.
New York: Drake Publishers, 1976. $14.95

House, Form and Culture, by Amos Rapaport. What a house is and how its form changes with time, with different cultures, with the availability of various materials, and with different climates. Plenty to think about in all that.
Englewood Cliffs, N.J.: Prentice-Hall, 1969. $3.50

The Architecture of Country Houses, by Andrew Downing. Although first published in 1850 in the language of the well-heeled, this book makes a lot of sense and has more than a little to say about well-built older houses.
New York: Dover Publications, Inc., 1969. $5.00

2. ENERGY VOCABULARY

This chapter begins with some basic definitions of heat processes that will be needed throughout the book. It continues by showing how these are used in various common forms of heating systems. Next we talk about the object of heating systems—human comfort. There is a brief discussion of human physiology, or how the human body reacts to heat, cold, humidity, and air motion. Then we speak of dwelling types of the past and how they took care of these needs with less resort to technical means and a greater use of natural energies. And finally we talk briefly of beneficial lifestyle changes that can easily be made.

DEFINITIONS

Heat has been thought about and studied for thousands of years. People believed it was some kind of object, one of the basic elements (fire, earth, air, and water), or a spirit that flowed in and out of objects. A fire was thought to release the spirit of heat from material, where it could be seen as a flame.

In the terms of modern physics, *heat is an activity* consisting of the motion of molecules of matter. The more movement, the greater the heat. In solid crystals such as salt, metals, and ice, the movement is vibration. When vibration gets out of hand, the molecules of the crystals jump out of place; when this happens, the solid melts and becomes a liquid.

Once in the liquid state, the molecules are free to move about, which they do in straight lines until they collide with other molecules. Remember that they are very small, and matter that might appear to be dense has quite a bit of free space, from the point of view of a molecule. As they rush about, ricocheting off each other, some of them may by chance be hit in such a way that

SOLID

LIQUID

GAS

Motion of a molecule

they develop a very high speed. If they happen to be at the top surface, they may be knocked right up into the space above. This is called *evaporation* and goes on all the time. As more heat is applied, more molecules take to the air. With enough applied heat, vapor pressure forms bubbles inside the liquid; the liquid is then *boiling*.

When molecules are free in space, they are considered to be *gas*. Gas molecules are free to shoot about as in a liquid but are much farther apart and collide much less frequently. A gas expands until it meets a solid barrier.

Temperature is a measure of heat intensity, of how tightly gathered the activity of heat is within a material. The heat of one match applied to a small piece of metal makes the metal hot enough to burn the fingers. The same match applied to a saucepan full of water will hardly raise the temperature at all. The resulting temperature is different, yet the same *amount* of heat is involved in both cases. Temperature, then, is related to mass. An object's mass affects how easy or difficult it is to heat or cool.

HEAT TRANSFER

Because heat is matter in motion, it diffuses through materials and transfers from one material to another. Heat transfer occurs in three ways—conduction, convection, and radiation.

When heat is applied to a pan of water by a gas burner, the molecules of the pan in contact with the flame vibrate more quickly, knock more vigorously against their neighbors, and set up a chain reaction. The metal molecules at the top surface transfer their increased motion to the water, which repeats the procedure. This process of heat transfer, where molecules convey a surge of energy while remaining in position, is called *conduction*.

Molecules of a liquid or a gas, on the other hand, are free to move about and transfer heat by *convection*. As water at the bottom of the pan is heated, it expands slightly and becomes lighter than the cooler water above it. Heated water then floats up toward the surface and is replaced by cool water, which sinks. A convection current of circulating molecules is thereby formed.

The third process of heat transfer is *radiation*. We experience radiation all the time yet it is the most mysterious of the three processes. Radiation is not a form of heat as we have described it; it is not an activity of molecules but an electromagnetic wave in the same family as light. Traveling through space at 186,000 miles per second, radiant energy waves turn into heat only when they strike a material and start its molecules vibrating. The sun with its surface temperature of 10,000° F is our greatest radiator and gets its rays to us across 93 million miles of empty space.

The sun is the basic source of radiant heat, but any object exchanges radiant energy with its surroundings, depending on their relative temperatures. Since your skin temperature is about

higher temperature to lower →

Conduction

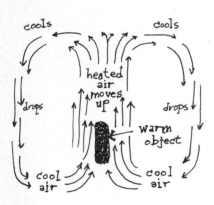

Convection (works same way with liquids)

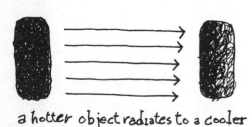

a hotter object radiates to a cooler

Radiation

90°, heat from it will radiate to a window pane, which is often at 40° in mid-winter, and you will feel cold. That is, you will feel the loss of heat. A surface hotter than your skin will radiate heat to you, and you will feel warm on the side exposed.

Things at a high temperature lose their heat to things at a lower temperature. Levels of energy in a system tend to equalize and eliminate the extremes. There is no way to stop this process, but there are ways to slow it down, such as the use of insulation. There are also ways to speed up this process of equalization, by means of a heat distribution system. Heat can be added to a system by burning fuel or by collecting sunlight, but there is no way to stop energy from seeking a level of equal distribution. The majestic operation of this natural law is evident to anyone who has tried to deliver a hot pizza.

MEASURING HEAT

We have described heat so far without using numbers, but we cannot get by without some means of measurement. Therefore, please greet the British thermal unit, or simply Btu: *the amount of heat needed to raise one pound of water one degree Fahrenheit,* or about the amount of heat generated by burning one match. (Your children will soon be telling you about the calorie, which is metric and is the heat required to raise one gram of water one degree Celsius.)

It takes a certain amount of energy to raise a given amount of material to a higher temperature, but it takes much more energy to make a material change state. The *change of state* from solid to liquid or liquid to gas is very important to an understanding of air conditioning, certain kinds of heating, and human comfort in general. Starting with a pound of ice at 0° F, we would need to supply about half a Btu per degree to raise it to the melting point of 32°. But turning that pound of ice into water takes 143 Btu's—without raising the temperature at all. All that energy goes into unlocking the crystal structure of the ice.

After melting is complete, water will increase in temperature 1° for each Btu of applied energy until at 212° (lower at higher altitudes) it reaches its boiling point. The temperature then stays at the boiling point until all the water has boiled away. Turning water into vapor requires 970 Btu's per pound of water without raising its temperature. All the energy goes into speeding up the vibration of the water molecules to the point where they can escape the surface of the water.

Water does not have to reach 212° for some of it to vaporize. *Evaporation* is common and occurs when individual molecules escape into the surrounding air. The air and water are both cooled in this process because the molecules that escape must attain a higher energy state at the expense of their neighbors. This is why you feel cool when a breeze increases the evaporation of water from your skin.

WHAT CAUSES HEAT TO MOVE?

1 Btu = 266 calories
1 lb = 456 grams

CHANGE OF STATE

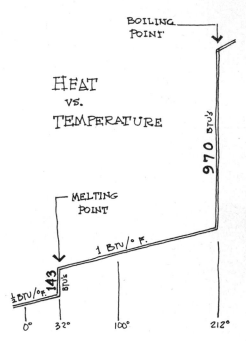

To change a pound of ice at 0° to a pound of steam requires 1309 Btu's, only 196 of which raise the temperature.

The reverse also happens. When a pound of water vapor turns back into liquid, it gives up the same enormous amount of heat—970 Btu's—to anything it *condenses* upon. This is how a steam radiator works. When liquid water freezes, it releases 143 Btu's per pound. This energy is called *latent* heat.

HUMIDITY

There is always some amount of moisture in the air. Humidity is water but it is also a gas. Individual molecules of water shoot about just like the oxygen, nitrogen, and carbon dioxide that make up most of the air. They are invisible and they don't "feel" wet.

WATER VAPOR

Water gets into the air by evaporation from the surface of every ocean, lake, river, and pot and pan of the world. As a drop or puddle, water clings to itself through molecular attraction. A higher temperature gives a water molecule the greater vibrational energy it needs to overcome this molecular attraction, burst free, and become water vapor.

RELATIVE HUMIDITY

Air has a certain capacity to hold water vapor, depending upon its temperature. Molecules of water vapor can be closer together at higher temperatures without uniting because they are vibrating faster. As temperatures fall, molecular attraction overcomes vibrational energy to form molecular clusters, which eventually become drops of rain or condensation on a cold surface.

In warm weather the air can and often does carry a lot of water vapor. In cold weather it cannot. Air at 70° has five times the vapor capacity of air at 10°. The ratio between the moisture air carries and what it could carry at that temperature is called its *relative humidity*. When air is reduced in temperature, its relative humidity goes up until the saturation point (100 percent relative humidity) is reached. If the temperature continues to fall, the "dew point" is reached and excess moisture must condense out of the air. It is rather like squeezing a partially soaked sponge.

Humidity has a pressure like any gas and it penetrates most materials. Among the benefits is the resilience it gives to wood; without it, the wood becomes brittle and flaky. Living creatures need to incorporate a great deal of moisture but lose it quickly in very dry air. However, too much humidity is not good either. It has a bad effect on many building materials because it encourages bacterial action such as mold and rot. High humidity with high temperature is very uncomfortable and difficult to modify. The right amount of humidity is variable but essential to well-being and comfort.

Hot-water system

HEAT TRANSFER IN BUILDINGS

The object of using a heating system, as opposed to simply using a fireplace, is to take heat from the furnace where it is generated and carry it to the remote parts of the house. Heating systems use all the methods of heat transfer that we have just discussed. These processes can be made to operate more efficiently once you know the system and how to control and assist it.

Most furnaces today use a distribution system of hot water in which conduction occurs inside the furnace and convection at the point of delivery in the room. Oil or gas is burned in the furnace to heat a boiler full of water by conduction. Hot water is pumped up to the room and heats metal fins on the water pipe by conduction. These metal fins then heat the room by convection.

Older systems were able to use convection itself instead of a pump. Water was heated and rose gently through fairly large pipes, was cooled (released its heat) in radiators, and then returned to the furnace naturally. In such a *gravity system*, the furnace had to be placed below all other parts of the system and near the center of the building.

Hot-air systems use sheet-metal ducts to bring warm air directly into a room. Air is still heated in the furnace by conduction, is moved from there by fans or through natural convection, and is circulated through the rooms by convection. Cold-air return registers should then capture drafts falling in front of windows and doors and bring this air back to the furnace to be heated.

Steam systems use the heat of vaporization to advantage. Water is heated to steam, which rises under pressure through pipes. The latent heat of steam is transferred to the room when the steam condenses within the radiators, giving up the heat acquired at the boiler. Liquid condensate runs back down, often within the same pipe, to the furnace. In this case, *radiators* are true to their name, reaching temperatures as high as 200°.

Electrical-resistance heating uses the properties of electricity to create heat by causing particles of metal to vibrate as an electric current passes through. An electric stove or light bulb generates heat the same way; a 1200-watt heat circuit in a room is like turning on twelve 100-watt light bulbs. Electrical-resistance units are usually mounted as baseboard units and heat by convection.

Systems of radiant heating have a number of advantages. The two systems commonly used have either hot-water pipes or electrical-resistance cables embedded in either a concrete floor or a plaster ceiling. The pipes or cables transfer heat to what they are embedded in, which raises temperatures to about 80° for floors and 90° or more for ceilings. These surfaces in turn heat the room by radiation and some convection.

Radiant heat from such large surfaces has a particular advantage because the source of heat is large enough to heat us all over. Instead of roasting one side of our bodies in front of a 200° steam radiator, we feel a broad wave of gentle heat that rolls over us. When we receive radiant energy directly from floors and ceilings, air temperatures can be left lower.

HOT WATER

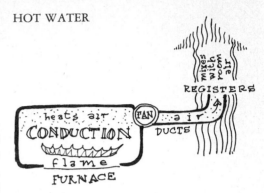

Hot-air system

HOT AIR

STEAM

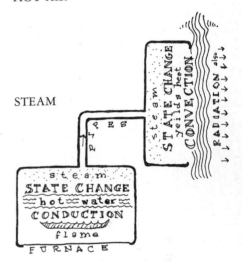

Steam system

RADIANT HEAT

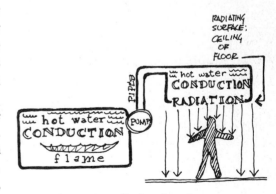

Hot-water radiation heating

COMFORT

Why do we heat buildings? Certainly not for their own sakes, nor for most of the objects in them. Even living things like plants and pets can withstand much more variation in temperature than people seem to want to tolerate. It is mainly for the comfort of our bodies that we go to such efforts; a great deal of expense in building construction is added just for that. We carefully build structures solid and stable enough to be sealed against the weather so that we can be comfortable standing, sitting, or at rest anywhere in the world and any time of the year. When you think of the number of buildings all over the world, that's a lot of investment in comfort.

What, then, is comfort? We define it as being able to forget our bodily needs and devote full attention to other things. This may seem obvious, but achieving it is not easy. Engineers, doctors, and researchers have spent and continue to spend a great deal of time measuring comfort and devising formulas so that designers will know how to produce comfort. As you might expect, the necessity to save energy complicates this task.

Comfort is, to some extent, personal and subjective. How often have we disagreed with others about the thermostat setting or how much the window needed to be open? It is almost like trying to agree on colors to decorate a room. Moreover, we disagree with ourselves from one time to the next, depending on whether we are cheerful or depressed, sick or well. However, there *are* standards and accepted ranges of comfort, and a good deal of agreement as to what produces them.

HUMAN PHYSIOLOGY

Human physiology determines how heat and cold affect us. In Chapter 1 we explained heat loss by showing a furnace as an object that supplies heat to a building, which in turn loses heat to the environment. If you substitute "metabolism" for "furnace" and "body" for "building," you can understand how hot and cold affect warm-blooded creatures. Our metabolism is the process of the body burning food to produce new body cells, useful work, and a lot of extra heat. That heat is continually generated inside the body, comes to the surface, and is lost to our surroundings. When we strike a balance between generation and dissipation of heat, the temperature of the body remains the same and we feel comfortable.

We are different from buildings in that they are not alive; it is possible to turn the heat off without killing them. We also differ from alligators and snakes, which *are* alive, but whose temperatures rise and fall with their surroundings. We cannot allow our own body temperatures to change in this way.

We are normally comfortable with an air temperature around 70°, which is a good deal cooler than our body temperature of about 99°. Our inner furnace is making heat all the time as a

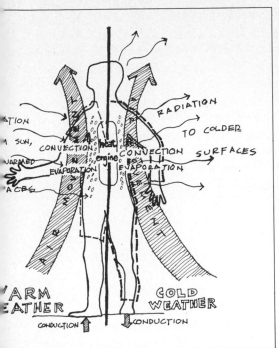

Types of body heat loss (and gain)

Interaction between body and environment

byproduct of staying alive, and surroundings of a lower temperature permit us to get rid of this extra heat easily. Our bodies have ingenious ways of doing this.

Under what are called "normal" conditions of light work, our heat engine burns 750 units of fuel, performs 250 units of work and releases 500 units of heat. This excess heat is carried from the center of the body by blood circulation to our skin surfaces where it is radiated and removed by convection of room air. As the air temperatures rise, extra blood is circulated to the surface to raise skin temperature too. We then experience a flush as the skin surface turns red with warm blood. Exercise, which increases the amount of body heat, often produces this effect; we feel our skin become hot.

If the air temperature continues to rise, or if a person's activity increases, the body resorts to *perspiration* as a way of releasing heat. Fluid is pushed out through the pores to the skin surface, where evaporation removes it. This fluid will evaporate slowly if the nearby air is already saturated with moisture, but a breeze improves evaporation by removing saturated air near the skin. In muggy weather the humidity is so high that perspiration is unable to evaporate, and it becomes visible as sweat. The same thing happens when we come to a stop after running; perspiration that was evaporated by the breeze generated in running soon covers the skin in a sweat that does not evaporate in still air.

This process of *evaporative cooling* operates in the winter as well. When cold air comes into the house and is warmed, its capacity to absorb water vapor is increased. Warm air leaving the house again loses this capacity to hold water vapor; it forms frost on very cold windows, where the vapor is chilled immediately to solid ice. This change of state works to convey heat from within the house to the surface of the glass, through which it is easily lost. A lot of this energy comes directly from you because dry air inside the house draws moisture out of you. As your body's moisture evaporates into the room and eventually makes its way out the window, your body loses 1000 Btu's for each pound of water you lose. You may lose as much as 5 pounds of water in a dry room each day. In addition to feeling unpleasantly dry, you will be cold and require higher air temperatures as your body experiences this constant evaporative cooling.

When the air is cool, the body responds first by decreasing blood circulation to the surface so that the skin becomes cooler, particularly at the fingers and toes. (Under severe cold the limbs may get so little blood circulation that they start to freeze, a condition called *frostbite.*) Another response is muscular activity, such as shivering and goose bumps.

Few of us will tolerate these more severe reactions to cold for very long, yet we are being asked to develop a tolerance to lower temperatures. The most common complaints about cold winters are low humidity and dry skin. The natural reaction of the body to evaporative cooling is to withdraw moisture from the surface of the skin; at the same time, it reduces blood circulation. It is not surprising that skin should dry out and crack in the winter because it is losing moisture from both directions. The answer to much of winter discomfort is to provide and maintain humidity in the room.

We have been talking about comfort for a person at rest or doing a leisurely activity. When the person is more active, the body generates more of its own heat and optimum room temperatures are not as important. Heavier activity allows comfort at cooler temperatures. However, any time that the body must make a substantial effort just to keep warm, the mind is apt to be distracted from other intended tasks. The harder we have to work just to be warm, the more distracted we become and the more uncomfortable we feel.

LESSONS FROM THE PAST

At this point we look at different dwellings through the ages to see how other people with less technology solved their shelter problems. A number of the ideas and processes of the past still are useful today.

THE VICTORIAN HOUSE

We can learn much from the way well-to-do Victorians used the space within their houses, although those houses were designed and built for a different sort of use than the ones we live in today. Victorians generally had a staff of servants to keep the fires going and the proper furnishings to keep the house alive and functioning as intended. The house was broken down into suites of rooms that were distinct apartments and functioned almost like separate houses. Each suite consisted of a central room with a fireplace plus a few service rooms. Only the major rooms with the fireplaces came near the level of comfort we expect today, and the halls were notoriously cold. Rather than heat the entire house, they would heat only the part they were using. Where there was no plumbing to freeze, any part of the house could be closed off when unneeded. This ability to divide the house into zones reduced the heating requirement.

A good house was zoned in a number of ways. In a large house, vertical zoning would be used. Heat moving upward through three stories of occupied space was lost twice to other rooms before it was truly lost. If only two of four major suites were being used, they would be two that were one over the other rather than two on the same floor. Such *vertical zoning* is still good practice. Bedrooms should be placed on the second floor to take advantage of heat rising from the first. This becomes more important as we learn again to keep the general temperature of the house lower and depend on local heating of rooms only when in use. Evening heat from the living room wood stove can then rise to heat the bedroom.

Each suite of the Victorian house was *concentrically zoned* around the fireplace in the sitting room, which was the only comfortable place to sit quietly. The heat for the entire suite spread from this one fireplace; this left the bedroom so cold that the bed had its own canopy and curtains to help keep in body heat.

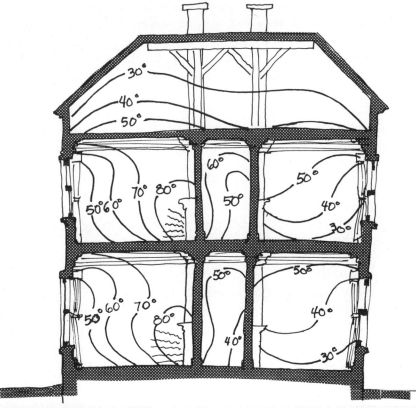

TEMPERATURE PROFILES OF A PARTIALLY OCCUPIED VICTORIAN HOUSE Heat rising from the downstairs suite makes it easier to heat the one directly above it. Notice the effect of the two fireplaces in use, the transmission of heat into hallways and attic, and the effect of leaky dampers in unoccupied rooms.

The large windows required to light these big rooms were carefully developed with so many layers of glass, shutters, and drapes that a Victorian window is often two or three times as well protected as a modern double-glazed window. A Victorian was very conscious of radiant energy flow and would sit facing the fire in a large overstuffed chair with his or her feet up off the drafty floor on an upholstered footrest. Cold exterior walls were blanketed with fabrics or tapestries. Furniture and hangings were placed to slow and divert drafts.

THE NEW ENGLAND FARMHOUSE

The form of the New England farmhouse is probably familiar to most of us, but its energy logic is still poorly understood. If less grandiose than the Victorian townhouse, it was no less complex and was probably a more efficient home. It typically had a single central fireplace and a simple order to its rooms. Farmhouses were not designed by architects but were merely built and allowed to grow as needed. The demands of a harsh climate strongly influenced the way they developed.

The basic house, oriented broadside to the south, was usually a heavy-timber frame box with one or two central fireplaces. The main rooms were organized around the first-floor fireplaces; the second floor contained the bedrooms. This follows the principles of concentric and vertical zoning. Our special interest in farmhouses derives from the way the entrances evolved. Most had formal entrances that were seldom used; the functional entrance was the side or back door. This entrance developed into a *buffer zone* between the inside and the outside and became a separate room with space to take off winter coats and workboots, room for a workbench to store a few handy tools, and a place to drop whatever you might have in your hand when you are called into the house. What in the city is called a *vestibule* is known as a *mudroom* in the country. If you are seriously considering the use

NEW ENGLAND FARM COMPLEX The farmyard is a sun trap. Note the pines to the northwest, the elm to the south.

of a wood stove, you should consider the addition of an entrance room to serve as a woodshed as well as a vestibule.

The *clustering* of farm buildings and landscaping was another way of reducing the exposure of each building. The barn was built, then a workshop, maybe a shed here and a lean-to there, and a farmyard was created within a cluster of buildings. Each building had its own particular purpose, yet taken as a whole they created something greater, a sheltered yard that enhanced the whole complex. A farmhouse with good landscaping became a settlement with its own shelter pocket backing up to the north and west and open to the south. In good weather a lot of activity happens in the yard, while in bad weather the whole settlement huddles together, each building protecting the other. In many farmhouse complexes it is possible to move from one building to the next without going out-of-doors. This is not only more comfortable but it saves heat.

Another important shelter is the prairie homestead, not for elegance, but for principles of shelter. Here the overriding concern was to cut down the impact of almost constant winds that blew across the flat plains with speeds of up to 50 miles per hour. The wind carried dust and could literally sand the surface off a wooden building. Wind exposure also puts a heavy demand on heating.

One response was to plant rows of *windbreakers,* trees planted between fields to prevent winds from removing newly plowed top-soil. Wind protection for the house developed into a system that would smoothly divert winds over the house. The function of wind protection for a building is to *streamline* the profile to avoid abrupt edges that create turbulence, thereby producing a body of relatively still air near the house.

When trees were scarce, homesteaders built sod houses by excavating into a hillside and building up the walls with chunks of sod. Timber beams carried a layer of sod and earth on the roof itself; the results were surprisingly warm. Because so much of the house was covered by earth or buried in the ground, there was little surface exposed to the air and cold. The *temperature difference* between the house and the ground was much less than it would have been between the house and the air. The thick sod walls were better insulators than the old wooden walls. Frank Lloyd Wright later used this principle of *earth berming* to create his energy-efficient prairie houses, and there is today a growing movement toward greater use of earth cover and underground shelter.

The pueblos of the Southwest, such as the ones at Acoma, New Mexico, represent a good way to cluster people into a settlement and they make good sense thermally. The climate is severe; at 5,000 feet of elevation they had to withstand both the fierce desert sun and very cold nights. One energy-saving proce-

THE PRAIRIE HOMESTEAD

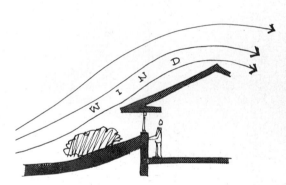

Berming and streamlining (an example by Frank Lloyd Wright)

THE PUEBLO SHELTER

dure was a *common wall* between houses, which reduces or eliminates much of the usual heat loss. Most urban buildings use this form of clustering and have as little as one-third the exposure of a freestanding house. Any form of compact clustering will have this advantage.

The rowhouses of the Acoma were carefully sited and constructed to gain maximum *solar exposure.* The rows of buildings were oriented so that a maximum amount of winter sun fell on broad south-facing walls and enclosed courtyards. The street was just wide enough so that one row of buildings would not shade the next. The walls were of heavy adobe brick, which caught and stored the energy of the sun and released it during the cold of the night. The thick walls delayed the effects of the heat from the sun until the evening when it was wanted. In addition, there were overhangs that helped protect these walls and the rooms from the summer sun. This sort of storage and timed release of heat is very important to solar heating.

The capacity for *mass storage and delayed release* of heat that was characteristic of the heavy adobe wall of the pueblo is common to most masonry construction. All shelters have some amount of mass storage capacity and the effect can be encouraged by introducing more mass into a building.

Another pueblo, at Mesa Verde, Colorado, is a special example of a natural shelter pocket that is an almost ideal *passive solar collector.* This settlement of almost twenty buildings developed in a large cave formation. Its siting was nearly perfect, in a recess high up on the side of a cliff, protected from winds, and easily defended from attack. The cliff overhang was just such that it provided shade from the high summer sun yet allowed the lower winter sun to penetrate all the way to the back wall. The dwellings formed an irregular semicircular row with advantages of good solar exposure similar to those of the Acoma pueblo.

The marvel of these ancient Indian settlements is that they were solar buildings without modern materials or equipment, with only correct orientation and use of materials. Modern buildings can be built using the same principles, and existing buildings can be adapted in ways that are both practical and economical. These examples merely indicate that solar energy need not be a complicated and expensive proposition.

DEVELOPING AN ENERGY-CONSCIOUS LIFESTYLE

The owners of the homes described above had very different relationships to their houses than we do to ours. Amidst our affluence we have lost many of the age-old sensitivities that enabled the Pueblo Indian and even the Victorian homeowner to develop highly evolved shelters. These were once the common-sense ways of doing things. If we retain our modern advantages and regain some of these old sensitivities, we can develop our houses in surprising ways.

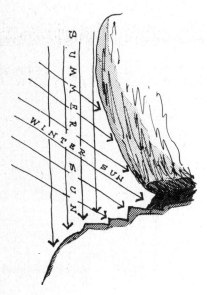

Living in a natural solar collector (Mesa Verde, New Mexico)

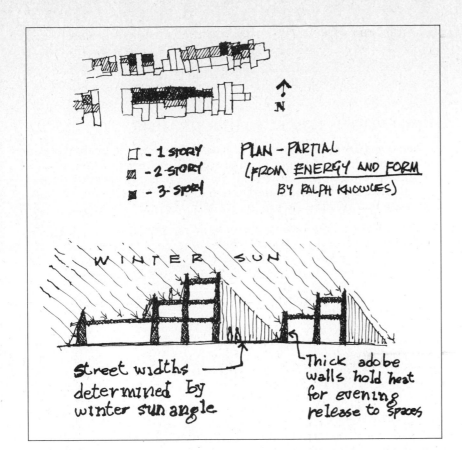

PLAN - PARTIAL
(FROM ENERGY AND FORM
BY RALPH KNOWLES)

☐ - 1 STORY
▨ - 2 STORY
▨ - 3 STORY

WINTER SUN

Street widths determined by winter sun angle

Thick adobe walls hold heat for evening release to spaces

Acoma Pueblo, New Mexico

Thermostat controls have narrowed our range of acceptable temperatures and we have come to believe that any deviation is a technical malfunction. On the other hand, the variations in temperature that occur with wood heating can be stimulating and in a short time one can develop a healthy tolerance for lower general temperatures. A slight chill will then be recognized not as a sign of something gone wrong but as a signal to control temperature yourself by closing shutters and curtains and feeding the wood stove. Living this way, people are able to heat a home comfortably for a season on a few cords of wood, are less prone to illness and colds, and stay in better shape generally.

Lifestyle adaptations in clothing and eating habits make a difference, too. You know to come in out of the rain and put on a sweater when you feel a chill, but what about starting out with warmer clothes to begin with? Natural fibers such as cotton and wool are generally warmer than synthetics. Slippers are more comfortable and warmer than street shoes. Do you change clothing to relax in the evening?

And what about the foods we eat? You can't expect your furnace to get good performance out of poor fuels. We each have different metabolic rates of food comsumption depending on what we do. A sleeping person gives off 250 Btu's of energy each hour, compared to 1500 Btu's while doing heavy work. A person who isn't active needn't eat as much as the one who puts in a full day

RANGES OF COMFORT

of hard labor. The active person, on the other hand, won't need as warm a room. We can change our *metabolisms*. Over time we can learn to eat better foods, improve our internal furnace efficiencies, and by so doing increase our comfort ranges.

SUGGESTIONS FOR FURTHER READING

Low-Cost Energy-Efficient Shelter, edited by Eugene Eccli. Culling from ninety years of experience among the contributing authors, Eccli has produced the basic text for any energy-conscious home-builder's library. A little dated but it's still essential.
Emmaus, Pa.: Rodale Press, Inc., 1976. $5.95

Mechanical and Electrical Equipment for Buildings, by William McGuinness. You don't have to be an engineer to read this book, but it helps. Everything you might want to know about choosing a system but very little about changing it. You've got to keep reading between the lines.
New York: John Wiley and Sons, Inc., 1971. $23.95

Physics of the Home: A Textbook for Students of Home Economics, by Frederick Osborn. You'll probably never find this particular book, but look for any *old* physics book for a straightforward discussion of energies around the home.
New York: McGraw Hill-Book Co., Inc., 1929.

Energy Primer, by the Whole Earth people. One of the best attempts to explain the bewildering range of energy possibilities available to all of us. Dense, technical style; most useful as a review and for access to other books, magazines, organizations, and key people.
Menlo Park, Cal. (94025): Whole Earth Truck Store, 1974. $5.50

Regional Guidelines for Building Passive Energy-Conserving Homes, by the AIA Research Corporation. Here is an excellent idea book that shows the range of climates we have in this country and what they imply for good building design. Nice little drawings with a lot of good information, but the text is very brief and choppy.
Available from the Superintendent of Documents, U.S. Government Printing Office, Washington, D.C. 20402.

3. THE DIAGNOSIS

After a couple of chapters devoted to theory and getting some perspective, this one gets down to brass tacks. The medical term Diagnosis is accurate; before doing anything else it is important to go over the house thoroughly and consistently in the manner of a doctor's examination. The findings of this examination will then indicate the treatments that are likely to give the best results.

The Map of Household Energy (page 28) is a device to further organize your thoughts. It attempts to show in one place all the different things that affect home energy use. It lists everything we could think of that might be found in a house to be modified, repaired, maintained, or created to save energy. It also shows how improvements change energy use. The arrows read "affects." For example, Window Location *affects* radiation (which is part of Direct Heat Loss), which in turn *affects* Energy Use. The map may look formidable but will become familiar and useful as you gain more information from this book and other sources. It isn't necessary to understand all the connections immediately for it to be useful as a guide.

We begin by noting that the Map is divided into three sections—the *house* itself, the *site,* and the *services.* The Diagnosis, a way of using numbers to focus on the parts of the Map most important to you, is divided into these same three parts. Each part is evaluated and scored separately. In general, a low score on a particular part indicates that there is advantage to be gained from a generally available improvement. Without laboring over particular details, the Diagnosis enables you to analyze the performance of your house and compare it to others. Use a pencil to mark your scores because you will want to come back and modify your scores in light of what you learn as you go further into the book.

The *House* section of the Diagnosis has a simple heat-loss calculation, which involves a quick measurement of the house. From this you will determine the approximate proportions of heat loss for the various parts of the building. The house is an easily measured object and its materials have been tested and rated by engineers. A statement of its heat losses can therefore be fairly

MAP OF HOUSEHOLD ENERGY

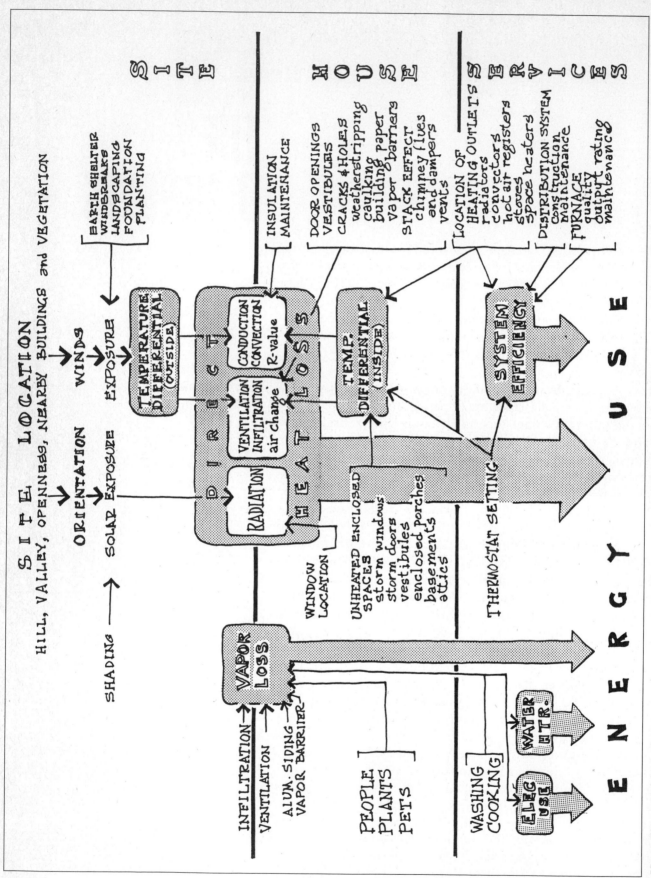

You will not understand everything on this map until you have read through the book, but you can get an idea right away of the number of factors that can affect energy consumption. Start with the small print around the edges, and follow the arrows, which should be read "has an effect on." Thus, for example: WINDOW LOCATION has an effect on RADIATION—which, in turn, affects ENERGY USE.

definite. The analyses of *Site* and *Services* are much more general and require a good deal of judgment. But evaluation there is just as important and profitable as for the House.

The evaluations of Site and Services are done with questionnaires. This part of the Diagnosis proceeds with a short discussion of the various elements of site and service to introduce a series of multiple-choice questions. The short explanation will help you to choose, from the range of possible answers, that condition that best describes your situation. Sometimes the same question is asked in more than one way. You don't have to answer all the questions to indicate your score for each series of questions. A consistent position on the table of answers (a vertical line that seems to center on your pattern of answers) is enough to indicate a score for that questionnaire; the score should then be placed on a scoring sheet, which can be removed from the Appendix. This same line on the table of answers may also indicate probable answers to the questions you couldn't answer yourself. In this way, the questions and answers may provide additional technical information about your home.

RELATIVE HEAT LOSS FROM VARIOUS PARTS OF THE HOUSE

As mentioned in Chapter 1, the amount of heat a building loses depends on the difference between the inside and outside temperatures. Yet each element of the house loses different amounts of heat at various rates. In the illustration, the gray blocks popping from the house represent the heat loss from the various surfaces—walls, windows and doors, ceilings, and floors. *The volume of each block represents the amount of heat lost from each part,* while *the distance out from the surface represents the rate.* Though small in area, a window loses heat at a high rate and is therefore shown with long blocks.

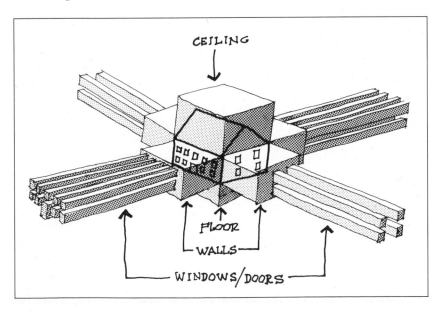

Heat loss can be reduced in a number of ways:

1. Lowering the thermostat. This results in shortening the projection of all heat-loss elements of the house in equal proportion.
2. Cutting down the rate of heat loss by means of insulation, etc. This shows up as a shortening of the projection of the heat loss from the particular element improved. In this figure, the attic has been insulated and storm windows added.
3. Closing off part of the house and not heating it. This in effect reduces the surface area of the house; the boundary walls between heated and unheated parts become, in effect, outer walls.

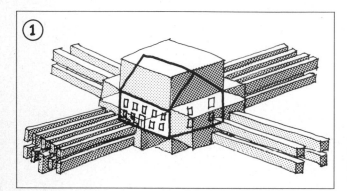

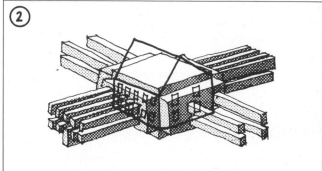

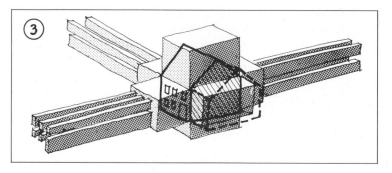

THE LEAKY BOAT

These gray block diagrams should illustrate something very important: There is only so much you can profitably do about any one area of the house before diminishing returns set in. Think of a boat with many leaks, both large and small. The passenger has only a certain amount of time and wherewithal to stop them up. Should he try to seal one leak perfectly, or should he spread his efforts around to attend to as many leaks as possible? The obvious answer is to distribute efforts among problems of greatest concern. A *balanced approach* will improve the seals for all the holes of the boat, beginning with the worst holes.

Compare the gray block for the uninsulated ceiling on page 29 to the block in figure #2, where the ceiling has been insulated with 6 inches of fiberglass. The squarish block has become rather like a pancake in #2. This corresponds to engineering statistics that show that 6 inches of insulation will reduce ceiling losses by 80 percent. Six more inches of insulation might reduce heat losses another 10 percent, and an additional 12 inches another 5 percent. No matter how much insulation you add to the ceiling after the first six inches, you are trying to reduce heat loss that has already been cut 80 percent, while the losses through the rest of the house remain unchanged. It is therefore more profitable to use the same money to improve the other parts of the house and get them into shape. The Diagnosis is a way to find the weakest and neediest elements of the house.

DOING A DIAGNOSIS

We will now quickly run through a heat-loss Diagnosis to clarify the concepts and vocabulary and to demonstrate the simplicity of the math. Because the attic and basement of our example house are unheated, the *basic heated envelope* consists of only the one floor of space between them. The heated envelope of a house is the part that is lived in and heated.

We want to figure out the relative heat losses through four elements of the envelope: *ceiling, floor, walls,* and *windows/doors.*

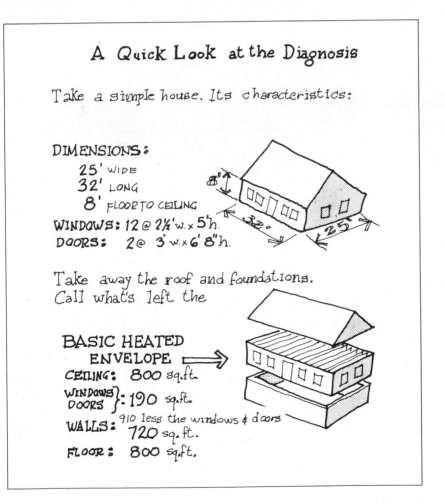

A Quick Look at the Diagnosis

Take a simple house. Its characteristics:

DIMENSIONS:
  25' WIDE
  32' LONG
  8' FLOOR TO CEILING
WINDOWS: 12 @ 2½' w. x 5' h.
DOORS: 2 @ 3' w. x 6' 8" h.

Take away the roof and foundations. Call what's left the

BASIC HEATED
    ENVELOPE
CEILING: 800 sq. ft.
WINDOWS
DOORS }: 190 sq. ft.
WALLS: 910 less the windows & doors
       720 sq. ft.
FLOOR: 800 sq. ft.

① R - VALUES

3 ← CEILING →

1 ← WINDOWS/DOORS →

4 ← WALLS →

2.5 ← FLOOR →

INFILTRATION

2 AIR CHANGES/HR
i.e, the number of times each hour that outside air replaces inside. Depend on tightness of windows, doors walls, etc.

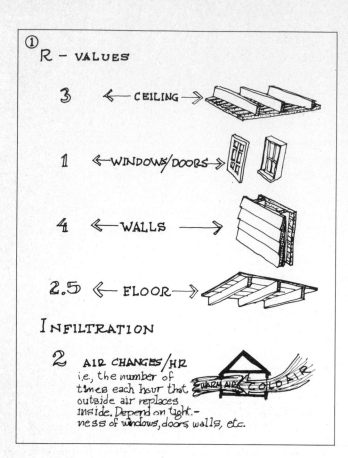

② EXPOSURE FACTORS

Heat loss from any surface of the Basic Heated Envelope may be reduced if it is partially protected from the cold. Exposure Factors vary from 0 (no heat loss) to 1.0 (fully exposed).

heat loss
inside temp.
intermediate temp.
outside temp.
less heat loss

ANY BLDG SURFACE
ANYTHING MODIFYING EXPOSURE

Exposure Factors

0.6 ← CEILING →
Attic protects ceiling from winds
vents

1.0 ← WINDOWS DOORS →
fully exposed

1.0 ← WALLS →
fully exposed

0.4 ← FLOOR →
bsmt partially heated by furnace, h.w. heater, pipes, ducts

doesn't apply ← INFILTRATION → exposure affects infiltration, but Diagnosis accounts for it in another way

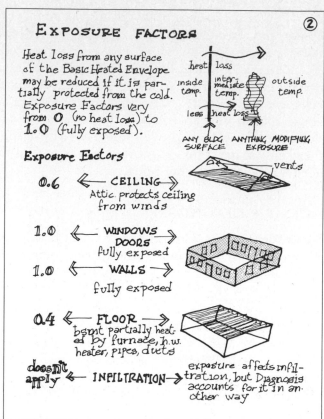

③ PROPORTIONAL HEAT LOSS in terms of $'s

Say the total heat bill last season was $500. This can be apportioned over each part of the house.

CEILING   17%   or $85

WINDOWS/DOORS   21%   or $105

WALLS   20%   or $100

FLOOR   14%   or $70

INFILTRATION   28%   or $140
TOTALS   100% $500

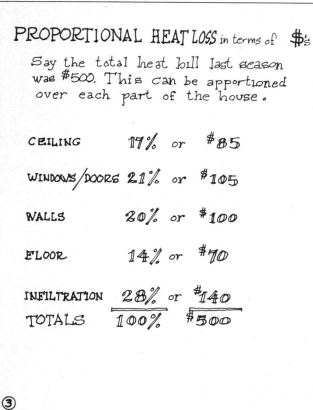

④ FIGURING PROPORTIONAL HEAT LOSSES

$$\frac{\text{AREA of surface (divided by 100 to simplify)}}{\text{R-VALUE of surface}} \times \text{EXPOSURE factor}$$

= HEAT-LOSS NUMBER

CEILING: $\frac{8}{3} \times 0.6 = 1.6$ which is 17% of

WINDOWS & DOORS: $\frac{1.9}{1} \times 1.0 = 1.9$ which is 21% of

WALLS: $\frac{7.2}{4} \times 1.0 = 1.8$ which is 20% of

FLOOR: $\frac{8}{2.5} \times 0.4 = 1.3$ which is 14% of

INFILTRATION* = 2.6 which 28% of
TOTAL HEAT-LOSS No. 9.2

* INFILTRATION EQUATION
$$\frac{\text{VOLUME of bldg} \times \text{Air changes} \times .02}{100 \leftarrow \text{to simplify}} = \text{HT-LOSS NO.}$$
ht. capacity of a cubic ft. of air

$$\frac{6400 \text{ cu.ft.} \times 2 \times .02}{100} = 2.6$$

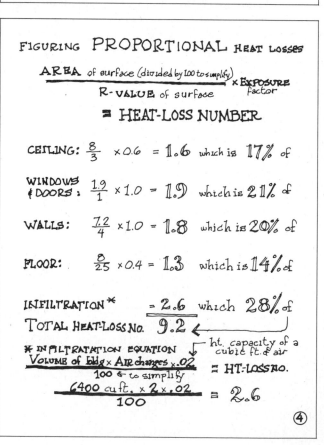

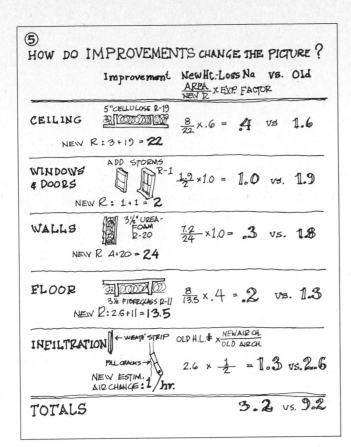

⑤ HOW DO IMPROVEMENTS CHANGE THE PICTURE?

Improvement		New Ht.-Loss No. vs. Old ($\frac{\text{AREA}}{\text{NEW R}}$ × EXP. FACTOR)
CEILING	5" CELLULOSE R-19 — NEW R: 3+19 = **22**	$\frac{8}{22}$ × .6 = **.4** vs. **1.6**
WINDOWS & DOORS	ADD STORMS R-1 — NEW R: 1+1 = **2**	$\frac{1.2}{2}$ × 1.0 = **1.0** vs. **1.9**
WALLS	3½" UREA-FOAM R-20 — NEW R 4+20 = **24**	$\frac{7.2}{24}$ × 1.0 = **.3** vs. **1.8**
FLOOR	3½ FIBERGLASS R-11 — NEW R: 2.5+11 = **13.5**	$\frac{8}{13.5}$ × .4 = **.2** vs. **1.3**
INFILTRATION	← WEATH' STRIP / FILL CRACKS → NEW ESTIM. AIR CHANGE: 1/hr.	OLD H.L.# × $\frac{\text{NEW AIR CH.}}{\text{OLD AIR CH.}}$ 2.6 × $\frac{1}{2}$ = **1.3** vs. **2.6**
TOTALS		**3.2** vs. **9.2**

⑥ IMPROVEMENTS ~ SAVINGS vs. COSTS

Difference	% of Old Fuel Bill	$ Saved per year	$ Cost	Years Payback
1.4	$\frac{1.2}{9.2}$ 15% of $500 → **15%**	$.30 × 800 **$75**	**$240**	$\frac{$240}{$75}$ **3.2 yrs.**
0.9	$\frac{.9}{9.2}$ 10% of $500 → **10%**	$25 × 12 / $30 × 2 **$50**	**$360**	$\frac{$360}{$50}$ **7.2 yrs.**
1.5	$\frac{1.5}{9.2}$ 16% of $500 → **16%**	$.80 × 720 **$80**	**$580**	$\frac{$580}{$80}$ **7.3 yrs.**
1.1	$\frac{1.1}{9.2}$ 12% of $500 → **12%**	$15 × 800 **$60**	**$120**	$\frac{$120}{$60}$ **2.0 yrs.**
1.3	$\frac{1.3}{9.2}$ 14% of $500 → **14%**	This material is cheap; say **$70**	**$100**	$\frac{$100}{$70}$ **1.4 yrs.**
6.2 ← TOTALS →	67% of $500	**$335**	**$1400**	$\frac{$1400}{335}$ **4.2 yrs.**

Infiltration is considered the fifth element of the house and is the difference between the envelope and the enclosure. A heat-loss number will be given to each of these elements, based on the area, R-value, and exposure of that part of the house.

The sum of the heat losses for these five elements equals the total heat loss from the house and may be compared to the fuel bill for the house. You can use the relative proportions of these numbers to figure out how much it costs to heat each element. As you consider improvements, you can then calculate how much difference each improvement will make.

About the Diagnosis

The Diagnosis uses a system of simple numbers and calculations to organize the decision-making process. The *relationships* between the numbers mean more than the numbers themselves.

If I tell you "A well-constructed wall has an R-value of 15," you receive a piece of information that by itself means little. If I then tell you "The window in the same wall has an R-value of 3," you can form a comparison, or *proportion,* that indicates that 5 times as much heat gets lost through each square foot of window as through the same area of wall. So, taking that window and a piece of wall of the same area, it would make sense to spend up to 5 times as much to raise the window's R-value from 3 to 4 (33

PROPORTIONAL ANALYSIS

percent) as to improve the wall's R-value from 15 to 16 ($6\frac{2}{3}$ percent).

That's one comparison and a valuable one. "But in actuality," you will reply, "there is almost always much more wall area to lose heat than window." True enough. You must also account for the *areas* of each to get a meaningful answer, one that allows you to make decisions. This is just what the Heat-Loss Numbers do— make it possible to compare not just two but ten things simultaneously: five R-values and five areas. For simple arithmetic, that's doing very well indeed.

SIMPLIFY But the simplicity doesn't occur automatically. It has to be made to happen. That is why we divide areas by 100: to make things *look* simpler and to concentrate attention on the "whole of the problem" before we get into the details.

You will need to measure your house. Define the basic form of the house and find the major dimensions before you follow the natural attraction to details. Learn to measure simply and approximately. Pace off horizontal distances and estimate ceiling heights. Use people for comparison to judge heights. One way to measure to the right degree of precision is to use a yardstick. Anything not
APPROXIMATE easily measured with this should be paced or estimated.

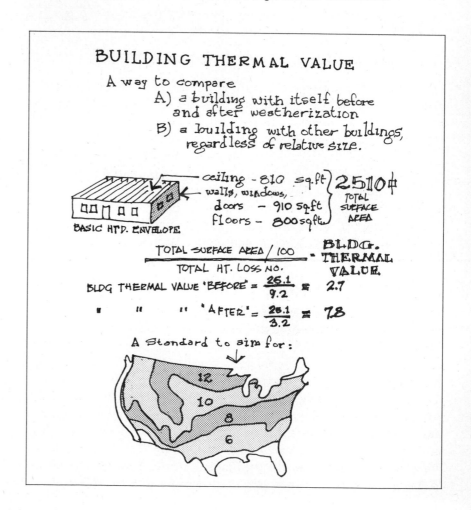

One long pace equals 3 feet
(or two regular ones equal 5 feet).

Estimate ceiling heights by comparison
with doorways.

$$\frac{15}{22} =$$ 0.68181818 !?!

THIS SHOULD BE ROUNDED
TO 0.7

Pocket calculators tell you more than
you want to know!

The Diagnosis is approximate. We will later discuss many other factors not included in the Diagnosis itself because they would only complicate it too much.

The scoring results are not supposed to be exact. One improvement affects another. For instance, putting on storm windows will not only cut window heat losses in half but will also reduce rates of infiltration. The numbers derived for payback periods are not iron-clad promises; they are merely indicators of the promise of one improvement relative to another. As a ranking of choices they are quite reliable.

An R-value is the resistance of a material to the flow of heat. It is used to describe the thermal value of a material. We use *thermal value* in a broader sense, however, to designate the worth of other improvements that, strictly speaking, do not have R-values.

We have avoided the use of U-values because they are more complicated and of little meaning to most homeowners. Technical literature and government regulations use U-values as a way of discussing the overall performance of walls and buildings; it is the reciprocal of the sum of the thermal resistances of an assembly. To complicate things further, some experts now group the entire heat-loss information of both wall and windows into an allowable U-value for a total wall system.

We develop this sort of overall performance information through the use of the Building Thermal Values, which is one number for the entire house. This number can then be used to compare a house to itself before and after improvement and also against other buildings, regardless of size.

The Heat-Loss Numbers found for each element of the house are, in effect, U-value descriptions. We have not bothered to provide the units for these numbers because we were only interested in comparisons in which the units would cancel out anyway. To ease the minds of the technically inclined, the units are British thermal units per degree Fahrenheit temperature difference inside and out.

R-VALUES

A U-value is an engineering expression for the overall performance of a building assembly.

$$U = \frac{1}{R + R + R \ldots}$$

$$= \text{Btu's/°F } \Delta t/\text{sq. ft.}$$

Heat loss numbers (HLN's) express the proportion of heat loss from each building element.

$$HLN = \frac{\text{area} \times \text{exposure}}{\text{R-value}}$$

$$= \frac{\text{Btu's/°F } \Delta t}{100}$$

Record data neatly and consistently. For those who will do more than one Diagnosis, it is important to get information down in a consistent form so that it can be referred to later and understood by the original diagnoser or somebody else. The Diagnosis worksheets (see Appendix) are devised to make this recordkeeping easier. The trick is to record all necessary details but no more. Write and draw clearly but be only neat enough for clarity.

RULES FOR THE DIAGNOSIS

Estimate dimensions by pacing off or other methods.
Round off any number to one decimal place.
Round off areas to the nearest 100 square feet.
(1,756 square feet becomes 1,800 square feet, or just 18.)
Record information neatly and consistently.

DIAGNOSING YOUR HOME

THE ANNUAL HEATING BILL — The first set of questions on the worksheet enable you to determine your heating bill for the year. In many cases, heating bills are combined with cooking and/or hot-water bills, so it is necessary to separate out the heating portion. The easiest way to do this is to add up the total fuel bills for an entire heating year from July to June. Then find a typical summer month when there was no heat on. This will show the fuel used for hot water and cooking only. Multiply this by 12 and subtract from the total yearly fuel bill to indicate the yearly heating bill.

Your house is probably not as simple as our previous example. It probably has wings or additions of various sorts. Some walls may have different R-values, and there are many other complications. These can be noted in various ways but when all is said and done, very little useful information will be gained by being

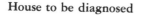

IF THIS FUEL IS DIFFERENT FROM THIS, NO PROBLEM IN FIGURING

HEATING

WASHING BODIES CLOTHES DISHES COOKING

SUMMER → FALL → WINTER → SPRING →

Some fuel gets used year-round.

House to be diagnosed

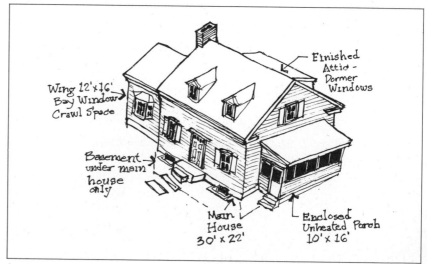

Wing 12'x16'
Bay Window
Crawl Space

Finished Attic - Dormer Windows

Basement under main house only

Main House 30'x22'

Enclosed Unheated Porch 10'x16'

concerned with minor variations, and the Diagnosis will become cluttered with little exceptions. Simplify.

Picture the Basic Heated Envelope in your head and then draw it step by step—the floor plan first and then the walls. Mark the outline of the heated envelope with a heavy line or a colored pencil on the sketches of the walls. Mark the windows and doors with dimensions to the nearest half-foot, noting whether they have storms or double glazing. Mark the parts of the envelope that have reduced exposure factors, as occurs in the example with the enclosed porch.

In most cases, variations from the normal box shape such as small jogs, bay windows, and so on may be safely ignored for the sake of simplicity. On the other hand, major additions to the heated envelope such as occupied basements and attics can be very important and must be dealt with properly.

An occupied but uninsulated basement may have considerable heat losses. In this case, the floor of the basement becomes the floor of the heated envelope. For masonry buildings, estimate the entire wall height from the outside and record the basement wall as only the depth of wall below ground level. For a wood house, it is easiest to record the entire basement wall as distinct from the wall upstairs. Beside this area measurement for the basement wall, estimate the percentages above and below ground level; for example, 50—50 percent, or 40—60 percent. This will later be entered into a table to determine the heat-loss rate for the basement walls. The volume of air in the heated basement should be included as part of the heated volume of the house.

The attic, like the basement, is usually outside the heated envelope. When it is heated, the ceiling of the attic replaces the lower ceiling as the cover of the heated envelope. Lump the attic walls and ceiling into one area number as the new ceiling area. With dormers and other projections, the surface area of the attic can be quite large and difficult to figure, so be kind to yourself and just estimate. The volume of an attic can also be cumbersome to figure, so simply multiply the floor area by the maximum ceiling height and use a factor from the table at the right.

Treat an attached garage or workshop like an enclosed porch since it helps to protect the walls of the house from severe cold. However, when these spaces are heated a good portion of the time they have to be included as part of the heated envelope. We will later describe the advantages of reduced temperatures for these parts of the house, but the best situation is not to heat them at all.

Unheated greenhouses and sunrooms on the south of the house are again much like enclosed porches, except that they often have a natural heat gain from the sun. To take advantage of this heat gain, these rooms are often opened to the house during the day and closed off at night. Analysis of this can get complicated, but it is safe to say that greenhouses and sunrooms well sealed against infiltration with two layers of glass will usually receive

The part of the wall protected by the porch gets an exposure value of 0.6.

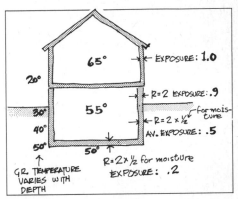

Basement heat losses are complicated: (1) Basement air temperature is lower than upstairs; (2) Typical concrete wall (R-2) loses half that because of contact with moist earth; (3) Temperature differentials, and thus exposure, are reduced deeper in the ground.

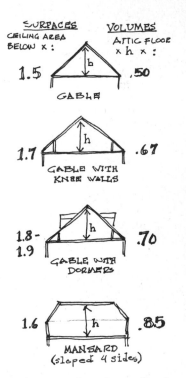

Volumes and surfaces of attics

more heat from the sun in eight hours than they lose over the course of a twenty-four-hour day. For our purposes, the wall between the house and such a greenhouse will lose no heat and its area may be subtracted from the wall area of the house.

COMMON WALLS

Many buildings in the city are placed one next to the other and share a common wall. This common or party wall is a surface with no exposure to the cold. This may also occur with the ceiling and floors of apartments. The area of any party wall, ceiling, or floor may be subtracted from the area totals for the building because it loses no heat.

HEATED VOLUME

We will need the volume of the Basic Heated Envelope to determine the amount of air in the house and the amount of heat lost by infiltration. The volume of air exchanged will include only the open spaces of the house and will not include closets and floor thicknesses where air does not circulate easily. To find the air-change volume, multiply the net height (the sum of the ceiling height for each floor) times the floor area of the living space (the interior floor area less 10 percent for closets, kitchen cabinets, furniture, and so on).

Building Construction and R-Values

What is a building made of and how is it put together? How well does the building do its job right now? This is the information needed to decide what improvements might be made. We get it by a more careful look at specific parts of the building. We can then figure the R-values and infiltration for the various parts of the house.

CEILINGS

The attic is the first and easiest place to check. If the attic is uninsulated and well ventilated, the only thing between you and the cold outside is a layer of lath and plaster. If the attic is poorly ventilated, its temperature might be halfway between house and outside temperature, and this air space will give some added protection. Yet there is no point in being more precise about attic constructions than to say that the R-value of any uninsulated ceiling is somewhere between 3 and 6, and we usually use 4. If this sounds imprecise, remember that with improvement this value should rise to almost 20. If your attic already has light pebbly vermiculite, fluffy gray rock-wool, or fluffy pink or yellow fiberglass insulations, you should estimate its thickness and add to the basic value of 4 the additional protection of this insulation as given by the table on page 39.

The R-values for walls are more tricky to determine. To begin with, there are two basic wall types in American homes. The first is the stud wall with a framework of vertical 2 × 4 studs spaced 16 inches apart. On the outside of the studs are placed sheathing, building paper, and siding, while on the inside you will find plaster, paneling, or any of various modern finishes. The importance of a stud wall for energy conservation is that it creates a 3½-inch air space in the middle of the wall for various kinds of insulating

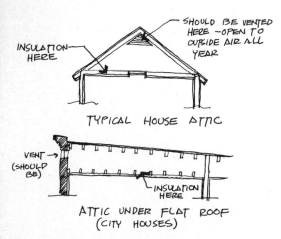

INSULATION HERE

SHOULD BE VENTED HERE — OPEN TO OUTSIDE AIR ALL YEAR

TYPICAL HOUSE ATTIC

VENT (SHOULD BE)

INSULATION HERE

ATTIC UNDER FLAT ROOF (CITY HOUSES)

Two different types of attics can have the same R-value.

R-VALUES FOR EXISTING CEILINGS
(total value found by adding components)

Finishes

¾" Lath and plaster	1
½" Drywall	1
¾" Acoustical tile	2
Air space	2
1" Attic flooring	1

Additional insulation per inch

Cellulose	3.5
Fiberglass	3.2
Mineral wool	3.0
Vermiculite	2.1

material. In very old houses, the studs may be 3 × 5's and spaced as much as three feet apart. There are other possible variations, such as plank walls with very few studs at all. One other thing to watch for in old houses is the practice of placing boards called *firestops* across the middle of these air spaces to keep fire from rapidly spreading up the entire length of a stud space. We mention these because they make it more difficult to blow new insulation down the length of this space.

There are many variations on the Great American Stud Wall. The sheathing of the wall is usually boards or plywood but may be panels of insulation in newer construction. The siding may be vertical boards, wood or asbestos shingles, fake bricks of asphalt, or vinyl and aluminum siding. The outside of a stud wall may even be plastered with stucco or veneered with a layer of brick. The interior of the house is a bit more conventional and will usually be either of plaster or Sheetrock. Over this may be placed interior finishes ranging from paint and wallpaper to wood and Formica paneling, or even brick and stone veneers. All these finishes, both inside and out, are usually as thin as possible and have little effect on the R-value of the wall.

The other wall type, more common in older buildings and apartments, is the masonry wall of brick. Concrete block and concrete block with brick are now used in modern masonry buildings. This construction may or may not have an air space, depending upon how the interior finish is affixed to the wall. *Furring* is a layer of wooden strips attached to the inside surface of the masonry wall to hold the interior finish away from the masonry, thereby creating an air space of ½ to 2 inches. A ½-inch space will help make the wall warmer but a minimum of 1½ inches is needed for blowing or foaming insulation into an existing wall.

How do you know what your wall construction is? Look at the outside; look at the inside; measure the thickness of the wall. A stud wall will usually be only about six inches thick overall and will have siding on the outside. Stucco (exterior cement plaster) on a stud wall will add 1 or 2 inches to the thickness. A brick wall

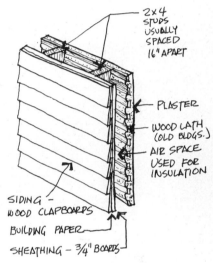

The great American stud wall

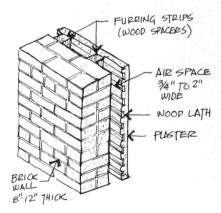

Masonry wall

will be visible on the outside and will be 8 inches or 12 inches thick (two or three bricks thick respectively) plus about an inch for the inside finish. An air space would account for another couple of inches, so an 11-inch or 15-inch wall will usually have an air space. A good Victorian house of about 1880 may have walls 20 inches thick with 12 inches of brick, 7 inches of air space and an inch of finish.

Thump the inside finish of a masonry wall. If it sounds and feels hollow, there is an air space. It will sound different as you thump your way along the wall and move across furring and over air spaces. Plaster placed directly on masonry will sound very solid. Stud walls, of course, always have an air space.

IS IT INSULATED?

Does your wall have insulation? How do you find out? If your home is more than twenty-five years old, it probably has no wall insulation, and some houses as new as ten years old were built without it. The easiest way to tell is to remove an electrical receptacle cover and look around the outside of the electrical box for fuzzy material. Very few masonry buildings have insulation and most of them don't even have room for it to be added, but we will get to that problem later.

R-VALUES FOR EXISTING WALLS
(total value found by adding components)

Interior air film	1
Wooden Stud Wall	
Interior finish	1
Air space inside wall	1
Sheathing	
¾″ boards	1
plywood	1
insulating panels	3
Siding	
wooden	1
asphalt	0
vinyl or aluminum	0
brick veneer	1
Masonry Wall	
Interior finish	1
Air space	1
8″ brick	2
12″ brick	3
8″ or 12″ concrete block	4
Insulation (per inch)	
Cellulose	3.5
Fiberglass	3.2
Urea-formaldehyde foam	5.5
Urethane foam	6.0
Styrofoam	3.5

Use the table on page 40 to determine the R-value of your present wall. Starting with the inside of the wall, take a value of 1 for the inside air film and then R-values for each layer component of the wall until you get to the outside. You should end up with about 4 or 5 for an uninsulated wall. A value of 5 is a safe average and will serve the purpose because an improved wall will be about 15. Again, measure and account for existing insulation.

The floor is treated much like a wall and R-values for various floor constructions are given in the following table. Unless your

R-VALUES FOR EXISTING FLOORS
(total value found by adding components)

Wood Floors	
One inch of wood flooring	1
Air space	1
Lath and plaster below	2
Carpet and liner	2–4
Concrete-slab-on-grade	
Insulation (per inch)	
Fiberglass	3.2
Styrofoam	3.5
Urethane foam	6.0

EXPOSURE FACTORS FOR FLOORS

This table gives temperatures for under the floor of a house on a day with winds of 15 mph, an outside temperature of 20° F, and an interior temperature 65° F. The table also translates this floor temperature to a percentage of full exposure.

	Temp. (F)	Exp. Factor
Building up on posts with floor directly exposed to outside air	20°	1.0
Crawl space enclosed but not tightly sealed	30°	.8
Slab-on-grade (colder near edges and warmer toward center)	30°	.8
Basement ½ below grade	40°	.6
Sealed crawl space	45°	.5
Basement ¾ below grade	50°	.33
Tight basement, ¾ below grade, with furnace and other heat-generating equipment	60°	.1

building is up on posts and open to the wind, the air under the floor will not be as cold as the outdoor air. This is accounted for through an *exposure factor* (see table on bottom of page 41).

The basement can be as much a problem as a help. Rooms in the basement that are used and heated must be analyzed and accounted for. The usual temperature of a basement is about 50° and it costs nothing to enjoy this shelter. The basement remains this warm in winter because it is directly connected to the earth, which has a lot of mass and is very resistant to changes in temperature. The earth is able to carry summer heat into the winter and winter coldness into the summer so that basement temperatures stay about the same year-round.

The trouble with heating an uninsulated basement is that you end up trying to heat up the entire earth below you. Heat applied to floor and walls is soaked up like a blotter and conducted into the ground with very little temperature rise at the wall surface. The thermal resistance of a 6-inch concrete slab in contact with the ground is only half that of a sheet of glass in contact with the air.

The R-value of concrete walls and floors in contact with earth is only about 0.6 for an 8-inch wall and 0.5 for a 6-inch floor slab. These values drop to about half these numbers when excess moisture is present, and we will later see how cold walls induce condensation and insure that uninsulated basement walls will be cold and damp. The exposure factors for basements are about 0.3 for floors and 0.7 for walls below grade.

WINDOWS AND DOORS

The last elements of the envelope are the windows and doors, and they are big losers of heat for their size. Their function is complicated by moving parts and they lose heat in a number of ways. For the moment, however, we will pretend that they are simple; we'll look into more subtle aspects later.

R-VALUES FOR EXISTING WINDOWS/DOORS

Primary window or door	1
Storm window or door	add 1
Insulating curtains closed half the time	add 1
Same kept closed 24 hours	add 2

To estimate heat losses through windows and doors, give an R-value of 1 for the primary window or door. To this add 1 for each additional layer of material that traps dead air; for example, storm windows or doors. After you have effectively stopped air infiltration, additional thermal values can be added by anything that slows convection. Shutters and curtains that are used only during the night hours should be added at half value because they are used half the time. These processes are discussed more fully in Chapter 4. R-values are shown in the table above.

The problems of energy conservation would be much easier if all heat losses were through the physical elements of the heated envelope as we have just discussed. Unfortunately, a lot of heated air sneaks out around and between these elements—as much as 50 percent of the heat loss of many houses. This devious process is difficult to calculate to achieve a precise number, yet it must be recognized and controlled through constant vigilance and a yearly program of maintenance.

Heating engineers figure that the total air volume of a normal building is exchanged for outside air once every hour through this process of infiltration; this gives an *air change rate of 1 per hour.* When the wind is blowing, cold air enters one side of the house and pushes warm air out the other side. Wind alone doesn't account for all infiltration; it occurs even when the outside air is still. Warm air will rise up the chimney if there is one, or will simply escape through cracks high in the building while cold air enters through lower cracks. In this way, vents, stairways, and any tall spaces act like chimneys and encourage the rise and loss of warm air.

Engineers who specialize in heating analysis have measured the amounts of air that go in and out of buildings, and have set up methods for calculating these amounts. One such method is called the "crack method." By judging how weathertight a window is, the length of a crack, and the wind speed, one can find in a table an estimate for the cubic feet of air that is supposed to pass through the crack (see the front cover).

This all takes time and patience and even then is not guaranteed to be accurate from one building to the next. A building in a windy location will have more infiltration than the same building in a sheltered area behind a hill or among evergreens or other buildings. The same building in the same location but twisted around to a different orientation will have yet another exposure value. The same building in the same location, with the same orientation, will have different infiltration for each winter, and so it goes. Once again, it is time to approximate.

A simpler method is to observe and compare the effects of infiltration. Because it is very hard to judge how much air is coming through particular cracks, it is reasonable simply to compare the general quality of one building against a range of others that have been carefully measured. Engineers have found that the air-change rate for most buildings is between $\frac{1}{2}$ and $1\frac{1}{2}$. From the table on page 44, choose the description and rate that seems appropriate to the condition of your house.

We have now completed the analysis of the house and should total up our figures to see how we have done. These are initial estimates and you may want to modify them, so work in pencil. For each part of the house you should have figures for area, R-value, and exposure. Heat-loss numbers are found by dividing area by R-value and multiplying the result by the exposure factor.

INFILTRATION

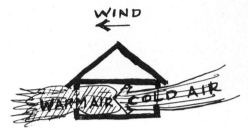
Air changes due to wind pressure

Chimneys draw in cold air.

These heat-loss numbers are compatible with infiltration heat-loss numbers and can be added together to arrive at a total heat-loss number for the entire house.

CONDITION OF BUILDING	NO. OF AIR CHANGES
Very tight building where the major air change comes from opening doors	$\frac{1}{4}$
New buildings, windows tight and well weather-stripped, doors with good storms and vestibules, no leaky fans, vents, or dampers, walls covered with building paper, and winds average 15 mph	$\frac{1}{2}$
Older buildings that are well-attended, windows rattle some, weather-stripping not perfect on doors but windows have good storms	1
Older building with very rattly windows, older storm windows and doors that are not tight, some caulking missing around window and door frames	$1\frac{1}{2}$
Same as above but no storm windows or doors. Other defects: holes in basement or foundation walls, leaky walls especially around windows and door frames	2 and 3
For each special item that leaks a lot of air, such as an exhaust fan, pet door, vents, loose dampers or double doors	add $\frac{1}{2}$
If wind speeds are higher than 15 mph the number of air changes may double or triple. Twice the wind speed gives three times the infiltration	3 to 5
Careful analysis of occupied urban homes in poor condition has discovered air change rates	up to 10

You may now compare your own building to others by computing the Building Thermal Value. This is found by dividing the surface area of the heated envelope (add floor, ceiling, and gross was areas) by the total heat-loss number. The table at the left gives percentile scores for the range of thermal values we have found for buildings in our area. (Readers who will kindly send the authors a copy of their scoring results will enable us to update this table for future editions.)

EVALUATING THE SITE

The conditions of the land on which your building sits will greatly influence your heating requirements. A house in Maine will certainly cost more to heat than one in Maryland, but we often forget that two houses in Maryland may have very different local conditions. You may have heard about "cold gulleys" or "warm hollows" that are only a few miles apart but are consistently 10–20° different in temperature. Even local Weather Service

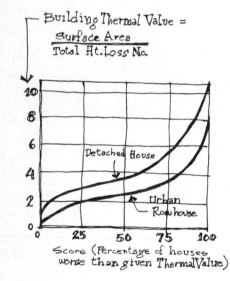

Scoring your house: If you live in a cold climate zone, the score had better be high.

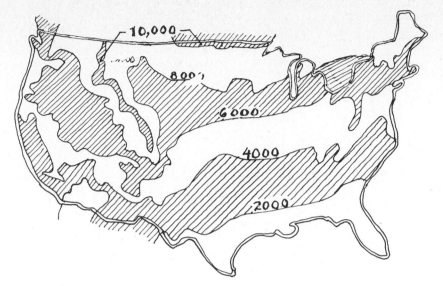

Severity of cold is measured in degree days per year. "Degree day" means the amount by which the *average outside temperature* for a given day is below 65°. Thus, a 30° average temperature over 24 hours yields 65 − 30 = 35 degree days. Degree days per year is the sum of degree days for each day.

statistics give only the large-scale picture; your home may experience a different "microclimate" altogether.

We have already begun to deal with site conditions in the Diagnosis through the use of *exposure factors,* which account for different temperatures in different parts of the house. As you quiz yourself in the following analysis of the site, you will discover a number of factors that affect your *overall* exposure. Your final score will be an indication of the extent to which you presently control exposure. A low score indicates room for improvement. Site improvements that reduce exposure will reduce heating requirements. Chapter 4 will develop this scoring system to indicate the cost/benefits of landscaping and good site planning.

There are two purposes for these quizzes: to attempt a comparative numerical evaluation of the site and in general to be thought-provoking. You will probably not be able to answer all the items because necessary information is further on in the book. Yet you needn't answer all the questions to get an idea of the general performance of your home. Answer the questions as best you can for a preliminary evaluation. You can always modify your estimates later as you gain a better understanding.

Exposure to cold is the primary cause of the heating requirement. A climatic atlas gives *degree-day* estimates of the amount of cold a building in different parts of the country is subject to, but these are regional averages. The *average winter temperature* for a given area is a more familiar number, but it is hard for a homeowner to average day and night temperatures for the entire winter. You can, however, call your local weather bureau and obtain both of these numbers over the phone. You should then readjust these numbers up or down depending upon whether your building is unusually exposed or protected.

EXPOSURE TO COLD

THERMAL DIAGNOSIS
2. Diagnosis

Name: _J. Anyperson_
Address: _Miller, MA_

Elevations:

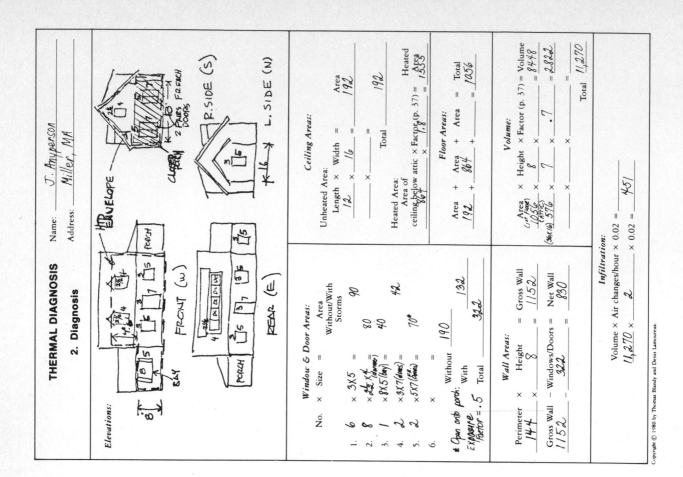

HTD ENVELOPE

P. SIDE (S)
L. SIDE (N)

CLOSET PORCH 2 PAIRS FRENCH DOORS

FRONT (W)
REAR (E)

BAY
PORCH

Ceiling Areas:

Unheated Area:
Length × Width = Area
12 × 16 = 192
_____ × _____ = _____
Total = 192

Heated Area:
Area of ceiling below attic × Factor (p. 37) = Heated Area
864 × 1.8 = 1555 = 1056
Total

Floor Areas:

Area + Area + Area = Total
192 + 864 + _____ = 1056

Volume:

Area × Height × Factor (p. 37) = Volume
(1st floor) 1056 × 8 = 8448
(attic) (36×16) 576 × 7 × .7 = 2822
_____ × _____ × _____ = _____
Total = 11,270

Window & Door Areas:

No.	×	Size	=	Area Without/With Storms	
1.	6	× 3×5	=	90	
2.	8	× 2½×4 (above)	=	80	40
3.	1	× 8×5 (bay)	=	40	
4.	2	× 3×7 (doors)	=	70*	42
5.	2	× 5×7 (doors)	=	70*	
6.		×	=		

\# Open onto porch:
EXPOSURE Factor = .5

Without: 190
With: 132
Total: 322

Wall Areas:

Perimeter × Height = Gross Wall
144 × 8 = 1152

Gross Wall − Windows/Doors = Net Wall
1152 − 322 = 830

Infiltration:

Volume × Air changes/hour × 0.02 = _____
11,270 × 2 × 0.02 = 451

Copyright © 1980 by Thomas Blandy and Denis Lamoureux.

THERMAL DIAGNOSIS
1. Description

Name: _J. Anyperson_
Address: _20 Cove Ave., Miller, MA_
Tel.: _248-3002_ Date: _11/2/79_

No. of units: _2_
No. of occupied floors: _2_

Building type: (1-family) 2-family apt. bldg.
Age of building: _1948_
Type of construction: (wood) masonry
Basement: (yes) no
Heating fuel: _oil_
Hot-water fuel: _electricity_ $/yr. _600_
Yearly heating bill: _$600_ $/yr. _200_
Remarks: _____

Plan of Building:

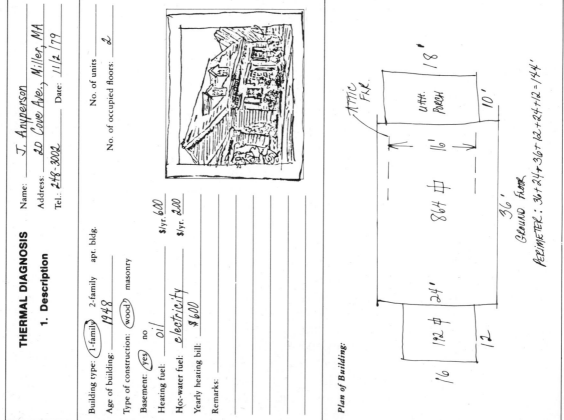

ATTIC FLR.
UTIL. PORCH 18'
10'
36'
864 ☐
192 ☐ 24'
12
16

GROUND FLOOR
PERIMETER: 36 + 24 + 36 + 12 + 24 + 12 = 144'

Copyright © 1980 by Thomas Blandy and Denis Lamoureux.

46 **ALL THROUGH THE HOUSE**

THERMAL DIAGNOSIS
4. The House in Context

Name: _J. Anyperson_
Address: _Miller, MA_

Evaluating the Site:

Exposure to cold	(1-40)	_10_
Exposure to wind	(1-30)	_15_
Exposure to sun	(1-30)	_5_

Exposure Percentile Score = _30_

Evaluating the House:

Building Thermal Value = $\dfrac{\text{Surface Area of Heated Envelope} (\div 100)}{\text{Total Heat-Loss Number (HLN)}}$

$= \dfrac{39.5}{12.9} = 3.1$ After Improvements: $\dfrac{39.5}{8.7} = 4.5$

Building Percentile Score (p. 44) = _25 %_   *Score After Improvements* _60 %_

Evaluating Services:

Heating Equipment

Furnace efficiency	(1-10)	_9_
Distribution efficiency	(1-10)	_4_
Temperature setting	(1-10)	_6_
Temperature setback	(1-10)	_2_
		_21_
Woodburning	(1-40)	_13_

Heating score (of 40) = _34_ ÷ 2 = _17_

Management

Space planning	(1-10)	_2_
Window management	(1-10)	_4_
Hot-water usage	(1-20)	_8_
Electricity usage	(1-20)	_12_
		_26_

Utility score (of 60) = _26_

Service Percentile Score = _43 %_

THERMAL DIAGNOSIS
3. Program of Improvements

Name: _J. Anyperson_
Address: _Miller, MA_

Diagnosis Summary:

Heat-Loss Number (HLN) = Area (÷100) × Exposure Factor / R-Value + Walls + Floors + Windows/Doors + Infiltration = Total HLN

Ceilings (unrated)

$\dfrac{1.9 \times 1}{3} \quad \dfrac{8.3 \times 1}{4} \quad \dfrac{10.6 \times .3}{3} \quad \dfrac{7 \times .5}{1} \dfrac{1.2 \times 1}{2} \dfrac{1.3 \times 1}{2}$

$.6 (+) 2.3 + 2.1 + 1.1 + .4 (+) 1.2 (+) .7 + 4.5 = 12.9$

Program of Improvements:

Ceilings: Add 6" fiberglass over wing. (Insulating attic is not feasible.)
Additional R-Value: $6" \times 3.2 / \text{inch} = 19.2$ New HLN: $(1.9 \times 1) \div (3 + 19) = .09$
Old HLN: .6 — New HLN: .09 = Change of: .5 Change: $\dfrac{.5}{12.9} \times 100 = 4$ % change
Area (200 sq. ft.) × $.30 /sq. ft. = Cost of change: $60
Total cost: $60 ÷ Total savings/yr: $12 = Payback: 5 yrs.

Walls: No change feasible.
Additional R-Value:
Old HLN: — New HLN: = Change of: Change: × 100 = % change
Area (sq. ft.) × $ /sq. ft. = Cost of change: $
Total cost: $ ÷ Total savings/yr: $ = Payback: yrs.

Floors: Insulate with 3½" fiberglass.
Additional R-Value $3\frac{1}{2}" \times 3.2 / \text{inch} = 11.2$ New HLN: $(10.6 \times .3) \div (3 + 11) = .23$
Old HLN: 1.1 — New HLN: .23 = Change of: .9 Change: $\dfrac{.9}{12.9} \times 100 = 7$ % change
Area (1060 sq. ft.) × $.15 /sq. ft. = Cost of change: $160
Total cost: $160 ÷ Total savings/yr: $60 = Payback: 2.7 yrs.

Windows/Doors: Add storms where none now (except French doors to porch).
Additional R-Value: + / for addition of storms   New HLN: $(1.2 \times 1) \div (1 + 1) = .6$
Old HLN: 1.2 — New HLN: .6 = Change of: .6 Change: $\dfrac{.6}{12.9} \times 100 = 5$ % change
Cost of change: $ 300
Total cost: $300 ÷ Total savings/yr: $ 30 = Payback: 10 yrs.

Infiltration: Reduce by half.
New HLN: $4.5 \div 2 = 2.3$
Old HLN: 4.5 — New HLN: 2.3 = Change of: 2.2 Change: $\dfrac{2.2}{12.9} \times 100 = 17$ % change
Cost of change: $ 60
Total cost: $60 ÷ Total savings/yr: $ 84 = Payback: .7 yrs.

New Diagnosis Summary:
Old HLN — Total of changes = New HLN
$12.9 - 4.2 = 8.7$
Change of 33 %

Overall Payback:
$\dfrac{\text{Total cost: } \$ 580}{\text{Total savings/yr.: } \$ 186} = 3.1 \text{ yrs.}$

Points:	10	20	30	40
1. What are the degree-day estimates for your region?	9000	7000	5000	3000
2. Is your site unusually warmer or colder than the regional average?	colder —— warmer			
3. What is the average winter temperature of your site?	10	20	30	40
4. How long is the heating season? (months)	9	8	6	5
5. Is your building settled into the ground or propped into the air? (pages 23, 77)	exposed —— buried			
6. Is your building sheltered by other buildings? (pages 23, 25)	no —— yes			
7. Is your building in the city or isolated out in the country? (page 25)	isolated —— clustered			

Enter _____ points onto scoring sheet.

EXPOSURE TO WIND

Wind affects local temperatures; it may also be a direct exposure factor. Charts of *wind-chill factors* indicate that winds in excess of 15 miles per hour will significantly reduce the apparent temperature. Ask your local weatherman for the typical and severe wind speeds of your region and again shade these numbers up or down depending upon the exposure of your site.

Points:	0	10	20	30
1. What are the typical wind speeds for your region? (mph)	30	20	10	5
2. What is their frequency?	often —— seldom			
3. What is considered a severe wind? (mph)	60	40	20	10
4. Is your site protected or exposed? (pages 74–77)	exposed —— protected			
5. Is the building protected by windbreaks? (pages 75–76)	no —— yes			

Enter _____ points onto scoring sheet.

The third major climatic factor is exposure to the sun, and this is usually a benefit in the winter. Local shelter pockets are caused by natural topography or groups of buildings that receive good sunlight yet are protected from the wind. You are very fortunate if you own such a property and are in an excellent position to turn your house into a complete solar home eventually; your heating bills are probably already surprisingly low. If, on the other hand, your building is in total shade, there may not be anything you can do to improve matters. We will later introduce methods that most people can use to improve the solar exposure and the wind shelter of a "neutral" site.

	Points:	0	10	20	30
1. Does your building receive winter sun or is it shaded by other buildings or evergreens?		shaded — exposed			
2. Does the building form create a suntrap? (pages 22, 24)		no — yes			
3. What proportion of the windows of the building face south?		few	half	most	all
4. How much southern window area do you have? (sq. ft.)		10	40	125	250
5. How many Btu's do these windows gather each day? (1000's)		10	50	150	300
6. What is this worth compared to oil heating for a season at $1 a gallon?		$14	70	140	300

Enter _____ points onto scoring sheet.

EVALUATING SERVICES

The relation between your building and its site determines how rapidly the building will cool and how cool it will get if the furnace is turned off. We must now analyze the heating system within the house to determine how well it performs it function. *The goal of this analysis is to determine the least expensive way to deliver heat to people in the home.* This breaks down into three systems: a system to create heat, another to deliver it, and a third to schedule the heating for those times when it is needed.

The centralized furnace is now the most common form of heat source. The efficiency of a furnace is defined as the percentage of heat energy made available to the house from the total energy produced by the combustion of fuel. Because some heat is always sent up the chimney, this efficiency is never better than about 80 percent, but it can drop to 50 percent or less as the furnace ages and deteriorates. Your furnace should be cleaned, tested, and adjusted at least every three years and preferably every year.

	Points:	1	4	7	10
1. What is the efficiency of your oil furnace? (page 80)		55	60	65	70%
2. How long since your oil furnace was cleaned and tested? (years)		3	2	1	this year
3. What is the efficiency of your gas furnace? (page 80)		65	70	75	80%
4. How long since this was cleaned?		10	5	2	this year
5. How old is the furnace? (years)		50	20	10	5
6. Is the furnace insulated or does it lose heat into the basement?			not —— insulated		
7. Is your furnace oversized? (page 82)				yes —— no	

Enter _____ points onto scoring sheet.

DISTRIBUTION EFFICIENCY

Distribution efficiency is a subject distinct from the operation of the furnace. Gas space heaters have a very efficient distribution system because heat is generated right where it is needed for 100 percent efficiency in delivery. As furnace systems move into the basement and require long systems of pipes or ductwork through cold spaces, more and more heat is lost before it arrives at a distant room. Some ductwork systems are so poorly designed that the air is cold upon arrival and efficiency of that part of the system approaches zero.

The placement of heating elements also affects the distribution efficiency. When heat is delivered to the center of a house, people and activities may cluster around the warmth and achieve comfort without having to heat the entire house equally. This differs from the usual practice, which places heating elements along exterior walls and especially under windows. This does produce more uniform temperatures throughout the interior of the house but assures greater heat losses through the envelope of the building. Homeowners will sometimes worsen this situation further by hanging curtains in front of the entire assembly and end up with their heating elements outside of the heated envelope altogether.

Accurate studies of the efficiency of distribution systems, as we define them, are unavailable. Most engineering solutions and procedures still encourage the creation of equally heated spaces even when this ignores the presence or absence of people who may or may not want the heat that is being delivered. We therefore estimate that modern distribution systems have efficiency values of 60–80 percent and may be as low as 40 percent. A truly central source of heat, such as a gas space heater or a wood stove, delivers heat at efficiencies of 80–100 percent. This is discussed in greater detail in the next chapter but we admit that this is an area of general ignorance and one of large potential savings as innovative work develops a body of knowledge.

	Points:	1	4	7	10
1. How efficiently is heat from the furnace delivered to you, the occupant of the home?		40	60	80	100%
2. Do heating ducts pass through cold spaces or exterior walls?			yes —— no		
3. Are heating ducts insulated?			no —— yes		
4. Is the house heated evenly or are the outer walls allowed to be cooler than central spaces? (pages 85–87)		evenly —— warmer in center			
5. Are heating ducts placed along exterior walls or located in the center?		perimeter —— central			
6. Are heat sources placed under windows?			yes —— no		
7. Does your house have 1, 2, or 3 floors? (page 88)		1	2	3	

Enter _____ points onto scoring sheet.

TEMPERATURE SETTING

The thermostat is the control device for most home heating systems and the setting of the thermostat has a major influence on the heating requirement of a building. Lowering the thermostat by 7° may immediately reduce fuel usage by 15 percent or more.

The lowering of the thermostat is still seen by many as a reduction of comfort. In the next chapter we will describe a number of other processes that function to create comfort. New homes are now being built with comfort systems that permit comfortable air temperatures as low as 60° and these systems may be developed in existing homes. The ability to achieve comfort at lower temperatures saves a good deal of energy and is a symbol of good energy management. As an incidental by-product, cooler temperatures are also healthier.

	Points:	1	4	7	10
1. At what temperature do you usually set the thermostat for the winter? (degrees)		72	68	65	60
2. Are large portions of the house allowed to have lower temperatures?			no — yes		
3. Are slippers and sweaters part of the usual evening clothing?			no — yes		
4. At what temperature are the bedrooms? (degrees)		68	65	60	55

Enter _____ points onto scoring sheet.

TEMPERATURE SETBACK

Most thermostats strive to maintain a particular temperature at all times. This is now acknowledged as a major waste of energy and has led to the marketing of timed thermostat setback devices that allow temperatures to fall during the night hours. This is one of several ways to time the delivery of heat to periods of occupancy. Another approach would be to allow lower general temperatures as the rule and then raise individual room air temperatures when and where needed with local heat sources (such as a wood stove). This second approach makes it unnecessary to raise the temperature of the entire house.

	Points:	1	4	7	10
1. Do you have an evening-setback thermostat?			no — yes		
2. How large is this temperature setback? (degrees)		1	4	7	10
3. Taking a different tack, do you maintain a low general temperature that is raised locally as needed?			no — yes		

Enter _____ points onto scoring sheet.

FIREPLACES AND WOOD STOVES

Anyone who burns wood is familiar with the processes of temperature variations and heat flow through the building. The final section of the heating portion of the test gives the woodburner a chance to account for the advantages of wood stoves and fireplaces. Despite all engineering statistics to the contrary, wood heating in both stoves and fireplaces can be used to reduce heating requirements; skill and experience in the art of woodburning will determine the amount of advantage that you obtain. Homes that are efficiently heated solely with wood may score a total of 40 points and may be excluded from the heating discussion altogether. Homes that are partially heated with wood should score that proportion of 40 points.

	Points:	0	13	28	40
1. What part of your heating is provided by woodburning?		0	30	60	100%
2. Are your fireplaces or wood stoves equipped with dampers?			no —— yes		
3. What is your woodburning efficiency? (page 89–92)		0	20	40	60%
4. Do your units heat by convection or radiation? (pages 89–92)			convection —— radiation		
5. Are your units located at the center of the room or against exterior walls?			perimeter —— central		

Enter _____ points onto scoring sheet.

MANAGEMENT

We have now analyzed every part of the house and home except what you, the homeowner, may be doing to help or hinder the process. If you wish to put a hand to it and invest some time, you can make a substantial difference in energy use simply by good or bad management. We have also chosen this part of the scoring sheet to indicate the effect of hot water and electricity usage on the total energy diet of the home. The need for efficient space heating has received plenty of attention, yet few people realize that *the annual energy for hot-water heating is often ⅓ the total fuel usage of a home* and *the energy needed to air-condition a modern* well-insulated *home for three months of summer is more than the energy needed to wood-heat many older houses for six months of winter.*

Space planning is closely related to heat distribution patterns, except that the distribution of heating elements is fixed while space planning is something you can change on a seasonal or daily pattern. In general, large amounts of space receive low efficiency values while smaller multi-use areas are more efficient. The ability to close off and individually heat smaller parts of the house permits major energy savings.

SPACE PLANNING

Points:	0	3	6	10

1. Are furniture arrangements for the winter different from those for summer?
   no —— yes

2. Is the source of heat in a room a conscious element of the furniture arrangement?
   no —— yes

3. Are the opening and closing of interior doors part of an energy-containment plan?
   no —— yes

4. Are portions of the house closed off the entire winter? (page 30)
   no —— yes

5. Are additional portions closed off for spells of severe cold?
   no —— yes

6. Is it possible to close off and heat individual rooms?
   no —— yes

7. How large is the minimal living area that can be isolated in severe cold? (sq. ft.)
   1000　700　400　200

Enter _____ points onto scoring sheet.

WINDOW MANAGEMENT

The variations of window treatments and use can greatly influence heating. The character of a room with large southern windows changes greatly with the time of day and the weather. Proper window management helps control such changes. Careful attention to evening protection gives a score of 3 while substantial amounts of southern glass, which provides heat for the house, may earn a score of up to 10.

Points:	0	3	6	10

1. Are large windows protected by insulated curtains or shutters?
   no —— yes

2. Are southern curtains and shutters opened and closed on a daily cycle?
   no —— yes

3. Are some non-southern windows sealed and insulated for the winter?
   no —— yes

4. Do you have a greenhouse or sunroom that catches solar energy and produces extra

Points:	0	3	6	10	*(Continued)*

heat for the house in winter?
(page 70)   no —— yes

5. Are windows protected from
the summer sun with
overhangs or blinds? (page
78)   no —— yes

Enter _____ points onto scoring sheet.

HOT WATER

Hot water can be a frightfully large expense for a larger family. The three major factors affecting your score on this item will be the temperature setting on the tank, the presence of insulation around the tank and long runs of pipe, and the pattern of use. A number of water-saving devices are available, but the cheapest change requires only a consciousness of the price we pay and a sincere desire to reduce consumption.

Points:	5	10	15	20
1. What is the thermostat setting on the water tank? (degrees)	160	150	130	110
2. Is the tank insulated?		no —— yes		
3. Are long runs of hot-water pipe insulated?		no —— yes		
4. What is the temperature of cold water going into the tank?	40	50	60	70
5. Do you make conscious efforts to reduce hot-water usage?		no —— yes		
6. How many gallons of hot water does your family use each week?	600	500	400	300

Enter _____ points onto scoring sheet.

ELECTRICITY USE

Electricity is a major environmental problem and is becoming increasingly expensive to produce. We all use many electrical appliances and it would be helpful to winnow out the least useful and most expensive.

Among the major users of electricity are 220-volt appliances; these include stoves, clothes dryers, large air conditioners, electrical heating circuits, water pumps, and some large pieces of workshop equipment. The other main categories of electrical use are the various electrical-resistance appliances, which heat up for use, and refrigerators, freezers, and small air conditioners.

	Points:	5	10	15	20
1. How large is the electric service bringing power into your house? (amps)		200	100	60	30
2. How many 220-volt appliances do you have?		12	8	4	2
3. How many electrical-resistance appliances do you own?		100	60	25	10

Enter _____ points onto scoring sheet.

SUGGESTIONS FOR FURTHER READING

In the Bank ... or Up the Chimney, by the Department of Housing and Urban Development. This booklet provided the starting point for our Diagnosis and is still very commonly distributed throughout the country. Very conscientiously done, but their procedure is all but impossible to follow through.
Available from the U.S. Government Printing Office.

Retrofitting Existing Housing for Energy Conservation: An Economic Analysis, by Stephen Peterson for the U.S. Department of Commerce. An overly precise evaluation that verifies common sense in a language most of us can't read. At least, it does indeed verify.
Available from the U.S. Government Printing Office.

Community Planning Guide to Weatherization, by Stephen Peterson. In this little pamphlet, Stephen summarizes his entire previous document in one excellent page of general guidelines, around which an entire national program of weatherization is organized.
Available from the Community Services Administration.

Applications of Climate Data to House Design, by the U.S. Division of Housing Research.
Available from the U.S. Government Printing Office; 1954.

4. IMPROVING THE HOME

IMPROVING THE HOUSE

Armed with a Diagnosis of your existing situation, we may now review various improvement options. Each improvement opportunity can be discussed and considered in relation to your own home and we can develop a unique series of numerical summaries to indicate the best options for your particular home. We will use a process of cost/benefit analysis that compares the cost of each improvement with how much energy and money it saves each year to indicate how many years it takes to return an investment. Improvements with the shortest *payback periods* are thereby indicated as first priorities. This method of analysis is useful regardless of the size of your building or the limits of your budget. For any budget there is an optimal program of improvements, which rests on a *balanced approach* that distributes available resources among the greatest elements of heat loss. Remember the lesson of the leaky boat.

This chapter will enable you to choose the kinds of improvements that are appropriate to your home, while the next chapter will provide the price and performance information for particular materials. While developing your program of improvements you will be flipping constantly between the two, but this seemed more useful than placing such information in the Appendix.

Reducing Infiltration

The first and most valuable way to improve the house is to reduce air infiltration. The benefits are obvious and the cost is low. If all you do about weatherization is to go around the building from top to bottom finding the places where those cruel drafts originate and correct them by whatever method seems practical, you will lower your fuel bill noticeably. You will also be much more comfortable because the body doesn't like handling different temperatures at different places which is just what a draft creates.

What we want to do in concept is to deal with infiltration by creating a container that permits as little air as possible to enter and leave the building. Stopping infiltration through a window allows you to get maximum benefit from the extra air spaces that you create with storm windows, shades, and curtains. The benefits of curtains, insulation, and most other improvements will all be drastically reduced if infiltration is not brought under control.

DETECTING INFILTRATION

On a cold day—the colder the better—examine each room of the building, looking and feeling for drafts. Stand still for a full minute in each space with your eyes closed and try to feel the drafts going by. By standing still you will be producing less heat yourself and will be more sensitive to differences in heat around you. Run the back of your hand around each window and outer door. Drafts are especially common in doorways, near windows, and in halls, stairways, and other passageways. When you find an especially mean draft, track it down and plug it up. Chances are very good that it comes from a big hole or even something left open.

There is such a thing as *exfiltration,* too. On a windy day the air piles up on the windward side of the house, but a vacuum is formed on the leeward side. This vacuum pulls warm air out of the house. You won't detect a cold draft there but cigarette smoke or a candle flame held next to such cracks will indicate air motion.

Diagram of infiltration

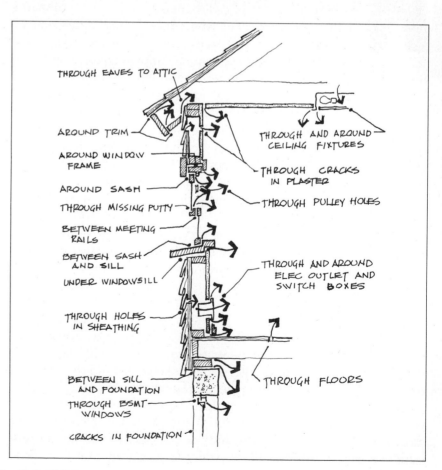

THROUGH EAVES TO ATTIC
AROUND TRIM
AROUND WINDOW FRAME
AROUND SASH
THROUGH MISSING PUTTY
BETWEEN MEETING RAILS
BETWEEN SASH AND SILL
UNDER WINDOWSILL
THROUGH HOLES IN SHEATHING
BETWEEN SILL AND FOUNDATION
THROUGH BSMT WINDOWS
CRACKS IN FOUNDATION

THROUGH AND AROUND CEILING FIXTURES
THROUGH CRACKS IN PLASTER
THROUGH PULLEY HOLES
THROUGH AND AROUND ELEC OUTLET AND SWITCH BOXES
THROUGH FLOORS

The same process occurs in the upper parts of the house; warm air leaves by way of the attic doorway as cold air enters the house downstairs.

The best way to create the container is to improve the interior finishes. There are several good reasons for this, the most obvious being ease and economy. Interior cracks can be easily located and filled using modern patching compounds that remain flexible. Interior materials are cheaper and easier to use, less likely to deteriorate, and the job can be done conveniently in any season.

By contrast, working on the exterior has a number of disadvantages. Trying to create a sealed container from the outside is much more difficult because there are so many more joints of materials that are subject to deterioration from the weather. Getting to many places outside the house involves climbing ladders and other inconvenient and dangerous operations.

However, the most important reason for not attempting to seal up the outside of the house has to do with moisture within the walls. Humidity that escapes from within the house, as well as any water that enters the wall from the outside, needs to be released to the outside. The interior wall, as the vapor barrier, should be the primary barrier to infiltration as well, while the outside weather barrier should be left somewhat permeable to allow for *cold side venting*. None of this is intended to imply that exterior maintenance should be neglected. Our point is only that the process of sealing up the outside of the house is a bad way to deal with *infiltration*.

A common source of cold air is through *breaks in the interior finish*. These breaks are created when old buildings settle and when builders poke new homes full of holes for electrical boxes, switches, and fixtures. Recessed ceiling fixtures are particular villains because they require ventilation and you are not permitted to place insulation near them; you should at least be sure the cover fits tight to the ceiling to slow the rush of air into the attic. Take a little extra time whenever you repaint to fill all the cracks in the plaster, and give special attention to the junction of window frame with wall. A little plaster stops a lot of wind.

It has become fashionable in the remodeling of old city houses to remove interior plaster to expose bare brick walls. This is often very handsome and we have done some of it ourselves. This practice should be limited to interior and party-walls because an exposed brick wall lets through an enormous amount of air, which the plaster stops quite well. The difference is in the order of 100 times, according to the ASHRAE book, which is the mechanical engineer's bible.

Once the walls, floors, and ceilings have been sealed against infiltration, the windows remain as the weak points of the container. Interior finishes and vapor barriers are apt to be open here at many points. The junction of the casing with the wall finish should be sealed (to the wall surface) as well as the various wood joints of the window frame itself. The best material for this

CREATING A CONTAINER

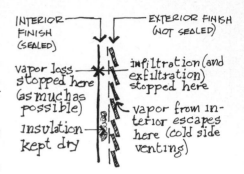

Infiltration control (incorrect method)

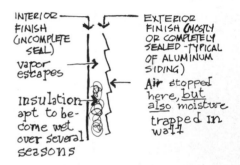

Infiltration control (correct method)

SEAL OPENINGS IN THE CONTAINER

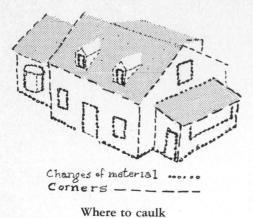

Changes of material ....
Corners − − − − −

Where to caulk

WEATHER STRIPPING

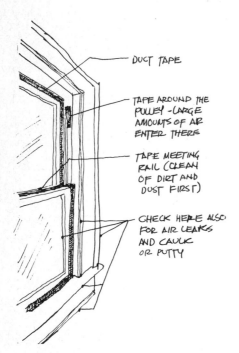

DUCT TAPE

TAPE AROUND THE PULLEY - LARGE AMOUNTS OF AIR ENTER THERE

TAPE MEETING RAIL (CLEAN OF DIRT AND DUST FIRST)

CHECK HERE ALSO FOR AIR LEAKS AND CAULK OR PUTTY

Taping windows is very effective.

is a latex-based patching compound, which adheres well to paint and wood and is flexible and durable. The way to seal operating windows is again from the inside either with tape or by means of a second layer of glazing, which is best placed and sealed within the primary window. This follows the above-mentioned *principle of containment—seal the innermost layer and vent the outer layer.*

Caulking can be helpful to control infiltration around windows and is very important in the control of rain penetration. Caulking is the great reconciler, the stretcher-and-shrinker that bridges gaps and keeps joints sealed. Important joints to caulk occur at changes of materials and at edges of a surface. Whenever window openings or doorways meet regular wall surfaces, walls meet foundations, frame walls meet masonry, or whenever things should be touching and are not, do some caulking. Openings for cold side venting are intentional and must be recognized and left open.

Which caulking material should you use? Better materials do a better job and last longer. There are materials that span up to half an inch and last up to twenty years. They are more expensive than ordinary materials but are worth the money for a job that lasts that long.

You cannot, of course, caulk parts that need to move. The operating parts of windows and doors call for *weather stripping.* Weather stripping also bridges gaps and reconciles the contradictions we impose on windows and doors. It is hard to make a seal on something that must be allowed to move, and these seals wear out after a while.

Doors are the big problem. They have about 20 feet of perimeter that must be sealed. A door that is opened and closed many times a day will wear, bruise, warp out of shape, and cease to fit tightly. It will expand with summer moisture and wear heavily, and then shrink in the winter and leave gaps. The threshold at the bottom must take foot traffic and not trip people and still fit tightly when the door is closed. Something durable, thin, and flexible has to be fitted between the door and the opening to make up these differences.

A permanent professional job of weather-stripping the front door that costs as much as $100 may still be a good deal. It may take a craftsman half a day to carefully install heavy-duty metal interlocking weather stripping, but you will have a job that lasts for years and will need no further attention. With savings of up to $35 a year, you will get your money back after only three years. A less expensive application of exposed weather stripping for only $5–10 may work as well for a while but may quickly deteriorate and need replacement.

Windows are easier to weather-strip than doors. They are generally smaller and receive less wear. Many of them need not be opened at all in winter and can be sealed with various tapes or rope caulk that can be removed in the spring. Severe infiltration around a worn window is a good reason to replace or rehabilitate the window; either way is economically reasonable. A number of

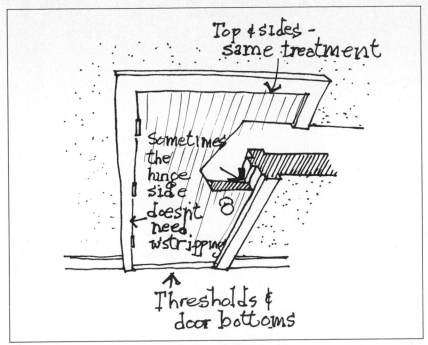

Weather-stripping doors

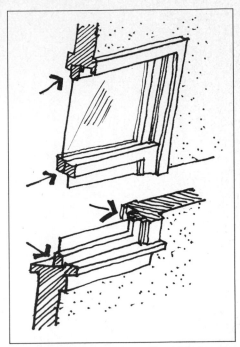

Windows leak air along four kinds of joints. Each requires a slightly different application of weather stripping.

new products make this process easier for the do-it-yourselfer.

An open door is a very large opening and its heat losses can be greatly reduced by introducing an *air lock.* This is simply a construction that allows you to enter and leave a building without letting precious heat escape. Air locks become more important as the climate becomes harsher. Imagine you are out in space and want to enter the Starship *Enterprise.* If you just parked your ship nearby, marched up to the *Enterprise,* and opened the front door, the entire contents of the spaceship would be blown out into space instantly.

The same sort of thing happens when you open the front door of a house in winter. In just two seconds 200 cubic feet of warm air rushes out and cold air takes it place. A *vestibule* can reduce this to a small fraction because it creates a large still air space that makes it possible to keep one door closed at all times and prevents winds from blowing directly into the house. When the door is not in use, it serves as a regular storm door.

The most commonly forgotten opening in the house is the chimney. It is a major cause of infiltration. A chimney is designed to draw warm air up and out of the house; the more effective the chimney, the greater will be the draft it creates. Warm air rising up the chimney causes a vacuum inside the house and encourages cold air elsewhere to fight its way in. Most fireplaces have *dampers* to control the draft; these should be kept closed when the fireplace is not being used. A glass enclosure placed in front of the fireplace is even better because it can be closed at the end of the evening before the fire is out.

Any fire in the house consumes oxygen and gives off smoke and gases that must be exhausted up the chimney. This exhaust

A VESTIBULE MAINTAINS A CONTAINER

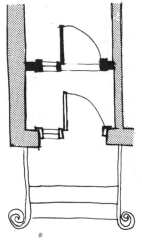

One type of vestibule created inside a large hall

CHIMNEYS

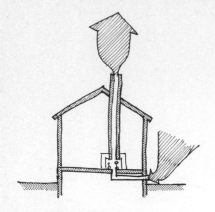

A ducted air supply for combustion reduces infiltration.

represents a lot of heat—often more than the fire contributes to the room—and can take with it a lot of precious room air. To preserve this valuable interior air, the combustion process of fireplaces and furnaces should be adjusted with dampers and measured air supplies to provide just the amount of air needed to support combustion. Ideally, outside air should be supplied directly to the fire by way of a duct. This system can be used for fireplaces, wood stoves, and furnaces.

Your chimney is not your only chimney; any opening through the ceiling is also a flue. A stairway to the attic functions this way; the door to it should be weather-stripped. Recessed ceiling lights are passageways for air, as are kitchen and bath exhaust units that vent to the attic or out-of-doors without dampers. Very likely to be overlooked are things like abandoned and uncapped plumbing vents, and roof ventilators that are concealed above suspended ceilings. Lightweight suspended acoustical ceilings generally func-

COSTS AND BENEFITS OF CORRECTING INFILTRATION

In our example house, infiltration accounted for 3.9 units of heat loss or about $\frac{1}{3}$ of all heat loss. If the fuel bill for the year was $750, then $\frac{1}{3}$ of that or $250 was the cost of infiltration. Cutting the rate of infiltration in half will then save $125 each year. The following is an example of what might be done to improve such a house to $\frac{2}{3}$ or $\frac{1}{3}$ its present infiltration loss.

	Heat-Loss Numbers		Savings	Cost of Improvement
Through the wall	0.8			
Filling cracks in plaster; exterior caulking	0.5		$20	$40
Putting gaskets on electrical boxes		0.3	$15	$10
Out the front door	1.3			
Weather stripping	0.7		$35	$15
Vestibule		0.4	$20	$150
Out the windows	1.3			
Weather stripping	0.8		$30	$25
Storm windows		0.4	$30	$150
Other openings	0.5			
Closing dampers and vents	0.4		$6	
Pet doors weather-stripped		0.3	$6	$2
	3.9			
	2.4		$91	$80
		1.4	$71	$312
Annual expense due to infiltration	$250		$162	$392
	$150			
	$85			

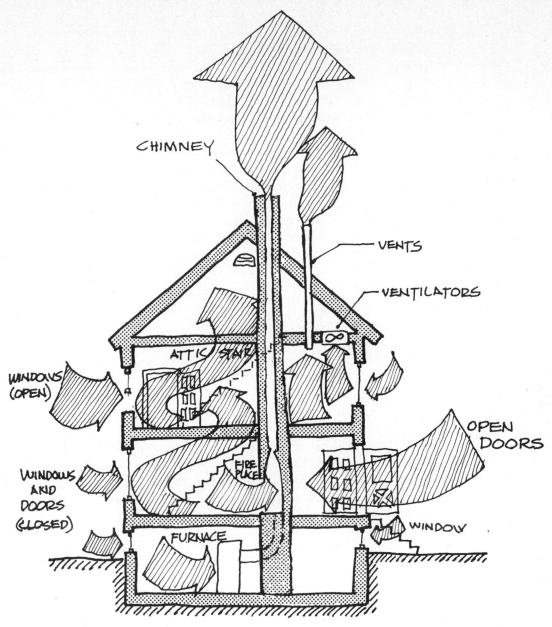

CHIMNEY

VENTS

VENTILATORS

WINDOWS (OPEN)

ATTIC STAIR

OPEN DOORS

WINDOWS AND DOORS (CLOSED)

FIRE PLACE

WINDOW

FURNACE

"Chimneys" of various kinds and other openings create huge infiltrations.

tion poorly as insulation because of the incredible lengths of joints that allow heated air to force its way up through. When air can escape through numerous openings such as these, the number of air changes per hour can be four, five, or even more.

Improving Windows

Windows have a major effect on the character of a room; the way you develop and equip them against the winter cold can be the most enjoyable and rewarding aspect of energy conservation. Very few people want to brick up half their windows as a way of cutting heat losses when they can get the same results by using available techniques and materials to improve the windows themselves. You can not only keep all your windows but even add more to pick up sunlight and still reduce your present window heat losses.

GLASS AND AIR FILMS

Glass by itself has almost no thermal resistance. The only things that prevent heat from rushing through glass are the thin films of still air on either side, with R-values of 0.85 inside and 0.15 outside for a total R-value of about 1.0 for a window. A single layer of glass with its air films has at least three times the heat loss of an uninsulated wall.

The way to improve the thermal resistance of a window is to increase the number of air films by increasing the number of layers of transparent material. These may be glass but any other transparent material will do as well. The main reason to use rigid materials is to provide protection from the wind and from handling. In fact, windows are now being constructed with many layers in which central layers are of thin and inexpensive plastic films. Each layer of glass or plastic creates an air film and provides a thermal resistance of 1. If air infiltration is brought under control, any additional layer of material added to a window will isolate more layers of still air and each will have a thermal resistance of 1.

The functional reason for double- and triple-layered windows is to create higher temperatures next to the inside glazing, which will therefore lose less heat, cause less discomfort, and have fewer condensation problems. Storm windows may be installed inside or outside the existing window, but in all cases the innermost layer should be sealed tightly to prevent both infiltration and loss of humidity. The outer layer should have a *small* amount of venting to let out any moisture that does escape from within. This is where triple-track aluminum storms are at a disadvantage compared to

1 Thickness
EXT. AIR FILM — .2
GLASS OR PLASTIC — 0.0
INT. AIR FILM — .8
R-VALUE APPROX. 1.0

2 Thicknesses
EXT. AIR FILM —.2
GLASS OR PLASTIC 0.0
AIR SPACE (¾"-4") 1.0
INT. AIR FILM — .8
R-VALUE APPROX. 2.0

3 Thicknesses
R-VALUE APPROX. 3.0
E, t, c.

The insulation value of windows comes from interior and exterior air films.

STORM WINDOWS

Comparison of triple-track storms with fixed (A sealed inner window is assumed in both cases.)

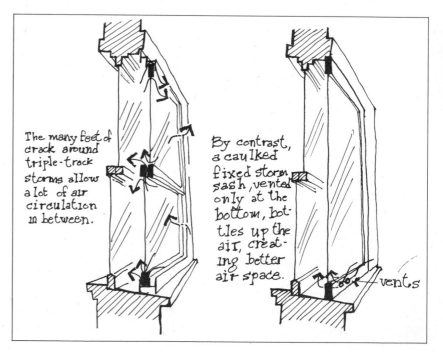

The many feet of crack around triple-track storms allow a lot of air circulation in between.

By contrast, a caulked fixed storm sash, vented only at the bottom, bottles up the air, creating better air space.

vents

a well-sealed nonmovable wood storm with a single vent at the bottom. The aluminum one, in order to allow convenient switching of storm with screen, has many feet of crack all around, which allows far too much air circulation. A sealed interior storm is the best of the three.

Wooden storm windows are still in use and, though a bit heavy and cumbersome to install and remove, perform at least as well as modern storms. The wooden frame is a much better insulator than aluminum and its seal to the house is apt to be better. They can be made in a home workshop or sometimes found secondhand. The process of putting up and removing wooden storms can be a good time to survey the condition of the house and make minor repairs.

The popular alternative to wood storms is aluminum. They are relatively inexpensive, easy to use, and easy to install. *Triple-track windows* come complete with screens and two sheets of glass, each covering half the window, and all of which remain within the unit year-round. This saves the trouble of removing the windows and provides safe summer storage. Aluminum will also relieve the necessity to paint the primary window frame as often. The disadvantages of aluminum windows are that they sometimes fit poorly, rattle in their tracks for greater infiltration, and conduct more heat through the frame.

An extra pane of glass can also be placed inside the primary window; this is called a *storm pane.* The main advantage of this interior storm is that it can be easily installed and completely sealed. Infiltration is effectively stopped and the problem of condensation behind the interior glazing is prevented. These storm panes come as rigid sheets of glass or plastic, or as plastic films.

Simple *roll shades* are used primarily to provide privacy and reduce summer heat gain, but they can be helpful when lowered on winter evenings and secured to the windowsill to trap a layer of still air. Roll shades are now available in clear plastic films with magnetic seals at the bottom, sliding tracks for the sides and an air-tight top closure. These shades are inexpensive, seal the window against condensation, and provide the same protection as a rigid storm pane. Roll shades are available with multiple layers of plastic film and with aluminum films to reduce radiant heat loss.

Curtains and drapes are a traditional solution to window heat losses. *Draperies* are usually thick and heavy, have good R-values, and are very good at stopping radiant heat losses. Good ones have an elaborate top enclosure and reach all the way to the floor to prevent air circulation, but they are also very expensive.

Modern *curtains* are lighter and less expensive than drapes. Many are foam-backed and have removable liners for easy laundering. They function to reduce radiant exchange with the surface of the glass, but careful detailing that closes off the top and bottom will allow these also to trap still air. Curtains are now being made

ROLL SHADES

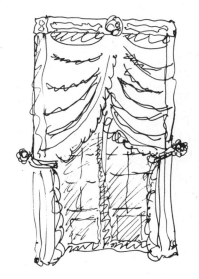

Draperies out of the past

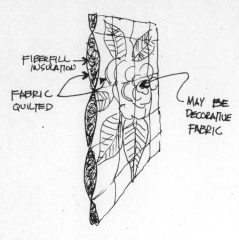

FIBERFILL INSULATION

FABRIC QUILTED

MAY BE DECORATIVE FABRIC

Curtains and shades may be made of quilted layers of fabric with insulation between.

SHUTTERS

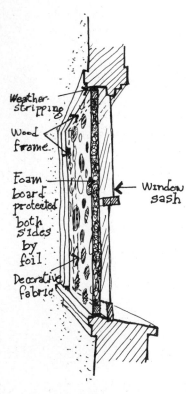

Weather-stripping

Wood frame

Foam board protected both sides by foil

Window sash

Decorative fabric

Simple interior shutter

by homeowners that are quilted with up to 4 inches of filler, a substantial amount of insulation. These are very effective at preventing heat loss but require special detailing to prevent severe condensation onto the glass behind. (In Chapter 5 we will provide instructions for making such quilted curtains.)

Shutters are yet another option for windows. Old houses often have handsome wooden shutters that fold into the wall thickness or back against the interior wall. Modern ones are available and are commonly sold as decorator items.

Insulating interior shutters are being made by homeowners and can turn a window that is not in use into something approaching an insulated wall. These can be made from rigid-board insulation, a wooden frame, weather stripping, and whatever wallpaper or fabric that you decide is appropriate to the decor. (Plans for these will also be found in Chapter 5.) It is important that such shutters close tightly to prevent condensation.

Exterior storm shutters have traditionally been placed on houses and closed in severe weather, but few are used today. They are

THE COSTS AND BENEFITS OF IMPROVING WINDOWS

A similar analysis to the one performed for infiltration can be easily performed for the wide range of window improvements; we will outline just how to do this at the end of this chapter. The following table gives the predictable thermal value of each improvement and an approximation of its *cost on a square-foot basis.*

	Material ($)	Labor ($)	R-value
The Window			
Replacing broken glass	1.50	——	1
Restoring old windows using			
new metal sliding track	1	2	1
Replacing the window	5–10	2	1
Storm Windows			
Wooden storms	2	1–2	1
Aluminum triple-track	2–3	1–2	1
Storm pane	1–2	1	1
Roll Shades			
Simple roll shades	1–2	1	1
Multiple-layer shades	3–5	2	4–10
Curtains			
Draperies	5–10	5–10	2–4
Curtains	1–3	2–3	2
Quilted curtains	2–4	2–3	4–10
Shutters			
Interior wooden	2–5	2–3	2
Insulating foam shutters	1–5	2	4–8
Exterior shutters	1–3	1–3	4–8

inconvenient because you have to go outside to open or close them or else use complicated and expensive mechanisms for closing them from within. Exterior sliding panels are quite likely to come into common usage as simple operating mechanisms are developed and mass-produced. The advantages of exterior shutters are the reduced need for precision fit and no problem of condensation.

Anything that impedes air motion around a window can thereby reduce heat losses. Deep reveals (wall thicknesses), both inside and out, and more frequent horizontal mullions will interrupt the path of cold winds and drafts coming across and down a window. A window with horizontal mullions twice as close will cut down the draft speed to less than half. French doors will therefore have a smaller heat-loss rate than the same area of plate glass. Elaborate woodwork around Victorian windows similarly reduced their wind exposure. By the same principle, some solar collectors use a honeycomb arrangement of thin plastic placed between two layers of glass to reduce heat losses by segmenting the paths of convection. These could also be used in windows. Windows filled with plants will similarly slow air motion and cut convection losses. The plants may, however, get in the way of the operation of shutters and curtains.

IMPEDE AIR MOTION

Insulating the Attic

The simplest home improvement is to insulate the attic. It costs very little, you can do it yourself, and you will feel immediate benefits. The usual materials are fiberglass or cellulose. You can carry them up into the attic in bags or rolls and put them in yourself, or rent a machine or hire a specialist to pump the stuff up into the attic through a large hose. If your attic has floorboards you will have to lift up a few and have the insulation blown into the spaces.

Attic insulation is one place where you don't have to worry about providing a tight vapor barrier if the attic is correctly vented. Moisture that passes through the insulation will simply be carried out-of-doors by air motion. If your attic is not ventilated, you should *provide a vapor barrier on the warm side of the insulation*. However, this is almost impossible below floorboards.

VAPOR BARRIERS AND VENTILATION

Attic ventilation serves the additional purpose of cooling the attic space in the summer to make the house more comfortable and prolong the life of the roofing. Natural ventilation is usually achieved by gable vents, but a modern development of ridge and eave venting provides a more even and effective flow of air. The size of these vents should be at least $\frac{1}{300}$ the area of the attic floor (about four square feet at either end of the path of circulation for most houses). Mechanical vents with electrical thermostatic controls are an alternative.

Insulating the attic floor leaves the attic space colder. If you want to use and heat this space, or anticipate doing so in the

INSULATING A FINISHED ATTIC

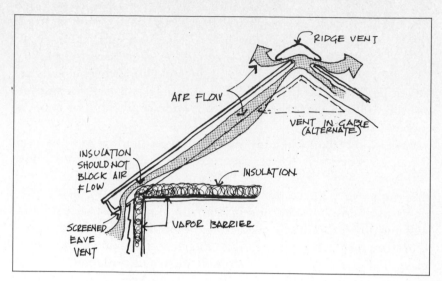

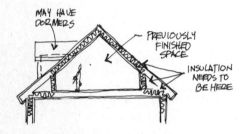

A finished attic—more difficult to figure, more difficult to insulate properly

HOW MUCH INSULATION?

future, you may decide to insulate the attic walls and ceilings instead. The wall studs and roofing rafters are usually exposed and you can easily provide vapor protection before installing an interior finish. This vapor protection is now very important because ventilation over the top of this insulation will be minimal. To be doubly safe, try to maintain an air space on the roofing side of the insulation so that a small amount of air circulation will allow roof boards to "breathe." Most insulation will settle a little to provide this space but if you have an 8-inch rafter it is better to only put in 6 inches of insulation than to force in 9 inches.

If you already have a finished attic, you should treat it like an uninsulated stud wall. The problem and solutions are the same and will be discussed in the section on insulating walls.

How much insulation should you put in the attic? Probably less than most people are recommending. If you already have 6 inches of insulation you should invest your money in other improvements before you further protect the attic. Wearing two hats won't keep you any warmer if you don't have a coat on or haven't buttoned it up. At the end of this chapter, we will explain the balanced approach to home improvements, which gives numerical support to this.

When you do decide to insulate, put in as much insulation as your budget will allow and your construction can safely hold. Insulation is not something you will want to add a little at time; the effort, preparation, and mess are not worth the results for just a small improvement. On the other hand, you will often have only a specific amount of space for it. A standard wall cavity will hold only $3\frac{1}{2}$ inches of insulation. It is possible to put more than 8 inches of insulation into an open pattern of ceiling joists, but you will end up with an ocean of insulation and no place to walk in the future. Such a process also runs the danger of blocking ventilation coming in along eave soffits.

Blocking ventilation to the attic with large amounts of insulation is one cause of icicles and ice dams on roof overhangs. These will sometimes grow large enough to back water up under roofing and cause water damage to interior ceilings and walls. The essential cause of icicles and ice dams is insufficient insulation, allowing enough heat loss to heat roofing boards and cause snow on the roof to melt and flow as water down to the exposed overhang, where it freezes. The trick is to prevent snow from melting and refreezing by maintaining roof boards at outside temperature. To do this, you should both stop heat loss into the attic and maintain positive ventilation of the roof. A polyethylene sheet attached to the underside of the rafters will help to keep them cool, reduce required ventilation, and permit a somewhat higher attic temperature for reduced exposure.

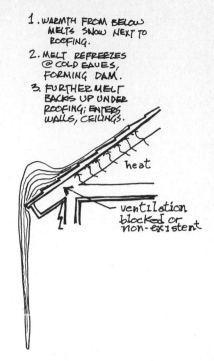

"When icicles hang by the wall . . ."

COSTS AND BENEFITS OF INSULATING THE ATTIC

The attic is fairly simple to insulate and the labor costs listed here can usually be neglected if you do it yourself.

	Material ($)	Labor ($)	R-value
Attics with open joists			
6″ of fiberglass batts	.30	.25	19
6″ of cellulose, bagged	.25	.25	24
Insulation blown in by contractor (especially under floorboards)			
6″ of fiberglass, blown	——	.65	15
6″ of cellulose, blown	——	.55	24

(For finished attics, look ahead to the section on insulating walls.)

For further discussion of material and labor costs of attic insulation, turn to Chapter 6. There you will find an analysis of the different insulations and a review of their properties. Costs and R-values are not the entire story.

Insulating Walls

Walls are the most difficult, expensive, and possibly dangerous part of an old house to improve. Some walls don't have space for insulation, and what space there is, is usually hard to get at. Moreover, spending money to insulate walls does not guarantee success. This is particularly true if the wall heat loss stems from infiltration rather than other causes. In these cases, insulation gotten one way or another into the cavity will help somewhat, but a much better solution would be a campaign against the air leaks themselves. Common suggestions are either to pump insulation unseen into the hollow space of the wall or to take off the interior finish, put in insulation, and install a new finish. A third possibility is just to add insulation over the existing wall and place a new finish over that.

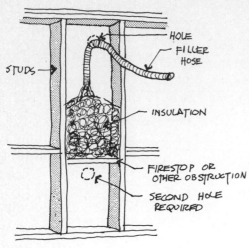

X-ray view of stud wall with
obstructions

OPENING UP A WALL

ADDING INTERIOR LAYERS

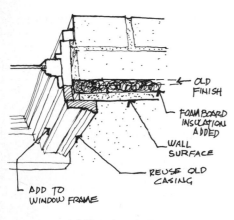

Adding insulation

Many companies now offer wall insulation services to blow in urea-formaldehyde foam, cellulose, loose fiberglass or mineral-wool insulation. They are all fairly expensive and may give problems. You can't tell how well the work is done because it is concealed. Firestops in the cavity can block the flow of insulation and leave spaces uninsulated. Special radiant heat detectors can be used to detect problems next winter, but that's not much help.

A very serious problem with all blown-in insulation is that there is no good way to install a good vapor barrier, although certain paints and fabrics applied to the inside of the insulated wall may do the job. If the job is not done properly or if the vapor barrier is weak, the wall space will become damp and the insulation will deteriorate. This can be a disaster.

It is more difficult but ultimately more satisfactory to strip off the old finish, put in insulation and a good vapor barrier, and then put on a few finish. This is a larger job, takes more time, and makes the interior unuseable during the process. It is also costly. It has the advantage of being more like insulating new construction, where you can see what you are getting and a good vapor barrier is very easy to obtain. This can be done a room at a time and you can do it yourself.

A variation of this procedure often used on historic buildings with elaborate interior finishes is to open up the wall from the outside by carefully removing wooden siding (most such buildings have no additional sheathing) and restoring it in its original position after placement of vapor barriers and insulation.

A third option, with all the advantages of the second, is to add insulation and a new finish directly onto the existing finish. It is somewhat less messy than tearing out the old finish but is a little more expensive; it involves new trim around doors and windows and bringing electrical boxes and switches forward, all of which is troublesome. This is a common and important procedure for the improvement of a masonry wall because a single inch of high-quality foam insulation may triple the R-value of the wall. Not only are heat losses reduced to a third but comfort is improved when the temperature of the interior surface of the wall is raised as much as 10°.

Yet another way to insulate is to add the insulation to the outside of the wall and place new siding beyond that. This is becoming increasingly popular in the city, since it has the advantage of preserving elaborate plaster finishes on masonry walls with no air space. At the same time, it brings a mass of masonry into the heated envelope, where it becomes heat storage. The disadvantage is aesthetic—a handsome exterior will be obliterated this way, although an attractive stucco finish may in some cases be nicer than the present wall.

Aluminum and vinyl siding are often sold as a solution to wall heat loss and they appear to fall within the above category. These sidings in fact provide little or no thermal benefit because the amount of insulation put behind them is negligible and the siding itself is a very good conductor. If applied tightly, they do cut infiltration—at the expense of cold side venting—and may trap moisture within the wall. For this reason, many sidings are equipped with venting, which then removes any claim to an insulating air space. Aluminum corner pieces and cornice details cover up and destroy the architectural character of an old building and may reduce its resale value. Beware when buying an aluminum-clad building; anything may be happening behind that shiny facade. The only virtue of aluminum and vinyl siding is that they do relieve the cost and tedium of repainting the house every few years and permit the owner to ignore the maintenance of hidden material.

Interior furnishings are not usually considered as a means of insulating a space, but they can achieve the same effect by cutting down air flow to the wall surface. Textured wall fabrics and bookshelves can affect the rate at which heat enters a wall. We will later explain why fabric walls are noticeably warmer than hard-surfaced walls. Although it is difficult to give cost/benefits for things like bookshelves and storage cabinets, it does make sense to make a habit of placing such things against outside walls whenever possible.

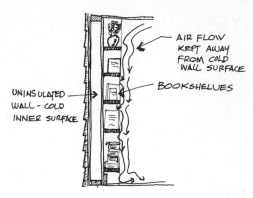

Storage or wall coverings separate and slow down the air circulation past a cold wall and cut down the heat transfer. Radiant losses are cut, too.

COSTS AND BENEFITS OF INSULATING WALLS

The following table gives an estimate of the thermal protection received for each of the mentioned improvements and an approximation of the costs on a square-foot basis.

	Material ($)	Labor ($)	R-value
Option 1: Insulation blown into a cavity (on a per-inch basis)			
Fiberglass		.15	3.2/in.
Cellulose		.12	3.5/in.
Urea-formaldehyde		.20	5.0/in.
Option 2: Remove old finish, add insulation, add new finish			
3½″ Fiberglass	.35	.50	11
3½″ Urea-formaldehyde	.50	.50	16
Option 3: Place insulation on old finish, add new finish			
3½″ Fiberglass	.35	.65	11
1″ Styrofoam	.35	.20	5
1″ Urethane board	.60	.20	8
Option 4: Insulation placed outside, with new siding			
2″ Styrofoam with wooden siding	.75	.50	11
2″ Urethane board with stucco finish	1.15	.50	16
Other considerations:			
Aluminum with ½″ of insulating backing.	.50	.50	2
Shirred fabric on interior walls	.50	.10	2

Insulating Floors

It is easy to forget that the floor is also a surface of the heated envelope and loses heat. A floor is usually easy to insulate and has a good payback, but you should keep in mind that this will result in a colder basement. Pipes may then have to be insulated and care taken to seal tightly all openings to the outside. In very cold climates there is even the danger that the ground near the house may freeze and expand to crack the basement wall. This severe case is unlikely if the furnace and other heat-producing equipment are down there to keep things warm and prevent the ground from freezing hard, but such a condition represents a relatively large heat loss. Energy is being used to solve a problem that is best dealt with through proper drainage and treatment of the soil, both of which are discussed later.

CRAWL SPACES   We highly recommend that you insulate the floor over a crawl space. There should be nothing under there that needs the heat and there is often a good deal of wind that chills the floor and causes infiltration up through the floor. You will be cramped for working space and may have to work around pipes and columns, but the savings and additional comfort will be immediately evident. Again, the vapor barrier of the insulation goes toward the warm side, in this case *above* the insulation. While you are there, insulate any pipes and heating ducts that might now be left outside the heated envelope. Crawl spaces usually have openings for summer ventilation that can be closed off in winter with stapled plastic, building paper, or panels. A sheet of polyethylene should also be placed directly on the ground to reduce summer moisture levels and prevent deterioration of the wooden floor structure.

SLAB ON GRADE   A concrete slab on grade can be insulated around the wall by digging a trench next to the slab and placing insulation down into the ground to a depth of at least three feet. This insulation should

Insulating the floor above a crawl space

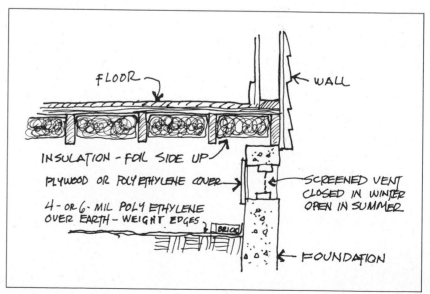

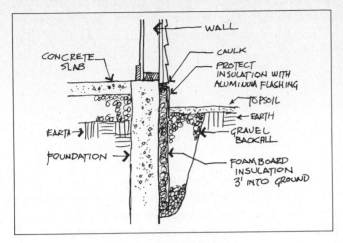

In-ground insulation below a wall
adjoining a concrete slab

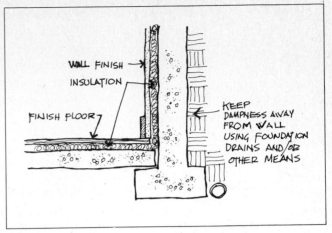

Insulating basement wall and floor

be closed-cell rigid-board insulation that will take the pressure of the earth and resist the penetration of ground moisture. Polystyrene and urethane boards are both commonly used.

Any heated rooms in the basement should be isolated from the mass of the earth by insulation. Even though the earth at 50° is a lot warmer than the outside air, it can take heat away quickly because earth is massive and a good conductor. *You don't need a lot of insulation to achieve isolation;* one inch is sufficient. Wall insulation is installed in a masonry basement by attaching furring

INSULATING A BASEMENT WALL

COSTS AND BENEFITS OF INSULATING FLOORS

This table can be used to estimate the thermal protection you should receive for improvements to the floor.

	Material ($)	Labor ($)	R-value
Insulating Crawl Spaces (estimate per sq. ft.)			
3½" of fiberglass placed up under floor	.15	.20	11
3½" of fiberglass placed around wall	.15	.10	11
Placing Insulation into the Ground (estimate for lin. ft. of wall)			
2" of Styrofoam placed 3' deep for slab-on-grade	.90	.50	10
2" of Styrofoam placed 6' deep for basement wall	1.80	2.00	10
Isolating the Heated Basement (estimate per sq. ft.)			
2" of Styrofoam and new finish on walls	.75	.20	10
2" of Styrofoam and new wood floor	1.00	.40	11
2" of Styrofoam and new concrete floor	1.00	.50	10

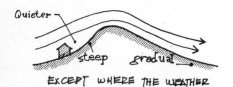

20% increase in speed

Winds

WINDS ARE HIGHER ON TOP OF A HILL.

Winds

Quieter

gradual   steeper

Often N or S, slope

THE LEE SIDE OF A HILL IS A GOOD PLACE FOR A HOUSE...

Quieter

steep   gradual

EXCEPT WHERE THE WEATHER SIDE IS MUCH STEEPER.

strips to the wall and placing foamboards between them. This wall is then completed with a polyethylene vapor barrier and then drywall or other paneling. Floor insulation is laid in a similar manner—furring and foamboards, the vapor barrier, plywood or other underlayed, and then the finish floor. In Switzerland, a double concrete floor sandwiching a layer of foam is standard practice.

IMPROVEMENTS TO THE SITE

Improvements to the site, or landscaping, have a major influence on the performance of a building. A good piece of land and careful placement of the house may halve its energy requirements. There are also many improvements for existing houses. We all spend a good deal of time and money on lawns and garden, trees and shrubs. These same elements of landscaping can be used to save energy for heating and cooling.

Building a house is itself a form of landscaping; the presence of the house changes the form of the land. The purpose of the house is to provide a distinct package of space with qualities differing from the outdoors. Judged by the laws of nature (which it will be), the form and functions of a house are rather abrupt. The practice of landscaping helps to make the house blend back into the natural flow of things. By easing the boxy shapes of houses, landscaping helps to reduce the energy demand of maintaining comfortable temperatures within the house.

Reducing Exposure to Wind

The effect of wind speed on the experience of temperatures is well documented in tables of wind-chill factors. As wind speeds go up, the apparent temperature goes down. R-value of 1 for a single pane of glass is based on an average air speed around buildings of 7 mph, but this average speed can easily be reduced to 3 mph to thicken the exterior air film and give a 20 percent improvement to the exposure. On the other hand, a 15-mph wind is also quite common and adds 20 percent to the effect of exposure. Higher speeds give results that are increasingly extreme. Wind speed has an even greater effect on air infiltration where the large surface areas of building walls create high air pressure and result in a tripling of infiltration with each doubling of wind speed. For these reasons, wind protection has long been a major function of landscaping.

Air motion occurs in two patterns; smooth *streamlined* flow and irregular *turbulent* flow. Modern vehicles all use streamlined forms to reduce air friction and allow more efficient travel. In effect, a house also moves through a body of air and air friction draws heat away from the surface of the house by reducing the outside air film. Broad surfaces that face the wind create greater turbulence, which can be reduced with proper landscaping. One

INFILTRATION THROUGH AN AVERAGE WINDOW

Wind Velocity (mph)	Cubic Feet per Foot of Crack
5	7
10	21
15	39
20	59
25	80
30	104

When wind speed goes up, infiltration goes up faster.

or two large trees are enough to divert the major impact of the wind.

Wind can be filtered to reduce its speed. One of the best ways to do this is to plant a *shelter belt* of trees, like those developed to control the high winds of the Great Plains. A large stand of trees diverts the winds up and over a house and creates a "shadow" of relatively still air. A house should be centered in the heart of this wind shadow, which occurs at a distance 5 to 10 times the height of the belt of trees. The complete shelter effect continues for about 20 to 30 times the height of the trees. At the center of the shadow the wind speed is usually reduced to about 50 percent and the reduction can be as great as 70 percent.

The effectiveness of a shelter belt depends on the density of the trees, the number of rows, and the penetrability of the shelter. Surprisingly, some wind penetration is necessary for best results. A solid building or fence of equal height will provide less shelter than a good stand of trees. The reason for this is turbulence: Wind passing over a solid object creates pressure on the windward side and a vacuum on the leeward side. Some of the wind blowing over a solid object is then drawn down into this vacuum and circulates as turbulence. On the other hand, allowing a small amount of air to filter through prevents this vacuum and permits faster-moving winds to continue smoothly over the top.

The principles of shelter-belt design should be well understood before attempting one. As an example of the sort of pitfall awaiting the unaware, a shelter belt that neglects to fill the air spaces among the tree trunks will not only permit the full force of the wind to pass right through but may actually channel the wind and increase its speed up to 20 percent. The details of shelter-belt design are excellently presented in a remarkable and inexpensive book by the Department of the Interior, *Plants, People and Environmental Quality.*

On a smaller scale, the house itself is necessarily a solid object and will therefore create turbulence. Trees and shrubs close in are therefore used to streamline the building. This process is similar to that of the larger shelter belt and works both independently or together with the larger system for additional benefits.

The general rule for *wind barriers* is to place them at a distance of twice their mature height from the house. Evergreens of full body down to the ground provide good winter protection, while

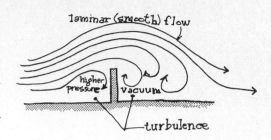

Turbulence in the air flowing around an obstruction destroys its insulating air film, increasing heat transfer. This is bad for buildings, but good for heat exchangers such as furnaces and convectors.

REDUCING WIND SPEED

DIVERTING THE WIND

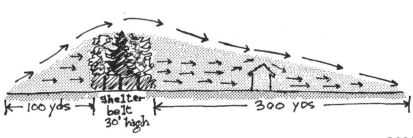

A shelter belt can reduce wind speed by 50 percent. Smaller-scale barriers work in a similar manner.

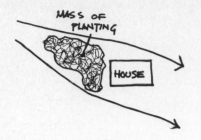

MASS OF PLANTING

HOUSE

Streamlining the building with planting

With thought and luck, the same landscaping can serve for both winter and summer.

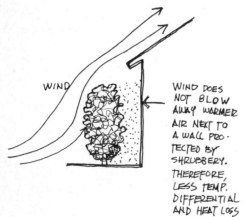

WIND

WIND DOES NOT BLOW AWAY WARMER AIR NEXT TO A WALL PRO- TECTED BY SHRUBBERY. THEREFORE, LESS TEMP. DIFFERENTIAL AND HEAT LOSS

Virtues of shrubbery next to house

a combination of large deciduous trees and low-lying evergreen shrubs is the best year-round solution. Dense plantings of fir and spruce near the house can reduce wind speed by 75 percent.

Dense evergreens planted next to the house can become in effect an additional layer of the wall. Used in this manner, they trap warm air escaping from the house and maintain relatively warm air there. Studies have indicated a fuel reduction of 20–30 percent for houses with such plantings. By our system of accounting, such evergreen plantings would have reduced the exposure to the wall to only about 20 percent (exposure factor 0.2).

It should be mentioned that air motion during the summer is usually an advantage and will save energy by reducing or eliminating the need for air-conditioning. The same principles of turbulence and streamlining, air pressures and air speeds can be used to encourage and direct air motion into the house in the summer. With luck, the seasonal direction of winds in your area will be different and one scheme of landscaping can be devised both to slow wind speeds in winter and to encourage breezes in the summer. The alternative is some form of adjustable or seasonal fencing.

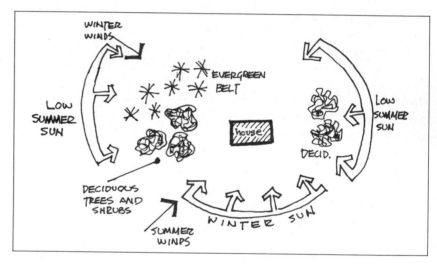

WINTER WINDS

EVERGREEN BELT

LOW SUMMER SUN

LOW SUMMER SUN

house

DECID.

DECIDUOUS TREES AND SHRUBS

WINTER SUN

SUMMER WINDS

Reducing Exposure to Cold

The warming of air trapped between dense evergreens and the house is one example of reducing exposure to cold. As wind speeds decline, the transport of heat from a building by wind conduction becomes less important than loss of heat by convection. Because convection is a relatively slow process, heat tends to loiter about the exterior of a building. The temperature of the air just outside the building wall is therefore higher than the "open field" temperature for that region and heat losses from the wall are significantly less.

An earth-sheltered house is another example of this approach. Placing a mass of earth against walls and/or roof slows the passage of heat and cold. Earth is a poor insulator as such; it requires 8 feet of earth to equal 4 inches of Styrofoam insulation. The value of the earth shelter lies in its mass and in its capacity to absorb heat and cold and dampen the effects of each. As heat is lost through the insulation of an earth-covered house, it is absorbed by the earth and continues to flow outward at a slow rate. In the process, the temperature difference between the inside and outside of the insulation is reduced and so is the rate of heat loss. This process is hard to describe numerically, but it works, as is being proven by dozens of successful earth-covered houses with heat losses that are much less than an R-value analysis would indicate.

Two aspects of earth shelters should not be overlooked. First, *the shelter of the earth does not replace the need for insulation.* The temperature of the earth about 8 feet into the ground approaches a constant 50, which is certainly preferable to the severer cold that is encountered above the ground. However, the earth has a tremendous capacity to absorb heat and it is important to install some insulation to interrupt the thermal contact with this 50° earth mass. You can't hope to raise the earth to room temperature.

The second factor is *the presence of moisture in the soil.* Aside from the inconvenience of water that might leak into a poorly constructed earth-sheltered house, the presence of moisture in the soil will greatly increase its thermal conductivity. Every effort should be made to drain the soil and keep it as dry as possible.

These principles of soil dynamics point to several possible improvements for existing houses. To begin, you can improve the insulating value of the earth around your present foundation by insuring that it is properly drained. If it is not, you may be well advised to pay an excavator to dig a trench around your house and install a system of drainage. This would also be the time to damp-proof the basement wall and install a couple of inches of closed-cell insulation. This may sound like a lot of work but it will save energy, rid you of a cold, wet basement, and may even add years to the life of your house.

A second improvement, if you have masonry walls, would be to bank or terrace earth up the wall to the height of the windowsills. This will require damp-proofing the wall but should provide an exposure reduction of up to 20 percent for the wall.

A radical alternative is to place earth upon the roof if it presently has a shallow slope. This will also require a system of waterproofing but need not require the strengthening of the roof structure if only a two-foot composition of lightweight mulch with good drainage is used. A number of different systems are being developed and tested. Architect Malcolm Wells, a leading authority on the subject, has already built dozens of homes and a number of other underground buildings and is soon to release a new book of his findings.

A very traditional way to reduce exposure to cold is to cluster buildings together and thereby reduce the percentage of walls exposed. The age-old practice of grouping farm buildings together to surround and protect a central farmhouse is an example of this.

Many homes have porches that could be enclosed to help

EARTH-SHELTERED HOUSES

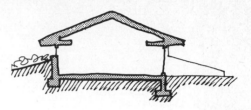

Earth-berm house (after Frank Lloyd Wright)

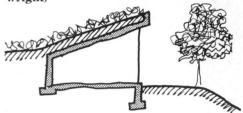

Buried-house design (open to the south)

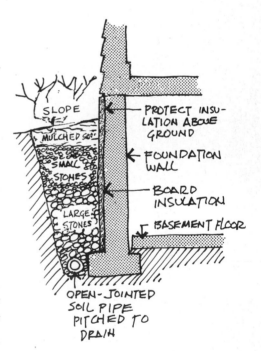

Foundation insulation, showing proper backfill and drains

CLUSTERING BUILDINGS

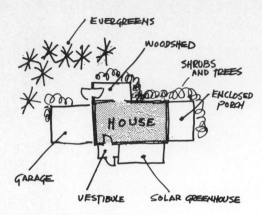

EVERGREENS
WOODSHED
SHRUBS AND TREES
ENCLOSED PORCH
HOUSE
GARAGE
VESTIBULE
SOLAR GREENHOUSE

Things that can be used, or added, to reduce exposure

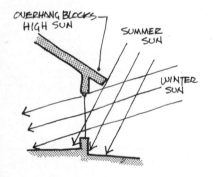

OVERHANG BLOCKS HIGH SUN
SUMMER SUN
WINTER SUN

The south-facing window—one of the best, most efficient solar collectors there is

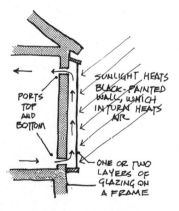

PORTS TOP AND BOTTOM
SUNLIGHT HEATS BLACK-PAINTED WALL, WHICH IN TURN HEATS AIR
ONE OR TWO LAYERS OF GLAZING ON A FRAME

A Trombe wall

reduce exposure. A large enclosed entry that could serve a variety of other functions can be added to a house. Many houses are going to be needing woodsheds and these can be placed against the house as a buffer. Garages, workshops, tool sheds, and greenhouses can all be added in such a way to reduce the exposure of the main house. Bit by bit and piece by piece a sheltered home can be created.

Improving Exposure to the Sun

A great deal of new thought has been going into the design of solar houses, and many of the same principles are applicable to older houses as well, particularly in the site-design aspects. The site should be opened to greater sunlight by eliminating objects like large trees that block the southern exposure, while trees and vegetation are left at the north, east, and west sides to cut wind exposure and to shade low sun in hot weather. The ground in front of the house to the south can serve as a sun reflector if light-colored; an expanse of snow is especially effective.

On the house itself, a great deal can be done to increase sun exposure in winter and control it in the summer. Most solar-house designs show angled collectors on the roof, but since the sun is so low in the sky in the winter even at noon, a vertical wall facing anywhere within 30° of south is in good position to collect.

Since an opaque wall stops sunlight that strikes it, it is good practice to maximize window area on the south side of the house. The south-facing window is the simplest, least expensive, and most effective collector of sunlight. High-intensity radiation penetrates the glass and heats opaque surfaces of the room. These surfaces then heat the surrounding air. In summer the sun is higher in the sky; it hits the window at a shallow angle, resulting in greater reflection and less heat getting through. This *change of sun angle* from about 20–30° in the winter to 70–80° in the summer (the higher angles in the southern states) can be used with overhangs calculated to block summer sun while allowing lower winter sun to shine in and heat the house.

More ambitious solar-collection schemes are possible and not very expensive but are beyond the scope of this book. We will mention only a couple that we find particularly promising in their simplicity.

One solution is to space a layer of glazing over all or part of the south wall. This allows solar energy to enter the space created and heat the wall, which is now painted black or some very dark color. A large amount of heat can be captured by this procedure and drawn into the house through vents. If the wall is of heavy masonry it will capture and store a good deal of the heat for later use. A very large and thick wall may even store heat for many hours, with the result that daylight energy is captured and becomes available to the interior of the house during the evening and night hours. This sort of collector is called a *Trombe wall,* after a solar scientist in France. A small one is now being built by the authors in the Blandy attic.

Another way to collect sunlight with a large southern wall of glass is to move the glass away from the house and create a new room that can be used as a *sunroom* or a *greenhouse*. Solar greenhouses are a development of the past few years. They differ from ordinary ones in having tighter enclosures against the wind and double glazing. They also have an insulated north wall, which reflects sunlight down on the plants. Plants get more sunlight than they would from a normal greenhouse and excess heat can be supplied to a nearby house. The solar collection of such a greenhouse is obviously secondary to the growing of plants for pleasure or food. In fact, the promotion of solar-greenhouse building has practically become a movement: Visionaries see the northern part of the country beating inflation by producing its own food supplies locally throughout the winter rather than importing vegetables from California and Mexico.

IMPROVING THE HEATING PROCESS

The goal of heating improvements is to squeeze more useful heat out of each unit of fuel. The efficiency of a system is the comparison between the energy the fuel contains and the amount of heat that actually arrives at the intended space. Regardless of what else is done to improve the house or site, there are great opportunities to raise heating-system efficiencies in three areas; the furnace itself, the distribution network of pipes or ducts, and the placement of heating outlets where heat is released.

"Solar" greenhouse

Furnace Efficiencies

The usual discussion of heating efficiencies is inadequate to a full appreciation of heating systems. By conventional description, the efficiency of an oil furnace is typically put between 50 and 80 percent, with 65 percent considered a good value for well-adjusted old burners. Gas systems are commonly rated at 70 percent. Electric systems receive up to 100 percent ratings because they can be placed directly into rooms where all the purchased energy is cleanly converted into heat without further losses.

However, none of these numbers reflects the actual performance of the whole heating system because they leave out so many places where losses occur. In the case of electricity, we must add the losses at the power plant and those of transmission, which bring the overall efficiency down to 20–30 percent. This is why a unit of electricity is more expensive than the equivalent amount of oil or gas. This efficiency expression leaves aside the pollution and hazards associated with power plants, which are eventually paid for. Similarly, gas- and oil-fired systems have losses that bring their overall efficiencies down to 30–40 percent. In this light, well-designed solar energy systems with overall performances of about 50 percent for active and 80 percent for passive begin to look more practical.

Of all the places that energy gets lost along the way, the furnace is the first stop. You will recall from Chapter 1 that the furnace is usually a fire chamber in which fuel is burned below a heat exchanger which collects the heat from the hot flaming gases. The heat exchanger is a metal device of two chambers with lots of surface to collect heat as it is transferred from the gases to the heating medium (water or air). In this way, air or water is warmed and sent through the distribution system to the living spaces.

In a completely efficient furnace all the fuel would be completely burned, there would be just enough air to provide oxygen for burning, and the hot gases would give up all their heat to the heat exchanger and be reduced to nearly room temperature before leaving for the chimney. In practice, fuel rarely burns completely, excess air tends to cool off the exchanger, and the burned gases are still hot when they go up the chimney. (Exhaust gases, in fact, must be somewhat hot to create a draft in the chimney.)

FURNACE MAINTENANCE

A furnace becomes less efficient as it ages and is left without maintenance. Yearly service of an oil burner can save up to 10 percent of a year's heating bill. A gas furnace can usually go three years without maintenance because gas has less dirt and impurities than oil. Over time, carbon, sulphur, and other nasty chemicals accumulate on the surfaces of the heat exchanger and not only corrode it but actually insulate it from the fire. Part of the autumn work schedule should be to open up your furnace before it is turned on and clean off the heat exchanger. There are special brushes for this with long handles, available at the hardware store. You should vacuum up what falls off to clean up the burner compartment. Every few years, during the spring and summer off-season, get a good serviceman to come and do the full job. In a couple of hours he should be able to:

- clean the heat exchanger;
- check the draft regulator for free movement and the smoke pipe/chimney for blockage;
- lubricate, clean, and adjust the burner, replacing worn parts;
- test the furnace for draft, smoke, carbon monoxide, stack temperature, and air leakage, adjusting and retesting until it runs at its best.

It is unfortunate that really good service is not easy to get. Fuel dealers will usually offer maintenance but they do not put the greatest enthusiasm into it. For many dealers it is simply a necessary evil of their main business, which is to sell fuel. The incentives work the wrong way: If a dealer does a top-notch job of maintenance, he sells less fuel! It is perhaps better to call in a good furnace supplier or installer for testing and maintenance.

Gas furnaces are similar to oil but much simpler. While oil is a liquid that must be pumped and atomized with a nozzle in order to mix with air before burning, gas is always ready to burn. A gas burner mechanism stays cleaner and in better adjustment, and burns with fewer pollutants. The heat exchanger still needs an annual cleaning and the burner needs the same sort of air and draft testing and adjustments.

Your furnace consumes a great deal of air in the process of the combustion of fuel—valuable conditioned air from the house itself that goes up the chimney and is replaced by cold air infiltrating around doors and windows. This air requirement of the furnace may account for more than half the cold air entering your building.

This problem may be remedied by ducting outside air to the furnace. A sealed furnace room with a 4-inch dryer vent to the outdoors, insulated from the rest of the house, is the simplest solution. Other systems use ducts that carry air directly to the combustion chamber of the furnace. In this type of installation, most systems join a second duct of outside air to the exhaust flue pipe as a barometric draft control to reduce the draft of an older heated chimney that was designed for a coal system and often draws up to 10 times the air flow necessary for modern oil and gas systems.

These simple modifications can improve furnace performances as much as 25 percent for oil systems and 15 percent for gas. You should have a trained furnace supplier or installer come in to reset the fuel-air balance after such modifications.

A common fault of furnaces is that they must turn on and off many times during the day. A furnace is most efficient when it burns continually, just as a car engine gets its best mileage when it gets warmed up and runs at a constant speed. Ideally a furnace should be just large enough to heat a building on the coldest day

EXTERIOR AIR SUPPLY

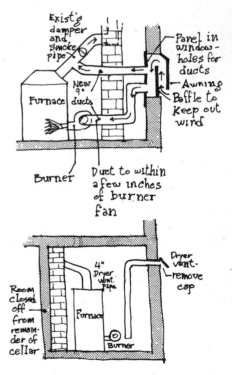

Bringing outside combustion air to the furnace (two tested schemes from *Popular Science*)

by running continuously. On warmer days, it will turn on and off a number of times. Each time it turns off, the heat exchanger cools down and must be reheated before it can pass on energy to the distribution system. This is unavoidable, but it is not good for efficiency. It is like heating a gallon of water every time you want a cup of coffee.

What's worse, most furnaces are *oversized* for the house and therefore cycle more often than necessary. The Rochester, N.Y., Gas and Electric Company surveyed hundreds of gas furnaces in its territory and found almost all of them oversized, some by as much as 350 percent, the average being twice as large as necessary. Chances are that furnaces all over the country are similarly oversized. The fault for this is shared by heating engineers (whose way of figuring heat losses is very conservative to begin with), furnace dealers (who commonly oversize the engineering requirement), and homeowners (who figure that bigger always means better). An accurately sized furnace may not be enough to keep the house up to 75° when the temperature outside goes down to 20° below, but that only happens a few days a year in the coldest places. A larger furnace may do the job on the worst days but will be very inefficient the vast majority of the time.

As you conscientiously improve your house and cut your heat losses significantly, your furnace will become even more oversized than it was before! This could develop to the point that burner inefficiencies consume much of your savings in heat loss. One solution to this problem is *de-rating*, which means replacing parts of the furnace to reduce its heating capacity and fuel consumption rate. The furnace will then be able to run more continuously and thus more efficiently.

Rochester Gas and Electric is doing this experimentally with five hundred of its gas customers. Some of the methods they are trying are illegal by present conservative safety standards, which require large amounts of excess air for combustion. These safety standards are being reevaluated under the impact of energy shortages to permit tighter control of the process and thereby greater efficiencies. This is a good example of the trade-off between safety and efficiency, between worst-case planning for conditions of poor management and efficient procedures for homes receiving close attention and knowledgeable supervision.

If de-rating becomes generally accepted and available, it will be a good thing for many people because it will be fairly cheap. The Rochester experiment averaged $150 per house and the paybacks are reasonably quick. For oil-fired systems, the burner can be replaced at some expense by units with *flame-retention nozzles,* which are more efficient at burning.

If de-rating is impossible, you might consider replacing the furnace altogether with a similar smaller one. This is an expensive proposition but may be worthwhile if the furnace is old and due for replacement anyway. When you ask for an accurately sized (smaller) furnace, expect an argument. Furnace dealers honestly believe they have been doing the right thing all these years and are not going to change their minds overnight.

Distribution Efficiency

Heat is normally transported through the house by means of ducted air or piped water or steam. The fan or pump that provides the motive power for the system must be properly sized and maintained to ensure good circulation. Circulator pumps of water systems should be oiled each year, and filters for hot-air systems changed two or three times each heating season.

The pipe or duct that carries this heat up to the occupied rooms will lose heat along the way. Uninsulated pipes and ducts within the basement can be tolerated since they tend to heat up the basement and temper the floor temperature, keeping other pipes and equipment from freezing. But if water pipes or heating ducts go through cold areas, such as crawl spaces, they should be insulated, especially if you insulate your floor and isolate the basement. Long runs should always be insulated no matter where they are located.

INSULATE PIPES AND DUCTS

Piping insulation should have an exterior vapor barrier, since during the summer, when the furnace is off, heating pipes will often be cooler than the air around them. The humidity will penetrate unprotected insulation, condense, and ruin the insulation. Air ducts that are used for summer air-conditioning should be insulated and provided with exterior vapor protection for the same reasons.

Heat is delivered to rooms by radiators, convectors, and registers. The most common convectors today are the fin-tubes used in baseboard hot-water systems. Most radiators, with the exception of steam systems, are actually convectors, since they do not reach high temperatures. A radiator sends heat directly to people and other objects, while a convector heats the air first.

CONVECTION SYSTEMS

A convector requires free air motion to function effectively. Two factors affect its efficiency: the surface area and the speed of the air moving past the surfaces. Surface area is hard to increase but air circulation is not. Air flow is frequently blocked by furniture or other objects, either at the floor or placed on top of the radiator. Poorly designed radiator covers and shelves can kill air circulation entirely. Dust blocks air circulation, too, so radiators and convectors should be vacuumed twice a year. The same kind of thing happens to hot-air registers if they are left closed or if furniture is put in front of them.

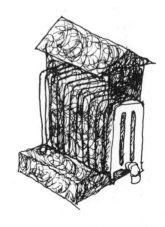

Air must be allowed to pass through a radiator or convector to make contact with its surfaces.

The heat exchange of the traditional radiator also depends upon the flow of water within the unit. The valve must be open; but equally important, air, which tends to accumulate in large radiators, must be bled off. *Bleeding* a radiator takes a little key available at a hardware store. At the beginning of every heating season, open the tiny valve at the top of one end of the radiator and let the air hiss out. Close it quickly as the water starts to

STEAM SYSTEMS

RADIATOR GETS HOT ENOUGH SO THAT IT DOES ACT AS A RADIATOR AS WELL AS A CONVECTOR

AIR VALVE— STAYS OPEN UNTIL HOT STEAM GETS TO IT

NO PIPE AT THIS END

STEAM RISES

CONDENSED STEAM RETURNS TO BOILER IN SAME PIPE (1-PIPE SYSTEM)

Steam radiator

emerge. (Hot-water baseboard systems have valves at high points that do the same thing.)

Air and hot-water systems are the most common modern types but steam systems used to be the norm and many older buildings still have them. Many furnaces may be used for either steam or hot water with only small modification of controls and furnace apparatus. Piping and radiation are similar but the method of heat transfer is different.

A steam furnace actually boils small amounts of water. In the *state change* from water to steam (see Chapter 2), enormous amounts of energy are absorbed by the steam. The steam is carried up to the radiators where it condenses, releases its heat, and raises the temperature of the metal radiator enormously. In this case, the radiator is hot enough to heat objects by radiation. In fact, it is often too hot to touch and somewhat dangerous for this reason. Steam is, however, a very effective system.

The controls for steam systems are different from those of hot-water systems. A steam valve should be either on or off, because closing it halfway interferes with the passage of the steam and the return of condensed water, which use the same pipe in most domestic systems. At the other end of the radiator from the valve is the *air valve,* a gadget that opens to let air out when steam first enters the radiator and then closes when steam reaches the valve. Some air valves are adjustable to control the output of the radiator. A radiator will not function properly if the air valve is not in working order. Special controls include an *anticipator* on the thermostat which helps to even out the temperature.

ELECTRIC SYSTEMS

Using high-grade electric energy for heating a house is considered a sin by energy conservation advocates and environmentalists; it has been compared to "cutting butter with a chain-saw." We agree with this, but add that there are degrees of sin depending upon how electricity is used in a given house.

The worst sin is *direct-resistance* baseboard heating, which has commonly been installed in new houses and apartments, because the cost to the builder was so low. Resulting heating bills are high in well-insulated buildings and astronomical in others.

Heat pumps are a lesser sin. Heat pumps are air conditioners in reverse; they use electricity to remove heat from the outside air (or water) and deliver it to a building. In any but the coldest weather, heat pumps do not use as much electricity per unit of heat delivered as would a direct-resistance system. They also reverse to air-condition in the summer. The initial cost of installing such a system is higher than most central-heating systems but lower than most combined heating and air-conditioning systems.

The most justifiable form of electric heating is for spaces that are only heated intermittently, where the installation expense of a regular system can be avoided. The heat is turned on for short-term and occasional use. Here the quick response of electric heat is an advantage while the amount of energy used in a short time is not great. There are various types of such baseboard and wall heaters. One of the simplest and cheapest is an infra-red lamp installed overhead in an ordinary light socket. This is very appropriate in a bathroom, especially as radiant heat is very effective and pleasant on bare skin.

Heating systems should deliver heat where it is wanted and at only the needed amounts. If some rooms are overheated in order to get enough heat to other spaces, there will be waste as well as discomfort. The process of adjustment is called the *balancing of the system.* Systems will usually have balancing valves or dampers directly on pipes and ducts to do this. Partial closure of a valve or damper will have the effect of increasing resistance on that one line and encouraging heat to go elsewhere. A heating expert can show you how to do balancing, but in a small house you can figure it out for yourself and get the desired results by trial and error—which is the same thing the experts do.

The location of the thermostat will affect the system's performance and fuel use, too. A thermostat next to a front door or cold window will experience lower temperatures and call for more heat than a thermostat located in a central area. Thermostats are usually located in hallways or living rooms and this is usually fine. Just be certain that they are protected from unusual cold drafts.

The supply of heat to a house should also be timed to periods of occupancy. This is made possible in automatic systems through the use of clock thermostats which provide for different settings at the various times of the day. They come as either two- or four-cycle devices. A two-cycle device is set to reduce the temperature setting at the usual bedtime hour and then return to the higher daytime setting shortly before you would normally rise in the morning. A four-cycle device allows for reductions in setting during the hours of the workday as well. Such a device may be the most profitable energy conservation purchase you can make.

The setting for a thermostat is one of your prime opportunities to reduce fuel usage. Lower settings cost nothing except the effort to learn other habits, which eventually include warmer clothes, more nutritional foods, and even the better kinds and locations of family activities. In effect, the thermostat setting is a measure of your success in adapting to this new age of energy efficiency. Efficiency is related to fitness.

The Case for Nonperimeter Heating

The desired *pattern of heat distribution* is not a simple subject, but it can be very important in determining heat loads and should receive special attention in the design of a new house or large alterations when the choices are still open. There is even much to improve in an existing house.

The conventional way to heat a house today is to distribute heat at the outside walls, and especially directly under windows. The reasoning goes that these are the coldest parts of the house;

if they can be made comfortably warm, then the parts within will be warm as well. This logic is correct if uniformly heated spaces are essential. However, putting the heat sources at the coldest points also means that heat losses are going to be the highest possible. The only way to make them greater would be to heat the walls from the outside—almost as logical from a comfort standpoint!

The alternative is to release the heat from the furnace at the building interior, well away from the cold outside walls, and allow the house to experience a range of temperatures from very warm at the center to relatively cool at the perimeter. This means that there will be less temperature difference between the two surfaces of the outside wall and therefore less heat loss. If the interior is heated to 70° and drops to 55° at the outside walls when it is 30° outside, the temperature difference is 25°, instead of 40° for a uniformly heated interior of 70°. The reduction in heat loss is more than 35 percent!

This form of heating scheme, however foreign to contemporary engineering, was the common solution in times past. The center-chimney New England house is a good example. Early hot-air systems also did just this kind of thing. Old towns are full of working examples of central hot-air systems. Ductwork emerges from the furnace and is brought up in the center of large rooms through a hole in the middle of the floor. Warm air rises from the heat exchanger without the need of fans and there are no horizontal runs. One has only to imagine the system to see the advantages.

There are disadvantages, as heating engineers will be happy to point out. Since the exterior walls will be cool and the windows even cooler, down-drafts will originate there and spread across the floor. There is considerably more air motion than in a

CENTRAL HEAT SOURCES

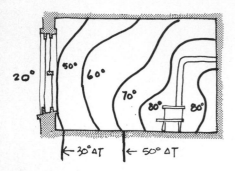

Nonperimeter heat can mean a lot less temperature differential.

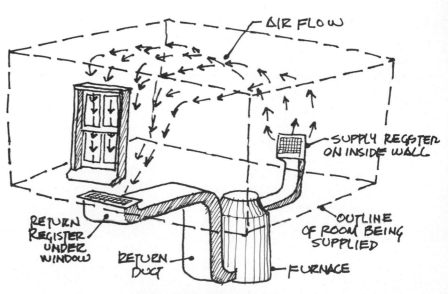

An older scheme of central heating

uniformly heated layout. Old systems accommodate this neatly by installing return air registers under the windows to collect the cold air and carry it back to the furnace. A hot-water system could not do this directly but cold air ducts under windows can still be led back under the floor and returned to the same room through registers placed under convector/radiators. A similar system can be used to provide combustion air for centrally located wood stoves and fireplaces.

Catching down-drafts from windows with cold-air registers prevents cold drafts on the floor. In fact, these registers create a slight vacuum, which pulls cooler air and dust from the floor, from baseboards, and from corners. The duct should therefore have a filter and cleaning port under the floor to catch the dirt that is pulled in—so you have a natural vacuum cleaner.

Another disadvantage cited for this system is severe condensation on windows. If windows are double-glazed, this should not occur until very low exterior temperatures are reached. When higher humidities are desired, triple-glazing and forms of insulated shutters or curtains with vapor barriers can be made to deal with most conditions. Our previous discussion of window and wall treatments comes into play here. Good draperies and insulated curtains direct down-drafts completely into registers; they also shield the cold window surface from your body's radiant view. Wall hangings and filled shelving systems similarly mask cold wall surfaces and improve radiant comfort.

How large are the advantages of centralized sources of heat? If these ideas are carried to their logical conclusion, a house would have rooms of high thermal demand at the center, around which would be clustered other rooms and storage spaces of lesser thermal demand. Such a design of *concentric zoning* would make it easier to maintain the warmth of the central spaces because heat would pass through two or three different spaces before it was truly lost. Such a house could maintain central zones at 70° with exterior walls at around 50° and could reduce the heat losses of the building by 30 percent. See Chapter 11 for a house design using concentric zoning.

Different areas of the house should support various activities at the appropriate temperatures. Kitchens and activity rooms would be comfortable with temperatures of 62–65°, while the living room might justifiably be 68–70°. Bedrooms would be warm at 60° and be allowed to fall to 55° when no one was there. All of this may be achieved naturally with careful planning and zoning.

Closing off *seasonal rooms* in winter is an effective way to reduce interior volume. This is most appropriate when seasonal rooms form a buffer as a sealed-off outer ring of rooms. In this way extra bedrooms, activity rooms, libraries, and so on, can be isolated from the heated house and become dead-air spaces, which help protect the prime central space from severe exposure. You should, however, be careful to monitor plumbing in isolated elements of

COLD-AIR RETURNS

CONTROLLING WINDOW CONDENSATION

CONCENTRIC ZONING

the house to prevent freezing in severe conditions. In my northern Vermont home, a whole fish tank was once inadvertently allowed to freeze solid during one cold snap. Extreme cold doesn't help plaster, either.

The lowering of ceilings is sometimes recommended to reduce volumes and save energy. In very tall rooms, heat will rise and leave cold air down where the people are, yet we don't recommend the lowering of ceilings to save energy because the same stratification of heated air occurs in the summer, when it is a blessing. It is much better to deal with the walls and ceilings in ways we've discussed and slow down the heat loss that causes the temperature stratification in the first place. Failing that, ceiling fans and special ducts can be used to bring warm air down from a high ceiling.

VERTICAL ZONING

The tendency of warm air to rise can be used to zone space on a vertical basis. *Vertical zoning* can operate in two ways. In the first case, a very tall room is used in such a way that activities of high thermal demand are located on high platforms while hardier activities are on a lower level. In this tiered use of space, convection currents are relatively fast and temperature differences are small unless draperies or other means of subdividing the space are introduced.

The other case of vertical zoning is where separated volumes of space are placed one over the other. Heat is introduced into the lower volume and is allowed to rise slowly up into the second. Heat lost through the ceiling of the lower room is reused in the upper before it is lost from the house. This is fairly common in two-story houses with second-floor bedrooms. Older houses have ceiling registers to allow heat from below to come up into the rooms above. When these upper rooms are insulated, the heat loss there is reduced such that they may overheat. The register should then be closed and possibly sealed up. Heat conduction through the floorboards themselves is enough to heat an insulated upstairs bedroom. If the temperature of such a bedroom cannot be reduced to 60° without opening windows to let out heat, it is time to insulate the floor with rugs.

Vertical zoning of a lofty space

Fireplaces and Wood Stoves

Wood heat is today a popular alternative and we recommend it for consideration. You may already have a fireplace that can be used and made more efficient. Burning wood is a simple and long-tested source of heat and recent advances in wood-heating technology now allow it to rival and often outperform most other heating systems. A well-built air-tight wood stove can achieve the same 60 percent efficiencies of the usual furnace, without additional distribution losses. Even a well-designed and carefully tended fireplace can achieve 30 percent efficiencies to rival the overall performance of many oversized heating systems.

Wood heat ideally complements simple solar heating because

it completes the daily cycle; unneeded during the daytime, wood heat is easily tended in the evening. Fireplaces and wood stoves do not lose efficiency by cycling on and off, as do furnaces. The thermal mass of a fireplace with an internal chimney works with the house by holding heat and releasing it slowly after the fire goes out. An air-tight wood stove needs only one or two loads of wood each day and can be set to a slow burn all night.

Wood as a fuel is economically similar to its alternatives. The cost of wood fuel is nearly the same as other fuels in most urban areas and only about half as much if you live in the country. The cost of wood disappears if you gather it yourself. It is also a renewable resource, unlike gas, oil or electricity. Trees *grow*.

There are three common kinds of fireplaces. The finest is the Rumford fireplace, which heats by radiation. Next in preference is the air-circulating type, which heats air by convection. The most common fireplace heats by radiation like a Rumford but lacks the correct proportions, so most of its heat is lost up the stack. These three types may be estimated at efficiencies of 30 percent, 20 percent, and, with luck, 10 percent.

The *Rumford fireplace,* developed by Count Rumford in the late eighteenth century, is still the best fireplace you can build because it develops the radiant-heat potential of the fire to its maximum. As described in Vrest Orton's book *The Forgotten Art of Building a Good Fireplace,* the Rumford is distinguished from

FIREPLACES

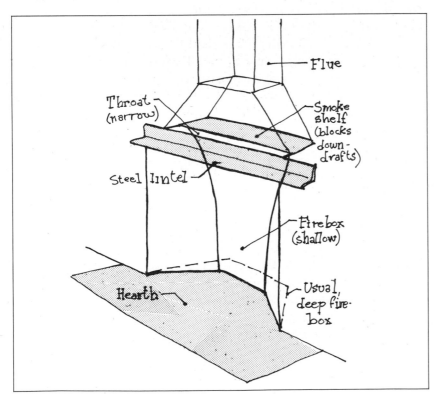

Rumford fireplace

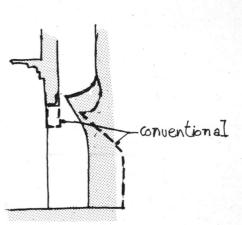

Comparison of the cross section of a Rumford with a conventional fireplace

most others by its high lintel, shallow firebox, and broad-angled walls. A Rumford has twice the heat-absorptive mass and twice the heat-radiating surface of a low and deep fireplace. It is designed to maintain a bed of coals, which is the most efficient phase of the wood-burning process. It requires the least amount of air drawn from the room yet radiates intense heat out to the room.

The greater height of heated masonry at the back assures a steady current of rising air that carries combustion gases up to a long and narrow throat that accepts this sheet of rising air at low velocities. Because the throat is smaller in area than that of most fireplaces and the air velocities are low, the heat loss is much less. The *draw* of a Rumford is just enough to capture all smoke and gases, even with a fire set as much as one foot into the room. One mason tests the draft of his Rumfords by releasing smoke from his pipe near the lintel where it should be "drawn gently, slowly, but completely up the chimney." It is possible to modify existing fireplaces to Rumford's proportions to greatly improve their performance and the Orton book tells you just how to do it. If you are considering a new fireplace, make it a Rumford.

Most fireplaces built today are *heat-circulating* fireplaces. They use a prefabricated steel firebox, which the mason covers with brick to make it look like a masonry fireplace. Most units have built-in ducts that draw air off the floor and through the walls of the unit; there it collects heat, which rises and exits at the top near the ceiling. It is safe, easy, and inexpensive. The firebox is low and deep and poorly designed to heat by radiation, so nearly all its heat is produced by convection. The steel walls of a prefab unit have little mass to hold heat and they are continually cooled by the air circulating around them. Because the walls are cooler, the fire must be more active to stay alive, in contrast to a Rumford's capacity to sustain a bed of glowing coals. The result is that more air motion is required to sustain the fire, more heat goes up the chimney, and more cold air must come into the house as infiltration. A prefab unit will also rust out in time; today's thin-walled units have a life expectancy of only about twenty-five years.

There are several methods to get more heat out of even the most inefficient fireplace. The now-popular *air-circulating grate* holds the wood on curved, hollow steel tubes. Air is heated in the tube, rises, and shoots out the top into the room while drawing cooler air off the floor. An air-circulating grate is a heat exchanger and there are various designs. One of the better designs was described by Vincent Shaeffer in *Home Energy Digest* as a steel-plate box that sits over burning logs. Piped openings at the front corners of the fireplace gather large amounts of cool air, which circulates through baffles within the box and is discharged as very warm air. Dr. Shaeffer claims that the fewer large openings make it superior to most grates but he is not manufacturing the unit, nor patenting it, so that anyone who wishes may make one.

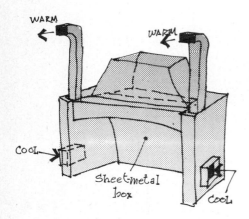

Heat-circulating fireplace

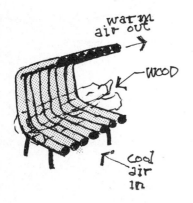

Common circulating grate

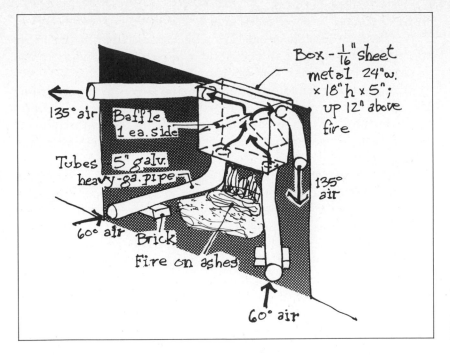

Box - $\frac{1}{16}$" sheet metal 24"w. × 18"h × 5"; up 12" above fire

135° air

Baffle 1 ea. side

Tubes 5" galv. heavy-ga. pipe

135° air

60° air

Brick

Fire on ashes

60° air

The "hot box" invented by Vincent Schaefer of Atmospheric Sciences Research Center, State University of New York, Albany

A two-level grate that holds logs in a set position to radiate effectively seems to be a good device. The fire area and thus the radiant production are always aimed toward the room. A traditional campfire technique is a variation of such a grate and requires no equipment in the fireplace at all. A large (8 inches in diameter) log is placed in a deep bed of ashes at the rear of the fireplace with a smaller log in front, and a fire is started between them. The front face of the big log radiates over the front log to the room while the smaller log radiates some heat back to maintain a high temperature and a good bed of coals between.

In the maintenance of any fire, two things must happen. First, several pieces of wood must be close together to radiate back and forth to keep up high temperatures and sustain combustion. This is why it is impossible to burn just one wood log at a time; the heat just radiates away and the temperature drops. At the same time there must be enough space between pieces of wood to give combustion gases a route to the fuel and to give the smoke an exit. A very effective way to put a fire out is simply to spread the wood out flat and let it dissipate its heat.

A very worthwhile investment for a fireplace is a combination screen and glass enclosure. The screen is a safety device to catch popping embers while the glass enclosure allows you to close off the fireplace opening at the end of the evening while the dying embers continue to smoke and require the damper to be open for the night.

A modern wood stove is really just a "parlor furnace" that burns wood; it has all the efficiencies of other furnaces without their distribution losses. With the recent development of insulated

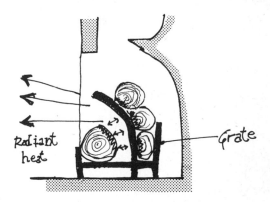

Radiant heat

Grate

Grate that holds logs in position to radiate

WOOD STOVES

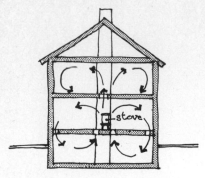

Air circulation from a stove

metal chimneys, a wood stove may be safely placed in the center of the house where air circulation and heat distribution are most effective. A wood stove is an excellent device for providing quick or sustained heat when and where it is needed.

There are an expanding variety of wood stoves to choose from. You may choose from simple or air-tight designs made in steel or cast iron. Models vary in size and wall thickness. You may even choose between an exposed radiant stove and an enclosed circulator version.

The first concerns in choosing a stove are its size and weight. Almost any stove can heat a room to a desired temperature; the questions are how hot does the stove get and what is the danger of overheating the stovepipe. In general, a heavy cast-iron stove has a greater capacity to hold heat, is less likely to overheat, will sustain a more even rate of burning, and will continue to radiate heat into the room longer into the night. A steel stove with thinner walls will rust through more quickly, but it costs less and will provide heat more quickly for rooms occupied intermittently, like workrooms. Steel stoves are sold on the basis of surface area, while cast-iron stoves are sold by weight. Cast-iron is somewhat susceptible to breakage, costs more, and usually performs better.

The size of your wood stove and how many of them you might need to replace your heating system are dependent upon the nature of your house and the pattern of heating you choose. A large wood stove is appropriate for open, interconnected rooms, while a subdivided house will need individual heating units unless special provisions are made for heat distribution with ducts or registers. A well-insulated house might need only one or two, while a typical home might need one for each major room.

Your next choice is whether to go with an *air-tight* stove or to stay with one of simple construction. A simple stove can deliver 40–50 percent efficiencies with careful use of dampers, while an air-tight stove can do as well as 60 percent. More important to most people who decide to buy an air-tight stove is its capacity for precise control of air supply to obtain a twelve-hour burn on a single loading. Careful construction to enable this control means more precision casting and fitting, and greater expense.

The higher efficiency of an air-tight wood stove must be balanced against the greater danger it presents of a chimney fire. Any chimney in use should be cleaned once a year and maintained in good condition, but a chimney for an air-tight stove should be monitored monthly.

CHIMNEYS AND FLUES

Whenever wood is burned, gases are given off and are exhausted out the chimney. These gases are actually unburned fuel vapors, which then condense on the cooler surfaces of a chimney and form a sticky substance called *creosote*. Since the condensing temperature of creosote is 250°, while the usual flue temperature should be 400°, it is common practice in a new construction to isolate the flue tile from the mass of the chimney with insulation to encourage creosote vapors to pass the entire distance up and out of the chimney.

The high efficiency of an air-tight stove now becomes a problem. When an air-tight stove is closed down for a long slow burn for the night, more unburned fuel vapors pass up the chimney while at the same time exhaust temperatures go down. The condensation temperature is reached and the chimney or stovepipe becomes coated with creosote. We have seen installations with a cleaning port and a bucket to receive the flow.

This creosote is very flammable. If at a later time you release exhaust gases at a higher temperature by failing to use the damper correctly, this creosote can ignite and cause a raging chimney fire. A chimney should be maintained in condition to withstand just such a fire, but it's a terrifying experience and a good many chimneys would fail the test. It is important that an air-tight stove exhaust *only* into a very well-constructed chimney or into an existing chimney that has been fitted with an additional steel lining that can be removed and cleaned. This accumulation of creosote is not peculiar to air-tight stoves but their mode of operation does aggravate the problem.

One method recommended to reduce creosote buildup is to deliberately have a hot fire each day for about thirty minutes to "burn off" the creosote before it gets a chance to accumulate. Our recommendation is to avoid the long slow burn that is the single largest cause of the problem. It is better to burn the fuel itself efficiently, get the heat out of the wood stove and into the room, and store it within the thermal mass of the stove itself. To this end, many wood stoves are now being clad in masonry.

In a similar fashion, we do not recommend the use of *flue-heat recovery devices.* Such devices may be used successfully to supplement the heat exchange of a wood stove or oil furnace that is operating inefficiently and works best at flue temperatures of 600°, which is the high end of acceptable temperature for any exhaust. It is better simply to have your furnace adjusted and get it working properly by itself. Heat-recovery devices should never be placed on the flue of an air-tight stove, nor should they be so large and effective as to reduce the stack temperature of any flue below 300°.

SUGGESTIONS FOR FURTHER READING

Weatherproofing and *Heating and Cooling.* Two of a series of *Time-Life Books* with detailed and practical information. High-quality illustrations. Moisture and furnace maintenance are especially well covered.
New York: Time-Life Books, Inc., 1976 and 1977. $11.56

Window Design Strategies to Conserve Engergy, in the NBS Building Science Series. One of the finest publications available in Washington, this summarizes research around the country and provides in an orderly and readable fashion the thermal benefits

of a wide range of improvements from landscaping to building interiors.
Available from the U.S. Government Printing Office. $3.75

Windows Beautiful, by the Kirsch drapery hardware people. A readable and useful ideabook to help you choose, plan, and make or order curtains and drapes—but does not estimate thermal benefits.
Available at fabric stores. 1972.

The Climate Near the Ground, by Rudolph Geiger. A classic, thorough discussion of microclimate—still the major text after thirty years. Packed with numbers and graphs; a bit heavy to read after supper.
Cambridge, Mass.: Harvard University Press, 1950. $18.00

Plants, People and Environmental Quality, by Gary Robinette, for the U.S. Department of the Interior. A remarkable publication with a sensitive and sensible discussion of landscape architecture. Very useful information delightfully presented.
Available from the U.S. Government Printing Office. $5.25

Earth-Sheltered Housing Design, by the Underground Space Center. A readable and well-organized discussion of the potential benefits and present difficulties of earth-covered homes.
Available from the University of Minnesota.

The Solar Home Book, by Bruce Anderson and Michael Riordan. Generally acknowledged as the primer to solar energy, this book covers the range from passive to active systems; it also scores on historical perspective and general readability. With its extensive appendixes, it is most useful as a source of tabled information.
Harrisville, N.H.: Cheshire Books, 1976. $12.95; $8.50 (paper)

Solar Dwelling Design Concepts, by the AIA Research Corporation. A commendable effort to present in brief but well-organized form the range of criteria to be considered in the design of a solar home.
Available from the U.S. Government Printing Office. $6.95

The Solar Greenhouse Book, edited by James McCullough. An extensive discussion of the entire range of issues, from theory through construction and into horticulture. A practical introduction to a promising new subject.
Emmaus, Pa.: Rodale Press, 1978. $8.95

5. CHOOSING MATERIALS

Choosing which material to use comes rather late in the game—after you have made the more important decisions, such as what to work on. For any particular job there are almost always two or more possible materials; you shouldn't lock yourself into choosing one material just because some advertisement calls it a "miracle of modern technology." Materials themselves don't do the job unless they are correctly installed, so choose a material that you can handle and understand. Above all, suit the material to the individual situation. Price is usually secondary unless you are thinking of a large project, such as insulating the walls. Availability is the third important factor. Sometimes a product you prefer is out of stock locally and you have a choice of waiting for a new shipment or substituting another product. The last excuse is called procrastination.

INSULATIONS

There are usually two or three suitable insulations to choose from. Thermal resistance is an important factor in insulation, but R-values are secondary to the quality of the installation. If you are doing the work yourself, use a process you understand and can control. Be certain you have the skills and equipment. If you hire out the work, follow the processes that the contractor recommends. It will be what he knows best and will give best results.

FIBERGLASS

The most common insulating process is to place rolls or batts of fiberglass between wall studs or ceiling or floor joists. Fiberglass is one of the best insulating buys (R-value per dollar), requires little equipment or skill, and introduces few problems. It is almost

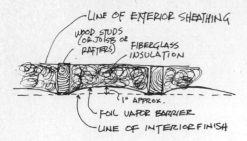

LINE OF EXTERIOR SHEATHING
WOOD STUDS (OR JOISTS OR RAFTERS)
FIBERGLASS INSULATION
1" APPROX.
FOIL VAPOR BARRIER
LINE OF INTERIOR FINISH

Fiberglass batts or rolls with foil backing. If polyethylene is used, it is stretched across at the dotted line.

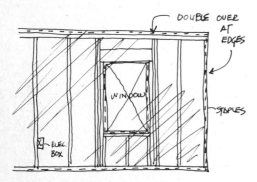

DOUBLE OVER AT EDGES
WINDOW
STAPLES
ELEC. BOX

Polyethylene is stretched over the entire wall surface. The holes for windows, doors, electrical boxes, and so on are cut out afterward, and the edges taped for a moisture seal.

CELLULOSE

N - 101 - 73
or
ASTM   C - 739 - 77
or
HH - I - 515D

Check cellulose bags to find one of these standards.

always preferred when the insulating space is easily accessible. Being a mineral, it will not burn, rot, or support vermin.

Batts are easily carried up to the attic and placed between joist spaces. Most spaces are either 16 or 24 inches wide, both of which are common sizes for batts. New wall construction maintains 16-inch stud spaces and insulation fits snugly within them. Batts and rolls come either with or without backing of aluminum foil or kraft paper. The aluminum foil works as a vapor barrier; the kraft backing is much less effective. The type with aluminum-foil backing should be placed with the foil on the warm side as a vapor barrier and stapled to the inside of the studs, leaving an inch of space within the cavity to create an air space between the foil and the interior finish. It is essential with plain batts, but good practice always, to provide vapor protection with a complete sheet of 4-mil polyethylene over the entire wall. The insulation will pass moisture and become soaked if installed without it. Secure the full sheet in place and then carefully cut an *X* at each opening for windows and electrical boxes. The fit should be taped tightly around the frame or box.

Some people find fiberglass very itchy and wear long shirts, protective gloves, and face masks. Others simply prefer to complete the task as soon as possible and get into a cold rinse and hot shower to sweat out the fibers. Greater protection is needed for longer tasks.

Cellulose is an alternative insulator for attics. Cellulose is a loose, gray material made from recycled newspapers, is organic, and must be treated with chemicals to be fire-resistant. Cellulose treated with ammonium or aluminum sulfate as a fire-retardant rather than boric acid should not be used because the sulfate reacts with moisture to form sulfuric acid, which can damage metal, wood, or stone. Cellulose is now widely used in attics because it is cheaper than fiberglass and has a better R-value per inch. It is used in walls, but it tends to settle over time and leave a cold air space at the top. It also tends to absorb moisture, rot, and support vermin.

For a time, cellulose was produced by small contractors who ground up newspapers and treated them with chemicals in their own workshops. This often resulted in the installation of inferior cellulose and led to a number of serious fires. By law, cellulose is now produced under careful quality control and must meet federal specifications. Each bag of cellulose should carry a certificate stating that it meets one of the standards shown in the table at the left.

Before pouring the stuff into your attic, be certain all your electrical wires are protected and securely taped. Build retainer walls around ceiling light fixtures to keep insulation a full 3 inches away from hot bulbs. These two problems are the main sources of cellulose fires. Also surround your chimney with a layer of noncombustible fiberglass and build fiberglass dams at the overhangs of the roof to prevent loose cellulose from covering eave vents. With adequate precautions, you will get good results from cellulose. Be certain that a contractor follows these same procedures.

Few attic installations have vapor barriers, but a better job will include one. There are two ways to do this. One is to cut strips of polyethylene and staple them along the bottoms of the joists, with the insulation fitting in above. This method has the advantage of leaving the tops of the joists exposed. The second method is to stretch one sheet of poly across the tops of the joists, stapling or fastening wood strips at the edges. This method is quicker and allows less moisture to sneak through along the joists. You do, however, wind up with an ocean of insulation that conceals the joists. If you ever want to work up there in the future, you must push aside the insulation in your path. Place a few boards down the middle to move around on.

All attics should be ventilated, and this is particularly true for cellulose installations with no vapor protection. Vapor trapped in the attic will be absorbed by the cellulose, turn to water, and cause the material to compress permanently, greatly reducing its thermal resistance. Condensation within cellulose may leach out the fire-retardant chemicals, leaving the cellulose unprotected.

Keep poured-in insulation at a distance from light fixtures.

Vapor barriers with attic insulation

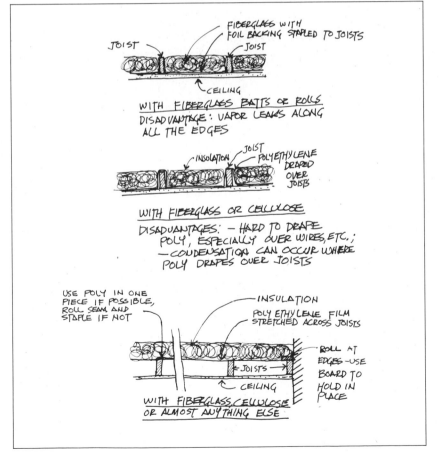

The particular problems of insulating existing wall cavities have led to the development of several blown-into-place insulating processes. Both cellulose and loose fiberglass can be blown into walls or attics for a quick job by a contractor, but are best used only in the attic. Another material for insulating enclosed wall cavities is urea-formaldehyde. Developed specifically for this use, urea-formaldehyde is injected into a wall or other enclosed space by way of small openings as a two-part liquid; once in the wall, it expands to the consistency of shaving cream to fill all the gaps and corners, which are often missed by other methods. Care must still be taken to recognize the obstruction of firestops.

Urea-formaldehyde is somewhat more expensive than blown fiberglass but has a better thermal resistance. It is fire-resistant and will not rot or harbor vermin. It will allow vapor to pass but will lose much of its insulating value if left without a vapor barrier.

There are, however, several objections to urea-formaldehyde. One is that it shrinks as it cures. After an initial set of about 45 seconds, the foam continues to cure and release moisture for as long as 60 days. As much as a full pint of water leaves each 16-inch wall cavity, so openings must be provided for this to escape as a vapor lest it settle and form puddles. With this loss of water comes a shrinkage of the foam. Proper installation will keep this shrinkage to 4–6 percent, but it can be as high as 10 percent if improperly installed. A full 10 percent shrinkage will leave $\frac{3}{4}$-inch gaps on either side of the insulation and gaps up to $\frac{1}{4}$ inch on each broad surface. Such spaces permit infiltration and allow convection currents within the cavity to bypass the insulation and chill the interior wall.

A more serious objection to urea foam is that, if not properly mixed, it may either disintegrate or produce noxious odors. There have been stories of houses becoming unlivable and sickening the inhabitants with the odors. At this writing the state of Massachusetts is seeking to ban its use there. The contractors who sell this service, naturally upset, claim that it is only a few incompetents among them who do the bad work and that government licensing will solve the problem.

Urea-formaldehyde *is* a good product when correctly installed. A competent contractor is therefore an absolute necessity. Such a contractor will test the mixture of his foam two or three times a day. The set time for foam should never exceed 60 seconds. The temperature of the foam materials should be between 60° and 80°. The optimum outside temperatures for foaming are between 50° and 80°, but it is okay to install foam down to freezing temperatures. Temperatures below freezing will delay the cure and there is a danger of freezing moisture inside the insulation and rupturing cells. Temperatures above 80° cause too rapid a cure and result in excessive shrinkage.

The necessity to place insulation in the ground led to the

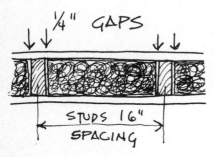

Urea foam shrinkage at 4 percent (Even an absolute minimum of 2 percent creates ⅛-inch-plus gaps.)

development of sheets of insulating foamboards. The most popular foamboard is *Styrofoam*, which is a closed-cell extruded polystyrene foam with good insulating values and a high resistance to water absorption and vapor transmission. Other polystyrene boards, like *beadboard,* have about the same resistance to heat transfer but little resistance to moisture penetration. Beadboard is useful as a sheathing material but is not recommended for use in the ground. *Polyurethane* panels have the highest insulating value per inch of the commonly available foamboards but have low resistance to moisture penetration. *Foamglass,* on the other hand, has the lowest thermal resistance of the common foamboards but has a total resistance to water absorption and vapor transmission, which makes it ideal for in-ground and roof deck applications.

The choice among foamboards depends on the moisture content of the ground into which it is to be placed, whether it is to be protected by an additional vapor barrier, and the desired thermal protection. As discussed in Chapter 4, in-ground insulations require less R-value than an open-air installation because the intent is more to isolate the house from the earth than to insulate it from the cold.

Styrofoam and other foamboards are now being promoted as a total sheathing system for a house above and below grade. Applied outside the wall studs and beneath the siding, they prevent heat transfer through the studs themselves and are

FOAMBOARDS

INSULATED SHEATHING

FOAMBOARD INSULATIONS FOR IN-GROUND USE

	R-Value/In. Thick		Moisture Absorption (perm-inch)	Installed cost/bd.-ft. (bd.-ft. = 12" × 12" × 1")	R-value per $		Remarks
	Initial (dry)	Final (wet)			(dry)	(wet)	
Styrofoam (Dow trademark)	5.0	4.5	0.6 (good)	$.16	31	28	Flammable—must be covered. No vapor barrier required.
Beadboard (expanded polystyrene)	4.0	2.8	2.0 (not good)	.11	36	25	Flammable—must be covered. Requires vapor barrier.
Polyurethane	6.5	3.0	2.0 (not good)	.19	34	15	Flammable—must be covered. Requires vapor barrier.
Foamglass	3.0	3.0	0.0 (perfect)	.20	20		Nonflammable. No vapor barrier required.

commonly used in addition to fiberglass within the cavity. A problem with this procedure is that it provides a vapor barrier on the cold side of the fiberglass and can lead to condensation without cold side venting. This venting can be provided through special details that allow some cold air to enter and leave the cavity and take with it excess vapor, but this undercuts the insulating value! Another disadvantage of insulating sheathing is the loss of the bracing usually provided by plywood, and not really provided by the small 1 × 2's that are now added.

Thermax, a derivative of urethane, is another product used in much the same way. It should be protected by polyethylene when used below the ground, yet its surfacing of aluminum foil provides good vapor protection in walls when the joints are sealed. Sheets of this material applied inside the stud wall before the Sheetrock serve both as a thermal break to the wall stud and as a vapor barrier for the entire wall system.

The interior use of foamboards is especially valuable in locations of little space. One inch of urethane insulation is worth 2 to 3 inches of fiberglass batt and is the only reasonable way to insulate a solid masonry wall. After removing $\frac{3}{4}$ of an inch of plaster and lath from the wall, a homeowner can install 1 inch of insulation and $\frac{1}{2}$ inch of Sheetrock and lose only $\frac{3}{4}$ of an inch of detail around the windows and doors. This amount of space can usually be sacrificed without having to rebuild door and window frames. This 1 inch of urethane will reduce wall heat losses by 66 percent.

Styrene and urethane foams are highly flammable and must always be adequately protected. When used on an interior wall, they must be covered with at least a half-inch of fireproof material, such as Sheetrock.

All the materials mentioned have been *mass insulations*. Mass insulations reduce heat loss by achieving low densities and low rates of thermal conductivity. The thermal values of all the previous insulations come from their capacity to create still air spaces with minimal amounts of material—in other words, fluff. The less dense the material, the better its R-value.

Moisture does terrible things to the insulating value of a material. Water will distribute itself along the fibers of a material and provide paths for heat conduction. In this way, *even small amounts of water can drastically reduce R-values*. If it can be vented away and the material dries out, its R-value may recover, but many insulations, such as rock-wool and cellulose, become permanently matted by moisture and never regain their original values. However, materials with low permeability values, such as closed-cell insulations, resist water penetration and retain their R-values.

By contrast with mass insulations, *reflective insulations* reduce heat transfer by stopping radiation. A highly polished metal surface

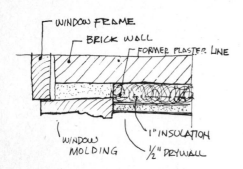

INSULATING A BRICK WALL   Use of only 1 inch of insulation board of high R-value plus ½ inch of drywall means the window molding can stay in place.

may reflect 95 percent of the energy that reaches it. Conduction within such material is high but only 5 percent of the heat gets in. Reflective insulating systems use multiple layers of polished metal to achieve thermal resistance values higher than mass insulation, since there can be many layers of aluminum in a small space. "Space blankets" have up to forty layers per inch to develop a very high thermal resistance.

A reflective system for buildings can be purchased as a material package or can be developed at the site by the builder. Simply recessing foil-faced fiberglass insulation into the stud space and covering the cavity with aluminum-faced Thermax or aluminum-faced Sheetrock will create a double-foil-faced air space. This space with a thermal resistance of 3 is totally lost if the fiberglass is applied flush to the stud face.

A system of three foil faces within a $3\frac{1}{2}$-inch space can achieve R-values of 21 in a wall. When placed in a horizontal position, the values are different for heat moving up or down with values of 15 upward and 29 downward. This resistance of 29 in a downward position is especially valuable in resisting summer attic heat gain. These values compare to an R-value of only 11 for $3\frac{1}{2}$ inches of fiberglass.

Carefully constructed reflective systems can be more effective than mass systems and deserve a good deal of further investigation.

VAPOR BARRIERS

Permeability has been introduced as a measure of the capacity of a material to permit the passage of water vapor. The table below illustrates the amount of vapor lost for various permeabilities and gives an indication of the humidity loss in older buildings with high permeability values.

Perm values below 0.5 should be sought for any existing building, while values of 0.1 or less are easy to obtain in new construction. It is often worthwhile to treat the insulation process

MOISTURE THROUGH A WALL ON A COLD DAY

Outside: temperature 0° F, relative humidity 35%
Inside: temperature 70° F, relative humidity 60%

Wall Surface	Permeability	Quarts/day/ 1000 sq. ft.
Unfinished Sheetrock	20	120
Clean plaster	10	60
Plaster and paint	2–3	12–18
Minimum vapor barrier	0.5	1.0
Preferred vapor barrier	0.1	0.6

of older homes like new construction simply to acquire these better permeability values.

Most walls have very poor resistance to vapor penetration and should be improved by adding new impermeable layers. The quality of a vapor barrier depends on the *continuity* of the barrier's surface. Polyethylene films are excellent because they have few seams and can absorb a good deal of wall motion without rupture. Paint vapor barriers applied to plaster or Sheetrock are apt to peel, blister or crack.

PAINTED VAPOR BARRIERS

It is possible to obtain vapor protection from a painted plaster surface if it is developed with special care. *The wall must be sound and secure;* it must have a good foundation and windbracing. Chances of maintaining a good vapor barrier in a poorly braced light-wood-frame building are very poor. Painted vapor barriers can be more easily maintained on the plaster of a heavy masonry building and can be of value even without insulation, because a good vapor barrier will allow masonry to dry to the outside to often double its natural insulating value. The need for artificial humidification can be totally eliminated because the moisture that occurs naturally is kept inside.

After the wall is stabilized, you should restore the surface of the plaster and give special attention to sealing all cracks around windows and doors and electrical boxes. This will at the same time help to reduce infiltration. Reinforce all cracks in the surface of old plaster with Sheetrock tape imbedded in compound to prevent cracks from reopening. Many of these cracks appear simply from ground vibration caused by street traffic and heavy trucks. A thin webbing of fiberglass cloth may also be papered over the entire wall to reinforce the surface for a superior job. This fiberglass web can then be filled with a thin layer of finish plaster.

When dry, this plaster should receive a heavy coating of primer-sealer. Don't be afraid to apply two coats of sealer if you suspect certain areas to be thin, and most certainly do so on surfaces of high interior humidity or severe exterior exposure. Onto this apply two coats of finish paints. Such a process can provide vapor protection that will approach values of 0.2. Careful preparation and thorough reinforcement of the wall will ensure long-lasting protection.

Oil-based paints provide a tighter initial seal than do latex paints, but they dry to a harder finish that is more likely to crack and peel over time. More experimentation is needed to determine the best materials for base coats. Insul-Aid is a primer-sealer marketed especially for vapor protection by Glidden. Waterproof paints can be used as primers as long as the final covering is compatible. Aluminum paint, vinyl, polyethylene, and silicone emulsions and sprays are all commercially available and might be applied to interior walls prior to finish coats of paint. As demand develops, these products will become available to the homeowner. They would have the advantage of producing a longer-lasting elastic surface.

After going through all this trouble to develop a painted vapor barrier, work to maintain it. Give window and door frames an annual check and applications of patching plaster as needed. Use adhesive hangers or picture rails to hang pictures and heavy paintings to avoid poking holes into your new vapor membrane. Even small openings allow for vapor escape and will lead to local deterioration of the plaster and eventual blistering and peeling of the surface.

SHEET MATERIALS

An alternative is to apply an actual sheet of vapor-resistant material to the surface of the wall. Papering kitchens and bath-rooms with quality *vinyl wallcoverings* will provide vapor protection as low as 0.1 with careful attention to overlaps and penetrations. A future concern may be the difficulty of either adhering new paper to this glassy surface or removing the old. Aluminum-

WATER-VAPOR PASSAGE (PERMEABILITY) THROUGH VARIOUS BUILDING MATERIALS

Insulations	
Fiberglass	70
Urea foam	26
Foamboards	3–0.6
Foamglass	0.0
Vapor membranes	
4-mil polyethylene film	0.1
Thermax	0.01
0.5-mil aluminum foil	0.005
Asphalt-saturated paper	0.3
Waxed paper	0.2
Interior-finish material	
Sheetrock	20
$\frac{3}{4}''$ lath and plaster	10
$\frac{1}{4}''$ wood paneling	2
Interior finish	
1 coat primer, 1 oil paint	0.9
1 coat primer, 1 coat latex	0.5
Rubber-based primer, latex finish	0.3
Vinyl wallpaper	0.1–0.9
Aluminum-faced wallpaper	0.05–0.5
Exterior finish	
Building paper	5
$\frac{3}{4}''$ plywood, oil stain	1
Plywood, 2 coats oil paint	0.2
Aluminum siding	0

backed fabric paper is more expensive but provides good protection with a soft-textured surface that will be more complementary to most rooms of the house.

The best place for a vapor barrier is within the wall, beneath a protective finish and just before the insulation. With new construction this is easy to achieve with a full sheet of *polyethylene* installed over the wall studs to enclose the room completely. This membrane should then be carefully cut with undersized X's for windows and electrical boxes, and these penetrations should be fully sealed with duct tape.

Aluminum is a total barrier to vapor and is used as a facing for some insulations, such as Thermax. The joints between sheets of Thermax should be taped with either duct or aluminum tape and openings around windows sealed by spraying in a small amount of foam for a positive enclosure.

VENT BEYOND THE BARRIER

If you have doubts about the strength of your vapor barrier, it is best to increase the amount of ventilation within the wall cavity to prevent problems of condensation. Sheathing, building paper, and sidings on the outside of the insulation may constitute a considerable barrier to vapor, which should be no more than $\frac{1}{5}$ the strength of the interior vapor barrier (i.e., these should have 5 times the permeability of the interior layers). Vapor barriers should not be placed outside the insulation except where summer heat and humidity are intense and air conditioning is being used; in such cases, consult an engineer.

CAULKING

Caulking is used to stop infiltration and provide an exterior seal against rainwater. Most caulking is sold in dispensable 10-ounce tubes. Materials range from simple oil and latex compounds to more elaborate latex, urethane, or silicone compounds. A study of thirty-seven products by a *Consumer Reports* testing lab in March 1976 revealed a wide range of performance among caulks and little correspondence between various materials, their expense, and their performance. In fact, a 51¢ tube of oil-based caulk was found to outperform many products that sold for $3 and $4. All products were judged useful and performed acceptably but some simply had superior qualities. The best ones do tend to be expensive.

The primary quality of a caulking compound is as a filler that adheres to the surfaces of an opening and maintains its grasp as neighboring materials move about. This motion can be produced by wind pressure, settling of the earth, or the impact of door and window operation. Materials that harden and become brittle are unsuitable as caulking because they crumble and fall out. Caulking, which started as mud and straw chinking around logs, is now sophisticated chemistry—compounds now adhere fiercely and remain flexible and rubbery for years. *Consumer Reports* found that the expensive *silicones* and *polyurethanes* performed best at maintaining flexibility, while *butyl* and *acrylic latex* were consistent performers at reasonable prices.

The method of application was found to affect the ease and quality of the job. Most caulks should be applied to clean, dry, and primed surfaces. The tip of the applicator should be cut at an angle to allow the operator to view the process of the work. Caulk should be gunned into a vertical gap, moving from the bottom upward so as to fill the space and maintain a small bead in front of the tube as the operation proceeds. Large openings should be prepared by inserting foam rope or oakum before the application of caulking. Silicone caulking cannot be painted but all other compounds were found to withstand aging better with a protective coating of paint.

Some caulks were found to bleed through paint and stain adjacent materials. Oils were particularly troublesome in this respect and should not be applied near light-colored masonry. Silicones that have spread onto adjacent surfaces during the process of application or leveling-off had the problem of spreading their resistance to paint. Abutting areas that are to be painted later should be carefully masked before the application of silicone caulk.

In general, caulking is easy with practice but is a tedious task if you have a lot of it to do. It can be dangerous as well, when you find yourself reaching out beyond the end of a ladder to fill an awkward joint. So work safely and treat yourself to a quality material, so that the application will last five to ten years.

WEATHER STRIPPING

Of all improvements, you will probably spend more time fussing with weather stripping than any other material. It is hard to acquire the right frame of mind to deal seriously and intently with something of so little size and weight. At a cost of only 5–25¢ per lineal foot, the material itself is quite inexpensive. Yet weather stripping does not just jump into place; it must be installed in *just* the right position if it is to function *at all.* There are a number of different products and each has an appropriate use and position. Each has its own skill level, too. While tilt-in window frames have been developed for the do-it-yourselfer, other processes that involve cutting an accurate $\frac{1}{4}$-inch groove down the entire length of a window sash demand the equipment and skill of an advanced home craftsperson or professional. It may at times be worth the additional expense to obtain a professional job. The complexity of the joint and the precision of the fit are just what makes weather stripping work.

The simplest material, and one of the most durable, is a roll of *metal tension strip*. These strips of steel in brass, bronze, or aluminum color are nailed on one edge to door or window frames. The free edge is then lifted and bent to create sliding pressure against the moving surface of doors and windows. These strips

TENSION WEATHER STRIPPING

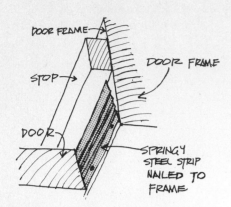

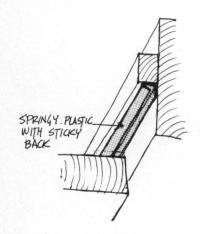

Springy steel strip may be used for doors or windows.

Schlegel Company's plastic weather stripping

work best with about ⅛ inch of space and a relatively straight surface against which to slide. They are the only weather-stripping materials designed to absorb sliding motion and can therefore be hidden within the junction of window and frame.

Schlegel Manufacturing Company has recently developed a series of very fine weather-stripping products including a set of springy plastic strips with adhesive backing, a variation of the metal tension strip. These products may be generally available by the time you read this or may be obtained by contacting the main office of Schlegel Manufacturing Company, 400 East Ave., P.O. Box 23113, Rochester, New York 14692.

An easier weather strip to install is compression weather strip, which is positioned tightly against the top and sides of doors and windows and nailed to the existing stops. One type is a *tubular gasket* of rubber or vinyl that may be foam-filled or left empty; the foam-filled is usually better. The flange of the gasket is sometimes reinforced with aluminum to help keep the weather strip in line and in firm contact with the door. It is sometimes necessary to caulk the existing doorstop to prevent infiltration from bypassing the tubular gasket. These gaskets may be ¼ or ½ inch in diameter, and are not very attractive. They may be placed around double-hung windows but should be reserved for the outside of the bottom rail of the lower sash (which has the greatest flow of air), where they will not be seen.

Felt weather stripping is probably the cheapest and most common form of weather stripping. The secret to proper positioning and long life is to glue it into place with a thin bead of caulking prior to stapling it. Felt should be placed within the closure of a door or along the top and bottom of a double-hung window. It is designed for compression and will deteriorate quickly if placed against a sliding surface. Because it is thin, it will fit into small gaps, but it cannot expand to fill large irregularities.

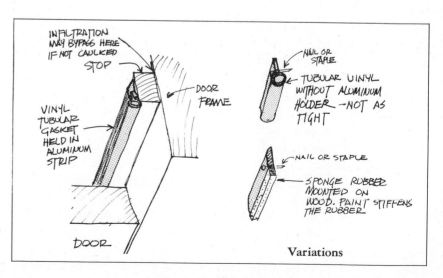

Contact weather stripping

Large spaces can be filled with a *foam strip* that functions much like felt but is available in a range of thicknesses and widths from ¼ inch to a full 1 inch square. These foams are highly compressible and usually come with a self-sticking backing.

Some of the finest weather stripping involves interlocking pieces that slide or close one into the other and provide a circuitous obstacle course for air. The wooden stops around the door and between the two window sashes are the most elementary forms. Many plastic products are now available but quality metal shapes have been used for over a hundred years. As the path air must take becomes more complex and the fit more precise, the performance of the weather strip improves. The special value of this form of weather stripping is its position within the door or window closure, where it can neither be seen nor be subject to abuse. Most factory-made windows come equipped with these products and modern materials are available to recondition an old window or door.

The simplest *interlocking weather stripping* is constructed by grooving the sides of a window sash and installing a tongue on the fixed frame for the sash to slide onto. The tongue may be of wood, metal, or plastic, but flexible materials are more easily installed in such a way that the sash may be taken out and returned without taking apart the entire frame.

Complete metal units of stops and spacers are available to fit existing sashes that tilt into the existing frame and provide weather-stripping protection simply and inexpensively. Such replacement tracks for the two sides of an old window can be bought for as little as $10 and installed in less than an hour. Another advantage of these metal units is that the expanding internal stop adjusts to the seasonal swelling and shrinkage of wood. Summer expansion of wood with humidity is permitted without creating high frictional pressures.

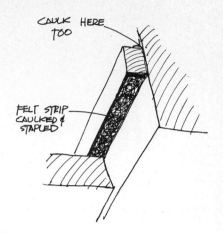

Felt weather stripping (only works for an even fit between door and frame)

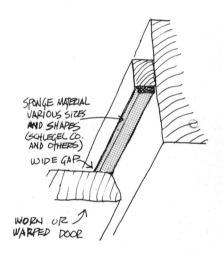

SPONGY STRIPS (stickum on them)   Care must be taken to use just the right thickness; otherwise there will either be a gap or the door may be all but impossible to close. If installed on hinge side, spongy strips may put a strain on the hinges.

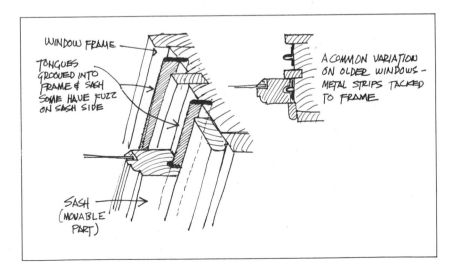

Interlocking weather stripping

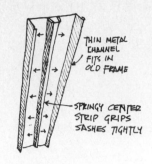

THIN METAL CHANNEL FITS IN OLD FRAME

SPRINGY CENTER STRIP GRIPS SASHES TIGHTLY

TILTING IT INTO PLACE

Light metal channels set into existing frames provide one of the cheapest, easiest, and best ways to recondition a double-hung window. Weather stripping for horizontal members must be worked out, too.

Weather Stripping for Doors

Doors are a tougher problem than windows because they must swing free of their frames many times a day. The simpler types of contact weather stripping mentioned above all work but are subject to considerable wear and tear and may break down and cease to be effective after only a short time. It is therefore a good idea to consider more elaborate and durable methods.

While the interlocking channels of windows are relatively easy to build and maintain because they are held in alignment by the window sash, similar items for doors and hinged-casement windows must be allowed to move apart and return in true alignment. Interlocking hardware for heavy doors must be of heavier-gauge material and protected from severe abuse. The door itself must be securely hinged and have good resistance to warpage for long-time benefits.

The simplest interlocking mechanism for a hinged door places a tongue on the face of the door; the tongue fits into a groove developed by adding a metal sleeve to the visible surface of the doorstop. Such hardware is easy to install but remains visible and may be damaged.

Better protection is obtained by placing the tongue on the closure of the stop and the metal sleeve on the edge of the door. The door must be cut back ¼ inch along the entire length to allow room for the sleeve, which remains visible. A fully professional job would be to cut out only a small corner of the door and place both interlocking channels deep into the recess where they would be safe from damage and out of sight.

THRESHOLD WEATHER STRIPS

Weather stripping for thresholds takes elaborate forms because it seals an area that is walked upon and must clear the surfacing

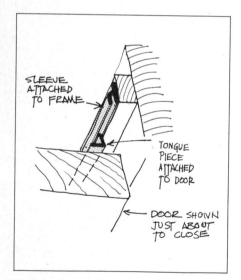

SLEEVE ATTACHED TO FRAME

TONGUE PIECE ATTACHED TO DOOR

DOOR SHOWN JUST ABOUT TO CLOSE

Interlocking weather stripping, surface-mounted

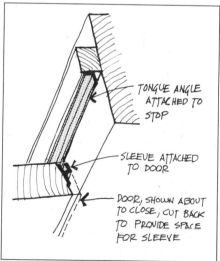

TONGUE ANGLE ATTACHED TO STOP

SLEEVE ATTACHED TO DOOR

DOOR, SHOWN ABOUT TO CLOSE, CUT BACK TO PROVIDE SPACE FOR SLEEVE

Door cut back to allow room for sleeve

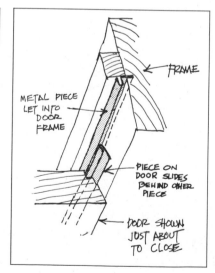

FRAME

METAL PIECE LET INTO DOOR FRAME

PIECE ON DOOR SLIDES BEHIND OTHER PIECE

DOOR SHOWN JUST ABOUT TO CLOSE

Old-fashioned interlocking-type weather stripping is often made of zinc (gray).

of the floor when the door is opened. One of the simplest designs is the sweep-strip, a heavy rubber or vinyl strip reinforced with a metal holding plate fastened to the bottom inside surface of the door. The rubber strip closes against the existing threshold and is wedged tightly as the door is latched. This works well when the threshold rises well above the surface of the floor to meet the rubber strip, and is required with a carpeted floor.

Another excellent closure for an aluminum threshold can be achieved with a *vinyl bulb* that rises to meet the bottom of the

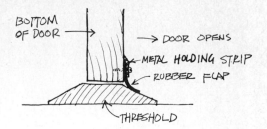

The simplest door bottom is the sweep strip. Unfortunately, it is usually no good with carpets and rugs.

WEATHER STRIPPING

	Cost per lineal foot ($)	Durability	Visibility
Metal tension strip			
brass	.20	excellent	very low
aluminum	.10	very good	very low
plastic	.15	good	low
Tubular gasket			
hollow vinyl	.10	good	high
foam-filled vinyl	.22	good	high
Felt			
wool	.10	fair	high
other	.05	fair	high
wool, reinforced	.12	good	high
Foam			
neoprene	.15	fair	high
urethane	.10	poor	high
vinyl	.05	poor	high
Interlocking window units			
simple tongue and slotted wood	1.50*	good	low
tilt-in aluminum frame	1.50	very good	low
tilt-in frame with expansion spacer	2.00	very good	low
tilt-in frame with tongues for slotted sash	3.00*	very good	low
additional fuzz strips	.10	good	low
Interlocking door unit			
exposed	.80	good	high
concealed	2.00*	very good	low
Threshold			
rubber sweep	.60	good	high
vinyl bulb in aluminum	1.50	very good	low
exposed hinged plate	2.50*	good	high

* Includes cost of professional installation.

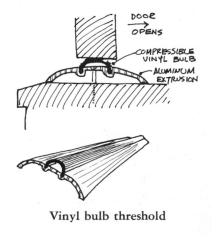

Vinyl bulb threshold

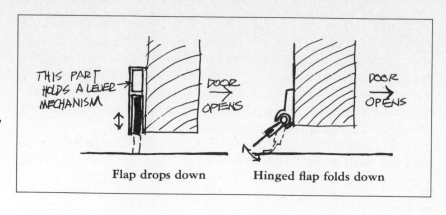

Flap drops down   Hinged flap folds down

Door bottoms of the Rube Goldberg persuasion: Flaps stay clear of rugs, etc., until the door approaches closure, at which point—by means of levers, etc.—they drop into place. Properly installed and adjusted, these can work remarkably well.

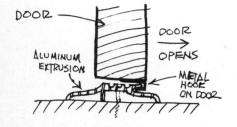

INTERLOCKING THRESHOLDS (There are several similar types and sizes.) These are generally not seen in hardware stores but must be obtained from architectural hardware firms.

door. As the door closes, the bulb compresses to assure a tight fit. Most bulbs compress only about $\frac{1}{4}$ inch, so the threshold must be installed reasonably parallel to the bottom of the door. This may involve some careful leveling of the threshold or trimming of the bottom of the door. The result is more attractive than the sweep-strip.

Other thresholds use moving and interlocking parts. One system includes a *hinged drop plate* along the bottom edge of the door that rides up the threshold during the closing of the door and then drops into a slot. This mechanism must be connected to the door handle to raise the bottom plate when the door is to be opened. Other systems involve hinged flaps activated by levers that come down just as the door closes. In some cases, the entire mechanism is enclosed within the door. An advantage of slotted systems is that wind pressure tends only to secure the door more tightly. Predictably, some of these are complex and expensive.

WINDOWS

The analysis of materials for the improvement of windows will be covered in three sections: glazing, frames, and curtains and shutters. This discussion will deal only with the properties of the different materials and will be highlighted by a few example constructions that you can make in your own home.

GLAZING   The individual pieces of glass in your window are called *glazing*. The most common glazing is glass itself and comes in three weights: single, double, and plate glass. A piece of glass larger than 60 united inches (height plus width) should be double strength; larger than 100 united inches, it should be plate glass. Two layers of glazing are now commonly used to reduce heat loss. Insulating glass is double glazing with a sealed air space between. Most weights of glass are available in a variety of tints to reduce glare and in patterns to provide privacy. Special tempered glass is more resistant to breakage and is used for greater safety and security.

The qualities of glass are now being rivaled by plastics and in some instances plastic is a more suitable glazing. Many plastics are now less expensive than glass and are less susceptible to breakage.

They are lighter, more flexible, can be sawed and screwed—altogether safer and easier to handle. The yellowing of most plastic glazings is now under control but many will scratch easily, marring appearance and transparency somewhat. Acrylic and polycarbonate are both quality plastic glazings that provide long service. *Acrylic* is less expensive and less likely to scratch but *polycarbonate* is more resistant to outright vandalism. (Polycarbonate is most readily available under the General Electric trade name *Lexan*.) *Styrene* is yet another glazing with similar properties that has just been introduced.

Both acrylic and Lexan are available as lightweight *double-wall sheets* that outperform Thermopane and are much less expensive. Because of their construction with closely spaced interior ribs, they are not optically clear but are now commonly used for solar-collector covers and as greenhouse glazing. They are also frequently used for large institutional applications. A translucent glazing of reinforced fiberglass produced by Kalwall is nearly unbreakable and less expensive than any other rigid glazing. Because it distorts vision, it is also used mostly for solar collectors and greenhouses.

Several new *glazing films* are now being marketed with novel installation procedures that stretch the films evenly and provide for clear vision. Two films produced by Dupont sell under the names of *Tedlar* and *Teflon* and both perform well as interior layers of a glazing composition. *Mylar* is an older product that is somewhat more expensive but is more durable; it finds many uses,

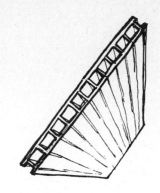

Double-wall plastic in sheets
¼ inch–1 inch thick × 4 feet × 8 feet

Kalwall
Solar Components Division
P. O. Box 237
Manchester, NH 03105
(603) 668 - 8186

GLAZING CHOICES

	Cost ($)/sq. ft.
Glass	
single weight	1.25
double weight	1.50
plate glass	2–3.00
sealed double glazing	4–5.00
Rigid plastics	
acrylic	1.60
Lexan (polycarbonate)	1.75
styrene	.60
Kalwall (fiberglass)	.75
Twin-wall glazing	
acrylic	
polycarbonate	1.50
Clear glazing films	
Teflon	.45
Tedlar	.45
Mylar	
Martin UV-X polyester	.75

SUN Catalog
Solar Usage Now
P. O. Box 306
Bascom, OH 44809
(419) 937 - 2226

$2; approx. 220 pages

ADDING LAYERS OF GLAZING

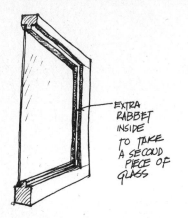

EXTRA RABBET INSIDE TO TAKE A SECOND PIECE OF GLASS

Adding another layer of glass

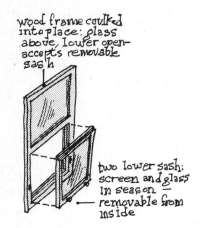

wood frame caulked into place: glass above, lower open-accepts removable sash

two lower sash: screen and glass in season — removable from inside

"Yonkers" window (discovered on a house in that town)

Temp-Rite Inc.
3934 N.E. Union
Portland, OR 97212
(503) 281 - 3434

or

Solar Usage Now
P. O. Box 306
Bascom, OH 44809

Two varieties of Temp-Rite's inside storm windows. Outside-mounted ones should have a vent near the bottom.

especially as a transparent roll shade. A new film by Martin that promises to become very useful is an ultraviolet-resistant polyester with a life expectancy of fifteen years in exterior use. Most of these products can be ordered from the SUN Catalog but you should first check your local suppliers and save as much as 20 percent on material costs and shipping.

Layers of glazing may be installed in various ways. Traditional glass is placed into a wooden recess, secured with little metal glazing points, and puttied into place. In some cases, an existing sash can be rabbeted on the inside to create a second recess into which another layer of glass can be installed in the traditional manner. This is advantageous for older homes where one may not wish to change the character of the window. It does, however, nearly double the weight of the window and may require a large set of counterweights. On the other hand, a rigid plastic glazing can be added with little weight increase.

Wood and aluminum frames for storm windows are both very common ways to mount a second layer of glazing. An unusual yet simple way to have the thermal advantages of wood storms yet gain the convenience of aluminum triple-tracks is to make a set of wood storms that are fixed permanently in place, with a removable lower sash that comes into the house and is replaced with a screen.

Interior storms placed within the primary window are a recent development. These storms are easier to seal against infiltration and vapor passage and are very inexpensive compared to conventional types. An interior storm may be glass in a wooden or aluminum frame, a sheet of rigid plastic caulked into place, or even a sheet of plastic film. All are equally effective if sealed at the edges.

The familiar plastic sheet stapled over the window, which is usually discarded in the spring, saves energy if installed tightly but tends to fill the window frame with hundreds of staples or nail holes after a few years; this leads to rapid deterioration of the wood. Temp-Rite has developed a simple vinyl frame that can be left permanently in place. Each winter a new sheet of film is installed by simply popping a wooden dowel into a slot to hold

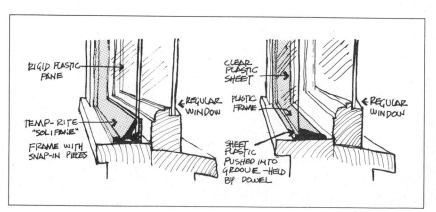

RIGID PLASTIC PANE

TEMP-RITE "SOLIPANE" FRAME WITH SNAP-IN PIECES

REGULAR WINDOW

CLEAR PLASTIC SHEET

PLASTIC FRAME

REGULAR WINDOW

SHEET PLASTIC PUSHED INTO GROOVE—HELD BY DOWEL

the sheet into position. The dowel and sheet can then be easily removed in the spring. These frames are inexpensive and may be installed either inside or outside the window.

Another simple yet very effective window can be constructed right at home with inexpensive materials. A simple wood frame is made of 1 × 2's to fit inside your existing window. Double-faced tape is then placed around the border of the frame onto which two people stretch and place a sheet of glazing film. On top of this is placed another frame of ¼-inch × 1-inch wood strips. Then tape, film, strip, tape, film, strip, etc., in as many layers as desired. The final assembly should be capped with sheets of rigid plastic glazing on either face, which can and should be caulked and screwed into place. In this manner you can assemble a window with a R-value of 6 in a space of only 2 inches. The unit is light, durable, and easily installed and removed with the seasons.

A roll shade can be a glazing film storage unit. Transparent glazing film is placed on a roller, drawn down, and attached to the windowsill. For maximum advantage the system is sealed on all sides. Some systems achieve this seal by adding curved side pieces against which the film is stretched. The bottom is often sealed magnetically and the top enclosed in a box. A similar device, but with straight side tracks, is marketed by Windo-Seal of Boston as a kit for $10 per window. For the price, it appears to be an excellent product.

A number of other systems include multiple rolls for additional layers of protection. Other systems use several kinds of materials

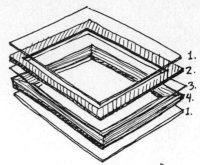

1. RIGID PLASTIC 0.1"
2. ¼" PLYWOOD OR HARDBOARD
3. PLASTIC FILM
4. 1 × 2 FRAME

Three-layer plastic
R-value: 3   Thickness: 1¼ inches
Each additional layer adds ¼ inch and an R-value of 1.

Windo-Seal
360 Washington St.
Lynn, MA 01901
(617) 599 - 2217

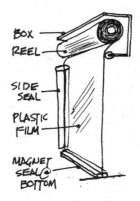

Windo-Seal

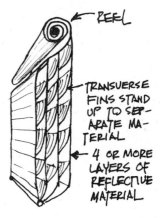

Multiple-layer systems keep the layers apart by means of transverse fins that unfold when the shade is pulled down.

GLAZING COSTS

	Cost of material per lineal foot ($)	Cost of labor per lineal foot* ($)
Traditional glazing		
glazing compound	.05	.30
wood strips	.10	.10
rabetted recess	.10	.50
Rigid storm glazing†		
wooden frame	.50	1.00
aluminum	1.25	.50
Temp-Rite vinyl	.65	.15
Film glazing systems**		
cardboard/staples	.10	.10
Temp-Rite vinyl	.75	.15
Windo-Seal	.65	.50
multiple rolls	2.50	1.50

* Figured for 3' × 4' window.
† Includes only framing material. Add cost of glass, etc.
** Includes glazing film.

on separate rolls to provide a choice of transparent material, opaque white for privacy, or aluminum film to cut radiant heat loss on winter evenings. One system includes no fewer than five layers of aluminum, for an R-value of up to 10. These multiple-roll systems require a fairly large enclosure above the window.

RADIANT BENEFITS

Most window treatments function primarily by the reflective principle of insulation. Any material placed in front of a window will reduce heat loss, but the most immediate result is to improve comfort by removing the cold window surface from the "view" of the human skin. Our evaluation tables quantify only the R-values of these materials but the advantage of radiant control should also be recognized.

CURTAINS AND DRAPERIES

Curtains and draperies are among the most exciting of all home improvements. The fashion magazines abound in novel and practical ideas but the Kirsch publication, *Windows Beautiful*, available at fabric stores, is the single most useful discussion of window options. It is full of well-organized information and instructions for ordering or making your own draperies or curtains, though it has no evaluation of thermal benefits. A more technical discussion is provided in the National Bureau of Standards' publication *Window Design Strategies to Conserve Energy*. The next few pages are based on these two publications. Because windows and their accessories will be receiving a great deal of attention in coming years, this discussion is intended only to assist you in evaluating and verifying from among a confusion of terminology and conflicting claims. Given the wide range of materials, styles, and applications, the numbers we provide are only an indication of relative costs and benefits.

Fabric materials range from $2 to $15 a yard and up; a variety of materials are available to meet different requirements. Most fabrics today are a combination of materials arranged to overcome the limitations of each element. The worst problems of draperies are fading from strong sunlight and difficulty in cleaning. Frequent in-place vacuuming, protection from the sun with liners or undersheers, and prevention of window condensation can relieve these problems.

The thermal value of draperies depends on the openness of the fabric itself, its thickness and weight, and the closure of the

CHARACTERISTICS OF DRAPERY FABRICS

	Durability	Fading	Washing	Fire
Acetate	fair	good	fair	fair
Acrylic	good	good	fair	good
Cotton	very good	fair	good	poor
Fiberglass	fair	good	good	good
Nylon	good	fair	good	good
Polyester	good	good	good	good
Rayon	fair	good	fair	poor

entire drapery system. A closely woven fabric placed to enclose a window can create an air space with an R-value of 1. A fabric of unusual density and weight, or a system of several layers, or an extraordinary number of pleats and folds can trap additional air spaces within the fabric to provide further R-value. Layers of foam bonded to fabric are of particular value, while aluminized fabric may provide a little vapor protection and a good deal of radiant benefit. These additional layers are usually detachable for ease in laundering the decorative surface.

The tightness of the drapery enclosure to the window frame becomes more critical as greater effort is made to improve the thermal quality of the drapery itself. A curtain will generally cover only the window itself while a full drapery will extend from floor to ceiling—the simplest way to seal the top and bottom of the enclosure. When high ceilings make this impractical, a top enclosure is introduced. A drapery should always extend down to and rest on the floor because a space as small as 1 inch will admit cold drafts into the room.

The value of a curtain is usually to provide privacy and shield those in the room from the cold surface of the glass. Very few curtains are enclosures for the window. However, a new kind of curtain is now being developed that is highly insulated and carefully sealed into its frame. The weight and bulk of these curtains are very visible and the mechanisms to secure them are displayed. *Alternative Sources of Energy No. 31* discusses three different variations of *quilted curtains,* which provide R-value protection of about 3 and can be made for about $2 per square foot of window. All three systems used Polar-guard filament fiber quilted into a thin bag of inexpensive liner material. This bag is placed into a removable and therefore washable case with an interior decorator face of 50 percent polyester and 50 percent cotton, and an exterior (facing the sun) face of off-white muslin. A useful variation would be to line the inside face of the quilted inner bag with an aluminum-faced fabric for radiant benefits and to ensure vapor protection.

Each of these systems uses a novel system to secure the curtains in place and to draw them aside into storage. Because the insulating fill is non-compressible, these curtains require a substantial storage space to the side of the window or up at the ceiling. An interesting system for a thick insulating mattress is described by William Shurcliff, in which the "curtain" is stored in a large box below the window (the top of which serves as a working surface to a greenhouse) from which the curtain is drawn up between two layers of glazing with ropes and pulleys. The possibilities are endless.

The best single cover for a window and one of the most attractive is *woven wood.* Slats of wood up to $\frac{1}{2}$ inch thick are laced tightly together with yarn to achieve a nearly solid membrane that remains flexible and can be folded when drawn to the side or rolled when hoisted to the ceiling in a system called a Roman

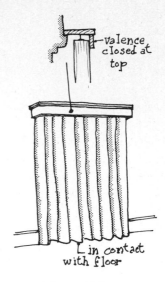

Thermal drape

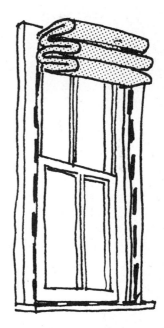

Heavy quilted curtains drawn to the top (from *Alternative Sources of Energy*)

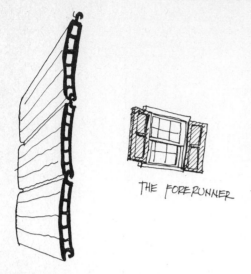

SHUTTERS

THE FORERUNNER

European-type exterior shutters constructed of precision-made hollow vinyl sections. The sides are held in channel sections. Reported to be very effective in reducing heat loss, they are also expensive and require a large housing.

shade. Woven wood is a transitional system combining the advantages of both curtains and shutters.

Another form of *rolling shutter* has been common in Germany for years and is now being marketed in America. Made of hollow, double-walled plastic slats, the system is very durable and as a storm-shielding device can be placed outside the window, where it provides insulating protection with no danger of condensation on the interior glass. Both this system and that of interior woven-wood are expensive.

For all the complication of today's shuttering mechanisms, the materials themselves are straightforward. The goal of a shutter, to provide movable insulating protection and high R-values, is easily achieved with today's rigid foamboards. The largest difficulty arises in attaining an adequate seal as the shutters are hinged or placed into position. Aluminum-faced foam is preferred for additional fire protection because simply placing flammable Styrofoam and urethane into window openings is a fire hazard.

A common procedure for the construction of a hinged shutter is to make a light wooden frame around a sheet of foam. The frame fits into the window opening, receives the hinges and screws, and is covered with fabric. A more attractive shutter can

EVALUATING CURTAINS AND SHUTTERS

	Improves MRT	R-value	Cost ($/sq. ft.) Material	Labor
Curtains				
left open	no	0	0	0
sheer	no	.3	.75	.40
foam lined	yes	.7	1.00	.50
aluminized fabric	yes	1.0	1.00	.50
Draperies (closed off at top and bottom)				
open weave	no	.7	1.00	.50
close weave	no	1.0	1.50	.50
foam backed	yes	1.5	1.70	.70
aluminum-faced fabric	yes	2.0	2.00	.50
½" fiber quilt	yes	2.5	2.50	2.00
4" insulated "mattress" (see *illustration, page 115*)	yes	12.0	4.00	3.00
Roll shutters				
woven wood	yes	2.0	2.00	1.00
hollow plastic slats (see *illustration above*)	no	2.5	7.00	2.00
Shutters				
1" foamboard	yes	4–6	.50	1.00
Thermax	yes	8.0	.75	1.00
wooden (solid)	yes	2.0	2.00	.40
aluminum foil on frame	yes	6.0	.70	1.00

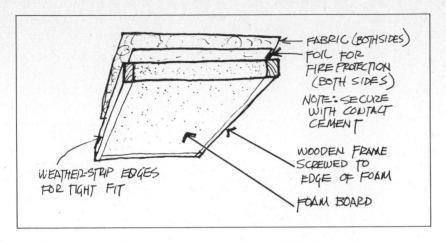

FABRIC (BOTHSIDES)
FOIL FOR FIRE PROTECTION (BOTH SIDES)
NOTE: SECURE WITH CONTACT CEMENT
WOODEN FRAME SCREWED TO EDGE OF FOAM
FOAM BOARD
WEATHER-STRIP EDGES FOR TIGHT FIT

Simple interior shutter

be made faced with inexpensive corkboard, and a cork/cardboard/cork laminate is both attractive and sufficiently strong to be used alone. Solid wooden shutters are still available and some even have the traditional adjustable louvers, but these are expensive.

SUGGESTIONS FOR FURTHER READING

Energy Saver's Catalog, by the editors of *Consumer Guide.* Covering the range of materials and products from insulation to lighting equipment, this catalog provides brand-name recommendations and addresses with high-quality illustrations and a well-worded text.
New York: G. P. Putnam's Son's, 1977 $6.95

Insulation Manual, by the National Association of Home Builders Rescarch Corporation. A generally useful document.
Rockville, Md. 1971.

Thermal Shades and Shutters, by William Shurcliff. Mine is a draft edition, two years old, but still the best source of information on the recent developments in curtains and shutters for large solar windows. Well-organized and loaded with addresses, prices, and performance information.
Write to Mr. Shurcliff, 19 Appleton St., Cambridge, Mass. 02138.

Blaine Window Hardware Catalog. One of the best sources of window hardware, invaluable when detailing sliding drapes and shutters.
Write to Blaine Window Hardware, Inc., 1919 Dr., RD 4, Hagerstown, Md. 21740 $1.00

The SUN Catalog, by Solar Usage Now. This is the Sears catalog of solar energy. Provides access to the basic materials, kits, and assembled components being developed around the country.
Box 306, Bascom, Ohio 44809 $2.00

6. GETTING IT DONE

f you have followed this book in sequence, you have done a Diagnosis on your house and have a good idea of what your improvement priorities should be. You understand the processes of heat loss and considerable specialized information about the various aspects of a building's performance. You have probably done more—talked to hardware-store people and contractors and have read other material. In short, you are well informed and know what you want to do, in what order to do it, and approximately how much it will cost.

This chapter carries you one step further into the ways and methods of accomplishing what you have set out to do. Almost everything said here could apply not only to the tasks of weatherization but to any home improvement. "Getting it done" covers doing it yourself or hiring someone else, such as a handyman or a contractor, to do it for you.

The first big decision after what to do is who shall do the work: you or someone else. This is a question of time, skill, and available money. If you have the inclination and the skill to do something yourself, it is unquestionably the best choice. You are more apt to get the job done to your satisfaction, even leaving aside the benefits of lower cost and self-education. There is just no substitute for knowing exactly what you want and then doing it. A less obvious advantage of doing it yourself is the savings in time. A good job demands planning, coordination, and communication to the contractor; for many jobs this takes longer than simply doing it yourself.

DOING IT YOURSELF

ARE YOU HANDY AROUND THE HOME?

Some people would answer the question "Are you handy around the home?" in the affirmative without hesitation because they are accustomed to dealing with the little repairs that are constantly needed about the house and have picked up a lot of know-how over the years changing faucet washers, fixing weather stripping, or repairing broken windows. They have also acquired a number of tools and gadgets that are useful around the house. In fact, the presence of and familiarity with a number of tools is an indirect indication that you are indeed handy. The tools don't do the work but they imply the interest and concern.

A lot of the skills required for handiwork are learned at the parent's knee; it is a great help to have watched a parent or handyman do a job and to have helped. It used to be that the cute little girl was barred from the workshop while the mischievous boy was watched whenever he stepped into the kitchen. Today these roles have broken down in the recognition that all activities are learning experiences, and a child should be encouraged to learn from any available workplace.

Aptitude is the most important thing. If you like to work with your hands and do the headwork required to do the job right, you can count on doing okay. If, on the other hand, the very thought of it all is irksome, then, by all means, have someone else do it. Somewhere in between are the willing but unconfident. In this case, if you try or at least ask a friend who did try, you will be surprised at what you can learn to do.

You need to have the time, the skills, and the necessary tools and equipment to do any job properly. Few weatherization jobs require much of any of these. A simple attic insulation job requires only a handful of tools, no previous experience, and only a day's time. At the other end of the scale, some wall insulation procedures require elaborate equipment and considerable experience. Most of the tasks in between can be learned. You will be slow at first but will pick up speed and skill as you go along.

Often the choice of who does the job comes down to money. If you have plenty, you can hire out the irksome tasks and perform the ones you happen to enjoy. For the rest of us it seems to come down to the brutal facts that the job needs to be done, we can't afford to hire someone else, so we guess we're elected. If the job is small and you know what you are doing, you should proceed and just get it done. But in today's world some tasks are so specialized that unless you are specially gifted and well equipped you cannot afford not to hire the appropriate tradesperson.

SHOULD I BE DOING THIS JOB?

How much is this going to take out of me? Do I have the time, equipment and skills to do what is required? If the job is rather large, can I keep up the momentum to get the job done over a reasonable period of time? Can I put up with living with a prolonged process?

Are my free time and working time more valuable to me than the expense of someone else's working time? Will my doing the work be a useful family experience or just a hardship? What might I get from a professional job that I couldn't get from doing it myself?

WEATHERIZING PROJECTS: DEGREE OF DIFFICULTY

(Note: All projects require your attention as you do them.)

	Infiltration	Windows	Attic	Walls	Heating plant	Exposure	Solar
Easy	• Installing self-stick weather stripping • Taping and puttying cracks	• Seasonal changing of triple-track windows • Changing storm-door panel	• Insulating an open attic • Installing poly vapor barrier	• Putting fiberglass in unfinished wall • Installing bookcases, fabric hangings	• Changing filter • Oiling motors	• Banking the side of the house for winter	• Opening and closing shutters, curtains, and drapes
Clumsy the first time	• Installing metal tension weather stripping • Caulking	• Installing plastic storms • Making curtains • Making and mounting Styrofoam shutter • Replacing broken glass	• Carrying insulation to the attic	• Installing poly vapor barrier	• Cleaning heat exchanger • Cleaning stove pipe and chimney from below • Adding glass front to fireplace	• Planting shrubs • Planting trees	
Takes time to develop skill	• Judging infiltration for Diagnosis	• Seasonal changing of fixed storms • Measuring and installing aluminum storms • Making drapes • Reconditioning old windows	• Installing an attic vent • Maintaining ventilation at the eave	• Installing insulation and new finish on old wall	• Maintaining an efficient wood fire • Installing combustion air inlet • Testing furnace for efficiency	• Berming earth against walls	• Making a solar greenhouse • Making a Trombe wall
Experience and demonstration needed	• Trimming a door for new threshold	• Replacing worn sills • Installing replacement windows • Making hinged shutters		• Reworking window trim to thicken wall • Tearing out old finish, adding insulation and new finish	• Cleaning chimney • Installing a safe wood stove	• Making earth-covered roofs	• Building an active air system

	Infiltration	Windows	Attic	Walls	Heating plant	Exposure	Solar
Very difficult for anyone who doesn't do it every day				• Installing foam in-place insulation	• Modifying a fireplace for efficiency	• Insulating basement and adding a drainage system	• Building an active water system
Needs special equipment	• Installing interlocking weather stripping (rabbeted)	• Rabbeting for second layer of glass • Other millwork jobs	• Installing blown-in material: borrow or rent machine (otherwise, "Easy" to "Clumsy. . . .")	• Installing exterior layers of insulation	• Testing furnace for efficiency	• Planting large trees	

Can I save part of the expense of hiring out the work by working with a hired handyman? Some handymen are willing to work along with a homeowner on a hourly basis and bring useful tools and experience to a job while you may still do the bulk of the work. Nearly any contractor is willing to define the scope of the work so that he contracts to perform a particular and more difficult task, leaving the cleaner (or dirtier) and easier work for the homeowner.

Will I do a better job than anyone else could possibly do? You should undertake some tasks simply because no one else could possibly be as fussy. It is, after all, your home. For many tasks the main ingredients are not skill or experience but devotion and patience. Inspecting an old house for air leaks and diligently stopping them up is an example of a task that takes hours but can be done little by little over several months. Another example is the reconditioning of windows.

The chart above is an aid to seeing if you can pull off a given task. Just as fancy dives in swimming competition are rated for Degrees of Difficulty, so we have rated the various improvement tasks. By comparing what you've done before to what you now intend to try, you get an idea of what you are getting into.

Get advice from people whose knowledge you trust as you prepare for a task. Salespersons in hardware stores are usually very helpful and knowledgeable. Go to a reputable paint store for advice about caulking and paint products. However, the salespeople of the hardware departments of large department and discount stores are not usually good sources of information—they are apt to know less than you do. A number of good home improvement books exist and are easy to obtain. In short, *don't assume you cannot do something just because you never have,* but *don't get into hot water trying to do what you should leave to others.*

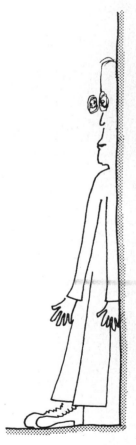

Just how much is this going to take out of me?

Organize the job. Measure the work. Make a list of necessary supplies and tools, then go out and get them all at once. Define the task to be done and how much you want to get done today or in a weekend. It takes a certain amount of energy to set the body into motion. Once a session of work is begun, the task will

Nobody else could possibly be as fussy.

carry you through to the end if everything is prepared. Having to stop to get additional tools or materials is wasteful of time and bad for momentum.

Buy good tools. For the time and trouble they save, tools are the best bargain around. This is especially true of hand tools; buy only good hammers, screwdrivers and paintbrushes. A good tool becomes a part of your hand and improves your production. Many people who don't like to paint have just never had the pleasure of working with a good brush. You will save the extra price of a good tool over a cheap one every hour you use it.

Don't buy gadgets. In addition to the basic set of tools there are myriads of little instruments for special purposes. A specially designed tool will make a job more efficient and more enjoyable and you should consider buying one for the job if it is not too expensive or if there is a large job to be done. But don't spend too much for a tool you will never use again. Try renting it instead, or improvise with what you already have.

Comparison-shop. It is hard to beat the bargain prices offered at discount department stores and they often offer quality items. Your local hardware store will have a better selection of tools of dependable quality but will be somewhat more expensive because it does a smaller volume of business. As a general rule you should support your local hardware store because it is more convenient, needs the business, and can provide lower prices as more people give it business. If you keep it in business, it will be there when you need it in a pinch.

Helpers are a big help. This may sound obvious, but someone to hold and fetch often means that two can do more than twice as much in a given time. A good team can even make an unfeasible project possible. This is even more true if the other person has a little more experience than you do. Children as young as five or six can help on some jobs and ten-year-olds can pick up a surprising amount of skill. They often want to help, and it gives them a big boost to be allowed to. Just suit the task to the age and

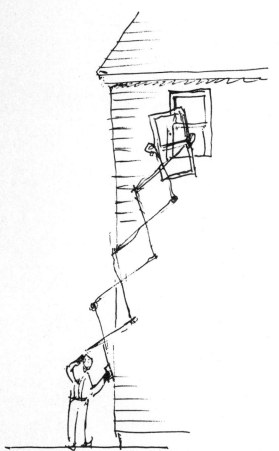

Doubtful gadgets . . .

don't expect too much efficiency or too long an attention span.

Pay attention. Many operations are extremely simple to do. They will not, however, do themselves; the material will not just jump into place. Be sure you understand the function of the completed assembly so that you will know what to think about as you perform the task.

Take your time. Basic organization will more than make up for the extra time you may take being slow and deliberate at an unaccustomed task. Better to be slow and at least get it done right the first time. Redoing work may take four times the effort of the original task.

Prepare a workplace. If you are going to spend hours doing something, take the time to organize the workplace. Find a reasonably comfortable position and provide good light and ventilation. Whenever possible, bring items of work to an organized worktable that you have cleaned off for the job. You won't lose parts on a clean surface. Cleaning up afterward is part of the job and should be scheduled into the working time. Stopping a half hour early to clean up makes it easier to start again tomorrow.

Don't be annoyed if things go wrong. Everyone makes mistakes; professionals just know better how to correct them. Most processes are reversible. If the first try is not right, you can usually take it off and try again. Whenever you buy a chemical or a solution, remember to get its thinner; it will be handy if needed while you are working, and you'll be able to clean up after you have finished. Where a process is irreversible, such as cutting a sheet of plywood, the watchword is "measure twice before you cut once."

Things usually get worse before they get better. You will usually discover more wrong with whatever you set out to repair than a first glance revealed. Or something won't go together properly and a twenty-second operation will turn into an hour-and-a-half project. Just persevere and eventually the job gets done. Walk away from it before you lose your temper—take a break or have lunch. The first go-round should be chalked up to experience and time lost will be regained some day in the future when you have to do it again and you know just what to do. If you make a mistake when repairing something small, it is sometimes easier and cheaper to just throw it away and use another piece.

Don't be overly fussy. Diminishing returns are inherent in perfectionism. Making it much better than average can take an additional third or half the time. Don't worry if the first-time results are not professional-looking. That's because you are not a professional. Adequate is enough. On the other hand, if it adds to your pleasure, then putter away. Just keep in mind that there are other things to get done.

Some days nothing seems to go right and you might as well admit that the stars are against you and try again tomorrow. Other days the weather will be just perfect and you will discover the

Both have their advantages.

Even five-year-olds can help.

proper rhythm of the work. You may get into the task at hand and find yourself enjoying it. It is good to work with your hands and a delight to see an accomplishment even if it is only replacing a pane of glass.

HIRING SOMEBODY ELSE

Having decided for any good reason that you cannot do something yourself and being convinced that the job still needs doing, you are faced with the prospect of getting someone else to do it. Now hiring someone is not like buying a loaf of bread; getting good help takes time and effort. You must decide whom to hire, what to tell them to do, and how to get them to do it as you like it. It is quite difficult to get other people to spend your money wisely.

THE HANDYMAN

For the smaller jobs or where there is plenty of time to do a bigger job slowly, a handyman may be just as satisfactory as a union carpenter while being a good deal cheaper. By limiting the scale of his work and usually working alone, a handyman is able to avoid the overhead, payroll, and expense of heavy equipment that comes with being a full contractor. Handymen tend to have more flexible hours and equable temperaments (else they couldn't keep getting work). Abilities vary a great deal; many have just one basic skill like carpentry or masonry. One may do one kind of job just fine and be mediocre or miserable at another. If he is a good worker, you may have trouble getting him to come over or, once on the job, to stay and finish what he has started. This is because everybody else wants him and he has made more promises than he can keep. If he is unsatisfactory, you can easily and tactfully say, "Well I've decided to wait on this other stuff" and then hire someone else.

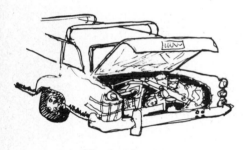

The handyman

Above all, you are dealing with an individual with all his idiosyncrasies who may have traded the opportunity for the larger income he could make working for a larger contractor for the independence he gets just working for himself. You may find the peculiarities of such an individual tiresome at times but if you find a good person, he is to be cherished. Dealing with such a person is a pleasure, and building a good working relationship is like money in the bank—you can use him in an emergency.

Rules for Dealing with a Handyman

1. The best way to find him is through a satisfied customer.
2. Make sure he is skilled at what you want him to do.
3. Make sure he understands what you want done and how. Make a list of the tasks to be done and the particular materials you want used.
4. Keep track, especially the first time around, as the work progresses, to correct things that don't seem to be coming out right. Don't hesitate to speak out about what you want, but don't expect perfection, either.

5. Politeness and consideration are always correct. This includes paying on time.

The line between handyman and contractor is indefinite, but in general the contractor is more of a businessperson as distinguished from an individual just picking up work for a living. He usually has employees and varying degrees of organization. He is there to make a buck and will be more expensive, particularly at smaller jobs. For the larger jobs, however, a more organized approach is desirable. Again, abilities vary tremendously; there are standards of workmanship that are generally recognized, but there is no such thing as a standard contractor. They may be competent or incompetent, honest or dishonest, expensive or inexpensive, and lazy or conscientious, and many unlikely combinations of the above.

Personalities vary. Some are cheerful and others gloomy, some are calm and flexible while others are excitable and rigid. Some are excitable and argumentative but are actually anxious to please and quite tractable once allowed to blow off steam. Occasionally you will meet a fanatic who does absolutely beautiful work but must do it his way. If his way is compatible with yours, okay; if not, you are in trouble. Dealing with these people, you will have to balance the good with the bad.

Remember that small contracting is often difficult and complex; the guy is likely to be overworked and harassed in a business that does not have large profit margins. Many of the people in the trades may be good workmen but are not trained in business methods. Such circumstances do not conspire for ideal relationships.

One thing that is *not* essential for a good contractor is an office. Some of the good ones we know do not answer their phones during the day because they are out working. If they are answered, it will be their home phones answered by their wives, who do the bookkeeping. This kind of operation is very common; it keeps overhead, and your costs, down.

The burden of proof is on the bigger company that comes on slick when you talk to them. Be wary of outfits with salesmen. A company that specializes, say, in insulation or aluminum will have specially trained people who sit in an office or even solicit door

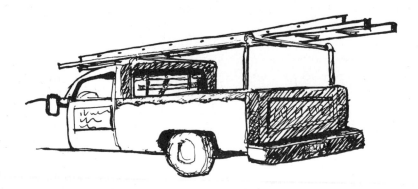

The small contractor

to door. These people are not necessarily bad folk but they have two things going against them. They are often trained only in salesmanship with only enough hard and useful information to get a sale; and they are not responsible for seeing the job through to a satisfactory completion. They can be very persuasive and if you are a person of good will, you may wind up signing up for something against your better judgment. Consumer laws in some states allow you a day or more to reconsider and cancel such a contract even if you have already signed. In any case, a decent business should allow you to back out of something you have second thoughts about so long as the work has not begun. If the job has begun, it becomes a very sticky matter.

Suit the contractor to the job. A specialized task like a heating system or blown-in insulation requires a specialist with unusual equipment. Other jobs, such as small plumbing or electrical work, may be done by non-specialists but probably should not be. Still others, such as carpentry or painting, can be done by organizations of various sizes with a range of results.

DEALING WITH A CONTRACTOR

Once a contractor has started, you lose most of your control over the job. It is very difficult to turn a sloppy workman into a good one and expensive to get someone who has started doing something one way to stop and do it differently. Your choice of contractor is one of the most crucial you will make.

Investigate at least three potential contractors and get work references for each. Don't rely on impressions. A good contractor expects to be investigated and should have a ready list of satisfied customers. Doing your homework beforehand will usually prevent having to stop a job in progress or having to pay for and live with a poor job.

A contractor does work by contract, sometimes verbal, but better written. A successful job requires that you know what you want and communicate it well to your contractor. Areas of confusion should be clarified before the contract is signed or any work begun. This means a bit of additional time spent in design and planning, but it also means that you can be sure to get what you want by having it down in writing.

Work should be supervised or at least carefully inspected before complete payment is made. Don't stand over a workman the entire day but don't give him free rein either. A good craftsman will rise to the occasion if a client provides a good working situation, pays well and promptly, and expresses an intelligent concern for good work.

Many of these rules hold for dealing with a handyman as well, but things are a bit more formal with a contractor. For work involving hundreds or even thousands of dollars, you are likely to want an agreed-upon price for the whole job. This is fine, but don't be surprised if tension builds when you delay the work by changing your mind or adding a little work here and there. Delays and extra work add to the expense of a job and the contractor may legitimately submit an additional charge if the little extras add up to an unreasonable burden. Most contractors figure in a few unexpected extras but can be flexible only up to a certain point. Take the time to determine just what you want from the start and you can save a lot of trouble and money. The more clearly the work is defined, the more closely the contractor can provide an estimate of the cost. An alternative is to work by cost-plus contract, in which case the contractor merely accounts for material, labor, overhead, and profit, and submits a bill at the end. This allows for flexibility in the course of the work but gives no guarantee on a top figure. Do this only with people you trust absolutely and keep track of the cost *weekly*.

Disagreements arise between reasonable people and construction provides ample opportunity for this to happen. There may be things that are not important to a contractor but are to you, and vice versa. A dispute arises, especially when it affects the quality and cost of the work. The best way to avoid this is to be very clear in the negotiating phase and to have a written contract. This can be very simple and short—a simple list of tasks to be done for so much money—but get *something* down in black and white.

It is legitimate for the contractor to ask for part of the money before he starts—from 10 to 30 percent depending on the size of the job. If he is small, he needs the cash to buy materials. By parting with some money you also demonstrate your intention to go ahead with the work and the contractor is then able to arrange his schedule.

On the other hand, it is also legitimate not to make the *final* payment until you are satisfied with the work. If you aren't happy with the way a job is left, you have a very persuasive argument for the contractor to return and set things right. If after being asked and asked he will not come, you may then use the money withheld to pay someone else to complete the work. A common trait of even the better small contractors is never to quite finish a job. It is like pulling teeth to get him back; weeks pass, promises and promises and nothing moves. It is not hard to see why this happens. As your job winds up, he and his men become busy elsewhere and the finishing touches that take time and extra trips to your house are just not very good competition for his attention. We don't mean to suggest that you hold back major amounts of money for minor omissions, but it is fair to get your money's worth.

With all this about the pitfalls of dealing with contractors, you could get the impression that it is all very unpleasant. This is not generally so, but one never knows what may happen. The point is to deal honestly and fairly with your contractor and demand the same from him. You will not always be dealing with a clear-cut situation and can always expect a few surprises. Take them in stride, share responsibilities for the unpredictable, and maintain good communication. Good workers take their jobs seriously for it is their life as well as their living. They will be sensitive about it, and a deserved compliment will make their day. A good job is a pleasure to behold. If you know what you want and go about getting it in a reasonable way, you can expect to enjoy your dealings with contractors.

Rules for Dealing with a Contractor

1. Be very careful in choosing your contractor.
2. Know what you want.
3. Write a simple contract, specifying:
      cost to the customer
      scope of the work
      quality of materials
      payment schedule
4. Check the work every day.
5. Expect good work overall but not perfection.

Ideal relations with a contractor

GROUP ACTION

COOPERATIVE EFFORT

All homeowners are in the same situation with their fuel bills and everybody should be doing something about it; this includes your neighbors. There may be advantages in planning and doing weatherization projects with them. First of all, it is a fine opportunity to work together and get to know one another in a working atmosphere. By cooperating to upgrade a group of buildings, everyone works to protect the investment of the others. You can pool information, skills, equipment, and labor and save money by cooperative buying of materials or group contracts for similar work for a number of houses in a small area.

To get an idea of how this might operate, we will sketch a scenario. You have just Diagnosed your own house and helped a neighbor do the same. Talking it over, you decide that it would be a good idea to try to get more people on the block involved. You find that about half the block people are sufficiently concerned to do something about it immediately. Those who are interested gather at your house, where you demonstrate how the Diagnosis works and what they can expect to achieve.

Everyone then returns home and performs a Diagnosis on his or her home. Meanwhile word has spread and a couple of more people want to participate so that you now have, let's say, ten households involved. Gathering again to compare notes, you find that six of the ten have little attic insulation and agree to cooperate putting it in. The insulation is ordered, delivered and, over a period of four weekends, crews of the people involved install it in the six houses. A work crew of homeowners has most of the advantages of an individual do-it-yourselfer while things get done faster and usually with more fun—even taking into account the inevitable difficulties of organizing a group.

Cooperative effort can also save money. By calling around to suppliers, you should be able to get a contractor's price of 20 percent off the usual retail price because you are buying a substantial volume at once. In this example, 6,000 square feet of insulation at 30¢ a square foot comes to an $1,800 order. A 20 percent savings means that each of the six houses saves $60. You might even find wholesalers to provide materials at greater discounts if you prepare a sufficiently large order. A discount of up to 40 percent is possible when the group picks up the material or provides a central place for delivery and distribution.

Cooperative effort can also be used to save money with jobs that require an outside contractor. Having a large number of storm windows made and installed is one possible example of this. Contractors working small jobs at scattered locations have to figure part of their cost in simply getting to the job, getting back from it, moving men and equipment during the day, paperwork, and so on. It stands to reason that a number of jobs at the same time and place will be more efficient for a contractor and will usually be reflected in a lower cost to the customer.

No matter the size or nature of the job, the price you pay for successful cooperation is in the effort of organizing. Some people are natural organizers and get a bang out of it but it is a real job; when large amounts of money hinge on it, it must be taken seriously by the individuals of the group. In the case of insulating or other straightforward do-it-yourself projects, the procedure is fairly simple once you have gotten the initial agreement among the participants. Someone has to be responsible for collecting the money, ordering the materials, scheduling work crews, and arranging with the families whose houses are to be worked on. Don't forget the support system—food, drink, and music. It all has to be attended to, but it still can be fun.

Close attention to finances is crucial. Potential participants are in or out of the process after a certain point where they must be willing to commit some money. As the moment of truth arrives, some people will be unable to come up with the money. These people should simply drop out of this round of activity. There should be no hard feelings but there should be no credit extended among the group.

When an outside contractor is to be involved, things become more complicated and provisions for payment have to be more formalized. It is not appropriate to make the payment all in one lump at the start of the job, yet the contractor is entitled to and will probably insist on some kind of guarantee that he will be paid by each and every member of the group.

One good way to work this out is for the group to have the contractor deal with each member separately but with a provision that if all the jobs go ahead, or a certain stated proportion of them, the contractor agrees to reduce his price by an agreed-upon percentage. Then the group as such has no responsibility for money matters—contracts are signed between individuals and the contractor—while everyone gets the advantage of the group action. This sort of business becomes even more complicated

ORGANIZATION

Some people are good at organizing.

when several contractors bid on the group work (as should be the case), and it might be wise to consult an architect or lawyer for advice, as these people have more experience with contracts. The expense of professional assistance should be easily absorbed by the various members and in the reduced costs of the job.

Rules for Group Action

1. *Choose one coordinator.* Find someone who is calm and organized and who agrees to be responsible *not* for doing everything but for seeing that everything is done.
2. *Plan carefully.* Schedule so that everything and everyone is where they should be at the right time.
3. *Keep the project reasonable* both in terms of money and time-span. The latter should be limited to 3 weeks maximum; after that, people begin to get tired and somebody gets left holding the bag.
4. *Keep everyone informed.* Just because the coordinator has it all in his or her mind doesn't mean that everybody else does.
5. *Keep plans simple and as flexible as possible.* Don't get any more complicated than necessary and don't let the plan depend on a lot of contingencies.
6. *Commitments are essential.* At a certain point every potential participant should decide to either be in or out of the venture by committing some money. Up to that point, people should be able to drop in or out without spoiling the plan for the rest.
7. *Make it fun* in the barn-raising tradition.

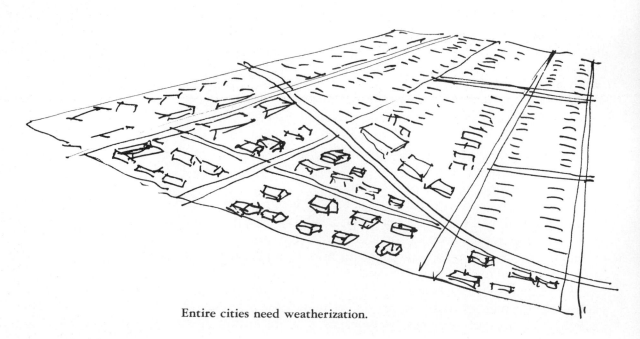

Entire cities need weatherization.

7. PAYING FOR IT

WEATHERIZATION AS AN INVESTMENT

While this section is on how to get the money to make the improvements you want, there is an important matter to deal with first. Is it worth it? In the first chapter we touched upon the subject of the investment value of a home, implying that it is a very good investment indeed. Among all possibilities, the returns you can expect from conservation expenditures are very favorable in comparison with anything else.

Repairs and improvements to the home are a good investment because they maintain the value of the property and restrain the ravages of time. If your neighborhood is stable, the value of your house is going up and the value of a recognizable improvement, say a new kitchen, is magnified. Maintenance does not add value but it does safeguard the value that is there. Weatherization improvements have the additional benefit of paying off the investment and actually make a profit in the business sense. You make money in the form of fuel dollars that you don't have to spend. This chapter will compare the value of weatherization to other investments one might make with the same money.

Amounts of profit are not the only relevant factor in economics. **PROFIT** In any business there are also the issues of the amount of money tied up in the investment, the amount of risk, control over how the investment is managed, and what bankers call "liquidity."

In all except the last of these factors, weatherization is apt to be a winner: the "profits" from weatherization are generally large; relatively small amounts of money are involved; the home-owner has close control over his investment; and the risk is small or nonexistent. The investment, however, is not very liquid. That is, the money cannot move in and out of the investment with ease. You can sell stocks and bonds or withdraw from a savings account to have cash as needed, but you can't sell insulation back to the lumber company.

While most of these items are easily understood, profit is not. To appreciate the profitability of home improvements, imagine a ceiling insulation job that costs $500 with an estimated $100 savings per year. The payback period is: $\frac{500}{100} = 5$ years.

INFLATION

This five-year payback assumes that fuel costs stay the same, which of course they don't. When inflation is taken into account, the payback period decreases. Using a conservative fuel cost inflation rate of 8 percent, the $100 savings for the first year would actually be $108, $117 for the second, $126 for the third, and $136 for the fourth. As the sum of these fuel savings is $487, the payback period with an 8 percent inflation rate is reduced to a little more than four years. Looked at another way, if the expenditure is not made, each $100 of fuel you use today will cost, at 8 percent inflation, $200 in ten years and $317 in fifteen.

At a 12 percent fuel-cost inflation rate, which many economists regard as more likely, the figures are frightful. The doubling time for the value of goods drops to only six years. In times of high inflation the investment into goods and property is very wise and profitable. Looking once again at the insulated ceiling for $500, the yearly savings are $112 the first year, $125 the next, $140 the third, and $157 the fourth, for a total of $535. The payback is less than four years. Remember that this has nothing to do with the enhanced resale of an insulated house; this is simply savings in operating expense.

Another way of viewing an investment is to determine its percentage annual return. A savings account that offers 8 percent

INFLATION versus INTEREST The shapes cover ranges of percent increases; savings and bank deposits don't look very good.

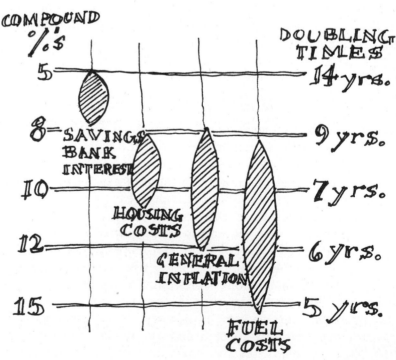

interest gives an 8 percent annual return. A home improvement that offers a payback of four years gives a 25 percent annual return! Consider the wisdom of leaving money in your savings account that could be earning three times the return right at home.

As this is being written, Congress has given even greater incentives for weatherization and solar heating. According to the American Institute of Architects *Journal* (December 1978):

TAX INCENTIVES

> The legislation gives a nonrefundable income tax credit of 15 percent of the first $2,000 expended for insulation and energy conservation measures (maximum $300) in the taxpayer's principal residence. The credit is available for expenditures made after April 20, 1977, and before January 1, 1986.
>
> Homeowners may also get a tax credit of 30 percent of the first $2,000 and 20 percent of the next $8,000 (maximum $2,200) for the installation of solar, wind or geothermal energy equipment in the principal place of residence. This is nonrefundable income tax credit, but a credit carry-over is provided to the extent that the credit exceeds the taxpayer's liability. The credit applies to qualified passive as well as active solar systems.
>
> Extended to 1980 is a grants program for states to buy and install materials to weatherize dwellings of low-income families, particularly the elderly and handicapped. Among eligible materials are insulation, storm windows and doors and clock thermostats. The maximum for any dwelling is $800. Both owner and renter-occupied residences are provided for. Appropriations are $200 million in fiscal years 1979 and 1980.
>
> The Government National Mortgage Association, under HUD, is directed to buy and sell home improvement loans for energy conservation measures, with priority given to elderly and moderate-income families. A loan cannot exceed $2,500. Also, GNMA is authorized to purchase up to $100 million of reduced interest loans to homeowners and builders for the installation of solar heating and cooling equipment in dwellings. Up to $8,000 per unit is provided.*

GETTING THE MONEY

Once you have decided to make a substantial investment involving more cash than you can part with at one time, you will usually be faced with going to a bank or some other type of credit institution. For those who are unfamiliar with these places, a short course in banking and loans will be helpful. Loans are a kind of game with somewhat complicated rules. As a novice, you will be at a disadvantage because the bank knows all the rules and you, to begin with, do not. If, however, you carefully read this chapter and ask around at more than one bank and at more than one *type* of bank, you can learn a lot and be better equipped to play the

---

* The last paragraph means that since a federal agency will buy various loans from banks, the banks will be much more willing to make such loans to the public.

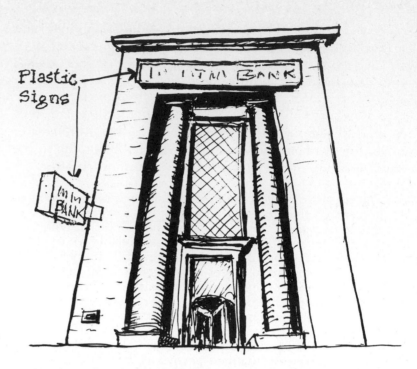

Plastic Signs

"Oh, the banks are made of marble, with a guard at ev'ry door . . ."

game shrewdly. Banks do, after all, want to lend the money; that's the way they make a profit.

LOANS   A loan is money that you rent and the rent is called *interest.* Just as you might be able to find equivalent apartments for different rents by looking around, so also do interest rates vary from bank to bank. More importantly, they vary among different types of loans, of which there are many. In general, loans for small amounts have shorter payment times (the *term* of the loan) than loans such as mortgages that may have terms of decades. Some loans require you to put up something valuable as security for the money. This is called *collateral* and it may be some personal possession of yours, securities such as stocks and bonds, or a savings account. For a real estate mortgage, the property itself is the collateral. Some loans have an indefinite time period for repayment while others have prescribed and definite monthly or quarterly payment schedules that you must meet or face a penalty. Some loans are *discounted,* which means you are paying interest for slightly more money than you actually are given to use; in effect, you are paying a higher rate of interest.

Banks, financing companies, and other lending institutions are regulated by state and federal governments and must adhere to certain rules. They may not deny a reasonable request for loan assistance and must be clear about loan characteristics and interest rates in particular. There are many ways to figure these and the unprepared and unsophisticated can easily be fooled by the jargon. A Truth in Lending Law now makes this more difficult for lenders by requiring them to quote the *effective* annual interest rate (APR). In this way, any loan can be compared with any other. On the other hand, banks must protect themselves and may ask questions and do a credit check on people who request a loan.

Different banks and bank personnel have different personalities. Some are pleasant and will go out of their way to help you; others will not. You have a right to be treated courteously and have your questions answered. Generally, you should start your quest for a loan at the bank where you have your savings and checking accounts. This is especially true in times of tight money supply when the bank is likely, as a requirement for a loan, to request you deposit your money there.

There are many types of credit institutions. The *commercial bank* exists to do business primarily with businesses but will deal with the average homeowner in several ways—checking accounts, domestic mortgages, and certain types of loans.

Savings banks and *savings and loans* are about the same. They give long-term mortgages on home and other residential properties. They obtain money for loans from the savings accounts of their members. Lately they have also begun to offer more commercial services such as checking accounts and home-improvement loans.

A *credit union* is an arrangement among a group of people to help one another meet financial needs. The employees of a labor union, for example, might set up a credit union into which members agree to deposit some of their savings, from which members of the credit union are eligible to borrow. The types of loans made available are the same offered by banks except that the rates and terms are more favorable. A credit union is a very good place to borrow money for those who are eligible.

Finance companies, such as Household Finance, Beneficial Finance, and Domestic Finance, offer more easily obtained loans with fewer questions. These companies therefore run a higher risk that a creditor will default, but they make up for this danger by charging higher interest rates.

Credit cards are sometimes called "personal lines of credit" and are a form of mass-produced financing. A credit card company is like a finance company and receives a high rate of interest on the unpaid balance of individual accounts. Because of their volume of business, large credit card companies can absorb many bad accounts and still offer interest rates lower than local finance companies. For home improvements, they are good for purchasing small amounts of materials but you won't find many contractors who accept them. Neither should they be used for purchases involving large sums of money or for loans with long terms.

Private lenders will make money available in special instances. These can range from perfectly legitimate and honorable people to the loan sharks of organized crime. No matter what the circumstances, arrangements with individuals should be very carefully studied before signing anything and should be reviewed by an attorney. The customer-protection regulations that apply to banks do not necessarily cover private transactions. You must protect yourself.

Over the years the government has developed a number of

programs to help homeowners buy and improve houses in the form of *guaranteed loans, insured loans,* and *grants.* The major programs have included Veterans Administration mortgage and loan assistance for members of the armed forces, Farmers Home Administration loans for rural places, and FHA (now HUD) loans for the general public. Under these programs, the borrower deals with a bank just as with an ordinary loan but the federal government agrees to insure the repayment of the loan if the borrower defaults. In this way, people who might otherwise be rejected can get a loan and in some cases the interest rate will be lowered. The rules and regulations controlling the eligibility for these loans are very complicated but it is worthwhile to ask the bank about them.

The above programs have helped veterans settle into homes, have helped victims of natural disasters, and have encouraged the public to move out to the suburbs. In recent years federal programs have attempted to help city neighborhoods. *Urban grant programs* are available in many cities under Neighborhood Improvement Programs funded by Community Development Revenue Sharing legislation. Grants are usually made to improve the appearance and the public spaces of neighborhoods. *Facade easement funds* make it possible for a homeowner to pay for the restoration of the facade of his or her building to its original character. Other programs make loans available for interior improvements by guaranteeing loans and reducing interest rates. The recent energy bill, outlined earlier, is another important program that homeowners should evaluate carefully and use to advantage.

FIELD GUIDE TO LOANS

Mortgages

Purpose	Long-term financing of buildings and other real estate. May be used for property improvements by adding improvement money to the mortgage amount at the time of purchase.
Amount	$5000 and up.
Time to repay	5–30 years.
Interest rate	8–12%.
Sources	Savings banks and savings and loans, commercial banks and credit unions; occasionally, seller of the property and private lenders.
Characteristics	Fixed monthly payments over a fixed term of years. The amount of interest is only on the unpaid balance, in contrast to other types of loans that load interest on the early payments. Early payment means a chance to avoid a lot of interest.

Characteristics (*cont.*)

Mortgages are almost always for only part of the purchase price. Purchaser must have cash (down payment) for the remainder.

Government agencies will sometimes guarantee the mortgage against purchaser default. (VA and FHA)

Availability of mortgages and size of down payment varies according to economic conditions.

Home-Improvement Loans

Purpose	Home improvements.
Amount	$1000–$10,000.
Time to repay	3–10 years; the larger the loan, the more time.
Interest rate	10–12% (1978).
Sources	Mainly through commercial banks, some savings banks, savings and loans, credit unions.
Characteristics	Fixed monthly payments over term of loan. Interest-heavy early payments, whereby over $\frac{1}{2}$ the interest is paid up after only $\frac{1}{3}$ the payments, $\frac{3}{4}$ after $\frac{1}{2}$ the payments—penalizes early payment.

Personal Loans

Purpose	Anything.
Amount	Up to $5000.
Time to repay	12–36 months.
Interest rate	11–13$\frac{1}{2}$% (1978).
Sources	Commercial banks, savings and loans, credit unions.
Characteristics	Similar to home-improvement loan. Available as secured or as unsecured loan.

Personal, Line of Credit, or Consumer Loan

Purpose	Short-term financing.
Amount	$1000–$2000.
Time to repay	Flexible.
Interest rate	18% (12% for larger amounts).
Sources	Credit cards and charge accounts at individual stores.
Characteristics	Minimum payment required each month; interest charged only on the unpaid balance of account.

(Continued)

Time or Demand Notes
(Note = Loan)

Purpose	Short-term financing.
Amount	$500–$5000.
Time to repay	30–60–90 days (may be renewed).
Interest rate	2% more than the prime rate to bank.
Sources	Commercial banks and savings banks.
Characteristics	Lump-sum repayment at the end of the term. A note may be "rolled over" by paying the interest due and taking out a new note to pay the old one. This process is not supposed to recur indefinitely.
	Available as secured or unsecured loan. A passbook demand note uses a savings account as collateral. The balance of the account may not be less than the amount of the note while the loan is in force.

Contractor Financing

Purpose	Medium-term financing.
Amount	$1000–$10,000.
Time to repay	According to agreement.
Interest rate	According to agreement.
Source	Through contractor who does the work.
Characteristics	Very much like a home-improvement loan.

Finance Company

Purpose	Short- and medium-term financing.
Amount	$100–$2500.
Time to repay	3 months to 5 years.
Interest rate	High—up to 36%.
Source	Finance companies, such as Beneficial, Household, and Domestic.
Characteristics	Highest interest rates of any method. Otherwise similar to personal loan from bank.

Life Insurance Loan

Purpose	Anything. Often used for home down payment.
Amount	Based upon, but less than, the sum of premiums paid in, called the "cash surrender value."
Time to repay	Flexible.

Interest rate	Very low, 3–5%.
Source	Insurance companies. Borrower must have a permanent policy in force for enough time to accumulate cash value.
Characteristics	Flexible repayment time. Very good way to borrow money.

Money from Your Own Savings Account

Purpose	Short- or long-term.
Amount	Any amount up to your total savings.
Time to repay	Flexible.
Interest rate	5% or whatever your account yields.
Source	Yourself.
Characteristics	This is not a "loan" in the true sense but is listed to point out that money left in a savings account loses value since the interest rate of 5% is less than inflation at 8–10%. By taking money out of savings to do weatherization, you would in effect be borrowing from yourself at a low interest rate to make an investment with a high rate of return.
	The disadvantage is that the money used is no longer there for an emergency.

8.
GETTING ADVICE

This book has not covered everything on the subject of home weatherization nor has it covered many things in great detail. You are probably still plagued by any number of questions: Am I forgetting something? How do I know if I really understand what I have read? Is this what I really want to do?

Just as some expenses are beyond your immediate cash reserve and some jobs beyond your technical competence, so also are some complications beyond the scope of this book. In such cases it is good to recognize these limits and obtain advice and assistance. There are many public agencies and private services that you should be prepared to use. You are only one of many homeowners in need of help and there is much experience to share.

It is important to develop confidence and *self-reliance,* but the often-expressed goal of *self-sufficiency* needs to be more closely evaluated. Exaggerated independence often merely isolates an individual from cooperation and a vital exchange of ideas and skills. We shouldn't undertake jobs for which we are unprepared when we can afford assistance. Self-sufficiency provides a grand excuse to delay getting things done into the distant and hazy future when we will all have the time and skills to do them.

There are times when economics will dictate that an individual simply cannot afford to do something himself. It may cost real money to have a specialist come and solve a problem but it often costs less than the value of the time and energy spent fussing over it in isolation. *Sub-contracting,* the skill of hiring just the right specialist to do a particular job, is at the heart of successful economics. It takes patience to locate the right person but it's worth the investment in time to look around. You might even discover that you are the best person for the job after all!

DOING YOUR HOMEWORK

In order to receive good advice, you must understand your own problem and be able to communicate it clearly. Having read this book, you now understand the language of energy conservation and are able to produce a competent description of your home.

You can now converse with a tradesperson or professional and ask specific questions instead of making a general request for help. If you later need additional professional assistance, a Diagnosis in hand will be worth several hours of professional time and save you money in preliminary services. But it is important to do your homework before seeking consultation. Talk with experienced friends and look in your local library for some of the other books we have recommended. The "U.S. Monthly Catalog" provides access to the latest technical reports that are available through the U.S. Government Printing Office, including many that are listed in our "Suggestions for Further Reading."

After doing a Diagnosis of your home, you can begin to evaluate some of the improvement possibilities. Look in the Yellow Pages under such headings as Building Materials, Contractors, and Insulation and make a few calls to local building-supply centers to verify the availability and price of materials. These stores will usually provide literature giving additional information about the installation of materials and the maintenance of equipment. Salespeople are usually too busy to spend much time on lengthy discussions but they can provide useful answers to straightforward questions.

The Cooperative Extension Service of your nearest state university can help you with regional homemaking and landscaping suggestions. Go to your local fabric supply store and landscaping nurseries to get ideas and estimates. Most such businesses will spend a little time with you and give advice and estimates freely. Your County Farm Agent can tell you the appropriate number and species of trees and shrubs for effective landscaping and sometimes make local species available free of charge.

Older buildings provide unusual difficulties and plenty of surprises and it becomes very important to talk to neighbors with similar houses to share experiences. The best technical literature on older buildings in this country comes from a series of small pamphlets from the U.S. Office of Archeology and Historic Preservation. "Preservation Brief #3" is a summary of recommended procedures and difficulties likely to be encountered. "Small Homes Council Notes" and the "Old House Journal" are two other good sources of information.

The SPNEA (Society for the Preservation of New England Antiquities) is one of many active preservation groups across the country that will guide you through the exciting but trying task of maintaining and improving an older building. Many communities and districts have local historic preservation societies that attract experienced people knowledgeable about local conditions. They can help you to place your house on the National Registry of Historic Houses, after which you become eligible to receive low-interest loans for restoration, which could cover weatherization improvements as well.

U.S. Government Printing Office
Assistant Public Printer
Superintendent of Documents
Washington, DC 20402

U.S. Office of Archeology
   and Historic Preservation
Heritage Conservation and
   Recreation Service
U.S. Department of the Interior
Washington, DC 20240

Small Homes Council—Building
   Research Council
University of Illinois at Urbana-
   Champaign
One East Saint Mary's Road
Champaign, IL 61820

Old House Journal
Dept. 7
69A Seventh Ave.
Brooklyn, NY 11217

Society for the Preservation
   of New England Antiquities
Harrison Gray Otis House
141 Cambridge St.
Boston, MA 02114

If you live in town, determine whether there is a federal assistance program for neighborhood improvement. You may be eligible for a grant or loan assistance if you comply with a few guidelines. Many cities have Neighborhood Improvements Offices funded under the Community Development Act where you can receive counseling or supervision of your entire improvement process. These offices often have small libraries of technical literature as well as salaried professional consultants. Many are equipped with tool-lending services and maintain records of local improvement projects as a means of sharing experience.

Large neighborhoods sometimes form independent corporations to accomplish goals far beyond the power of an individual. The problems of urban apartment dwellers faced with absentee landlords and powerless public agencies were one cause of the deterioration of urban neighborhoods and the rapid growth of the suburbs in the 1950s. The rising costs of commuting and the energy disadvantages of isolated suburban houses have now slowed this trend; in some cases it has been reversed, as neighborhoods have organized themselves to fight the forces that have drawn off rental profits of apartments while maintenance was neglected and buildings allowed to deteriorate. The People's Development Corporation in the South Bronx of New York City is one example of a cooperative that people successfully organized under the worst possible conditions to gain control of their own dwellings and bring them back to conditions of respectable habitation.

Institute for Local Self-Reliance
717 18th St. N.W.
Washington, DC 20009

The Institute for Local Self-Reliance in Washington, D.C., has assisted many neighborhoods in this process and lobbies for greater federal assistance to programs that help the urban dweller. Professional community organizers assist groups in preparing themselves to receive financial assistance and to conduct well-managed programs of neighborhood improvement. Energy conservation is often a central concern of these neighborhoods and is a useful issue around which to organize successfully. This workbook itself developed from our involvement with just such an urban energy conservation program in the Central South

Metropolitan Area Housing Alliance
1123 W. Washington Blvd.
Chicago, IL 60607

neighborhood of Troy, New York. The Metropolitan Area Housing Alliance in Chicago has a school for community organizers called the National Training Institute.

LEGAL QUESTIONS

A building permit may be needed for a major improvement to your home but this added complication may work to your advantage. The Building Department at the Town Hall will review your plans and inform you of potential building problems. This review may prevent trouble in the future and these people should be able to guide you to sources of technical assistance.

You have been advised to review carefully the work of potential contractors through a survey of their past performance. In some states local utility companies have developed weatherization programs for their clients and have prepared lists of suitable contractors. These lists may be helpful but many capable smaller contractors and most handymen will not be on the list even when qualified to do the work. As you choose a contractor, be certain to *define all details of the work in writing before any work begins.* Should legal problems arise you may turn to your local Consumer Protection Board. They will assist you in making a case for small-claims court. Larger problems will be directed to the State Attorney General's Office, especially if your case seems to represent a prevailing pattern. It is very important in such cases to have clearly specified in a written contract the quality and extent of the work promised. Multiple complaints to a utility against a contractor are enough to have his name removed from the recommended list but a written document is usually required to press charges.

If you have more general legal questions, twenty-four states have Public Interest Research Group (PIRG) offices ready to help. The NYPIRG offices at the State Universities at Albany and Buffalo have been helpful to us and are active in helping home-owners with energy questions; the office in Buffalo is now using our Diagnosis in a program involving thousands of houses.

National PIRG Clearing Office
Suite 1127
1329 E Street N.W.
Washington, DC 20004

APPROPRIATE TECHNOLOGY

Many ideas of this book differ from established and conventional ways of doing things. In some cases, new technologies and materials outperform and are replacing materials and methods that have now outlived their usefulness. In other instances, relatively new changes have failed to fulfill their promise and are being displaced again by the older techniques of proven value. Everything has changed so quickly in recent years that we now find ourselves with the difficult task of making *appropriate* choices from a wide selection of available *techniques.* The Diagnosis is itself an example of this process of Appropriate Technology at work.

The Appropriate Technology (AT) movement is a reevaluation of the way things are being done and allows greater opportunity for the development of alternatives. In an AT perspective, an enterprise is not valued by size, but by measures such as the degree of its pollution and the *real* usefulness of its product. Work done at home is as valued as work at the office and dollar income is not the only measure of worth. Wood gathered with your own hands provides heat as well as oil paid for with cash and must be accounted for by national planners and policy makers. Leisure in the backyard with friends can be as recreational as an expensive vacation in the Bahamas. AT people in general are learning how to slow down and spend less rather than running about trying to earn greater amounts. They are regaining control over their lives.

Although AT concepts can be applied to all aspects of our lives, the strongest efforts are being made toward the development of systems of local food production, simple programs of health care, and sources of alternative energies. Many individuals around the country are working on such alternatives as solar power, wind energy, and methane fuels, and the National Center for Appropriate Technology (NCAT) is working to monitor this activity. NCAT supports individual hands-on experimentation and is doing its best to keep track of the many networks of local talent that spring up daily. AT often takes the form of adult-education

The National Center
  for Appropriate Technology
P.O. Box 3838
Butte, MT 59701

programs and NCAT can help you locate such experts and activities.

SOLAR ENERGY

A look at solar-energy activity in this country reveals a growing industry of a few large corporate investors in competition with a large field of small-scale appropriate technologists. While appropriate technologists concentrate their efforts on energy conservation to produce tight homes that require small amounts of energy from simple and inexpensive systems of collection, corporate industry produces elaborate systems with expensive hardware for use on any building. It is unfortunate that "solar energy" activity is most easily recognized as the visible roof-top hardware of *active systems,* while most efforts at energy conservation and careful design of *passive systems* are taken for granted. Like the tip of the iceberg, most surveys of solar buildings and lists of solar designers are biased in favor of active systems while passive work has been less noticed to date.

The recognized center of technical development is the International Solar Energy Society, of which the American Section has over thirty regional chapters. These chapters promote the development of solar energy through meetings, publications, and information centers. Membership is open to any interested individual and includes a subscription to their newsletters and magazines.

The Department of Energy is becoming increasingly involved in solar energy and has sponsored a number of demonstration programs to encourage its commercial development. The National Solar Heating and Cooling Information Center in Rockville, Maryland, speaks for the government for these projects and prepares the results for government printing. Their toll-free number provides access to files of operating solar buildings around the country and lists architects and contractors involved in solar work. Their technical division is available to answer short, specific questions that arise as you develop a solar system for yourself but they obviously cannot engineer a total system over the phone. This information center is biased in favor of hardware solutions and has not kept abreast of developments in passive systems.

Efforts are underway to improve the gathering and distribution of information on solar energy through a larger national information center. The national Solar Energy Research Institute in Colorado is now being developed, as well as regional solar centers. Regional centers will be responsible for commercialization activity while the national center will do research and development.

A substantial portion of this budget is intended for the development of a "comprehensive and accessible solar-energy information data base." It appears that this data base may respond to and reveal a greater share of the nation's passive and AT activity than is presently the case. Such a system could develop into a network of computer information terminals at most major libraries to receive and dispense the latest information. The system will

The American Section of the
    International Solar Energy Society,
    Inc.
300 State Road 401
Cape Canaveral, FL 32920

National Solar Heating
    and Cooling Information Center
P.O. Box 1607
Rockville, MD 20850
Toll-free number: (800) 523-2929

Solar Energy Research Institute
1536 Cole Boulevard
Golden, CO 80401

The American Institute of Architects
1735 New York Avenue N.W.
Washington, DC 20006

Mid-American Solar Energy Complex
1256 Trapp Road
Eagan, MN 55121

Northeastern Solar Energy Center
70 Memorial Drive
Cambridge, MA 02142

Western Sun
To be located in
Portland, Oregon

need to be understandable to laypersons in their own terms if it is to represent the entire solar energy effort responsibly. This will not be an easy task but efforts to date have been promising. An example of SERI work is a little "Solar Energy Information Locator," available free from the Rockville Information Center, which is the finest brief survey of national and regional information services we have seen.

Every state now has an Energy Office that monitors and develops programs to control energy use. Although it is difficult to generalize about the programs of fifty different states, all are actively involved in programs of energy conservation, many have developed their own audit programs, and all can be helpful in guiding homeowners in locating information about local groups and activities. Many maintain records of innovative projects within the state and may assist groups in securing grants and aid in developing nonprofit programs. Call your State Energy Office to learn which local groups are conducting projects in which you might participate and from which you may gain useful information and experience.

Southern Solar Energy Center
  Planning Project
Exchange Place
Suite 1250
2300 Peachford Road
Atlanta, GA 30338

The authors, as you know, are architects and have written this book to impart some of the things they know about one aspect of architecture. We would like to believe that the basic ideas of this book will soon become common knowledge to homeowners. However, home-improvement projects will sometimes develop into complicated problems that require planning and design, and at this point you should consider professional assistance. A few dollars for competent advice can actually save money and yield results far better than following a haphazard and untrained approach can. Many people undertake design without understanding that it requires more than just knowing what you want as an end product. Design involves a process of analysis that benefits from experience and developed talent.

There are many good architects and many of these have small, even one-man or one-woman operations. They will often be able to make a breakthrough for you and come up with an idea for an alteration that is better and often simpler than you might have imagined. It may come as a surprise that many architect-designed houses are now selling for less than the national average.

The process of selecting an architect is *very* important and similar in every way to the choice of a contractor—look at his or her previous work and find out who has satisfied customers. There is an additional difficulty. In general, our profession has not made itself available to the homeowner at reasonable prices because many perfectly qualified architects will not bother with small jobs. But competent and economical architectural assistance can be found and the availability of such service will increase with demand. Contact your state office of the American Institute of Architects to consult such an architect before making major changes in your home.

9.
ACHIEVING
COMFORT

MAKE YOURSELF COMFORTABLE

The need to save energy seems always to compete with the desire for comfort. We have presented various ways to save energy throughout the book with little discussion of their effect on the comfort of the home. This chapter is therefore devoted to a discussion of the factors affecting comfort.

There are several different processes that affect comfort and many ways of balancing them. Most people agree that a comfortable room is one of warmth, light, and good air; unfortunately, it is hard to proceed upon such a general basis. Engineers have therefore devised systems to evaluate the levels of illumination, temperature, humidity, and ventilation. Leaving illumination aside, we will now explain some of the intricacies of humidity, ventilation, and radiant heating. Recent advances in these three areas now allow systems of home heating that differ greatly from our common experience. We hope this discussion will stimulate you to undertake some of our improvement alternatives that might have seemed a bit far-out to you. It is very important, however, that you understand the processes before you undertake the improvements.

HUMIDITY CONTROL

Humidity is apt to be a confusing subject. It is not much discussed because it is invisible and its effects are subtle. We have mentioned its relation to many other things but it warrants a section all to itself. Before reading on, you should review the discussion of humidity and water-vapor characteristics in Chapter 2.

Heat, humidity, and living processes are all interrelated; most buildings have an unhealthy lack of humidity in winter as a result of dry heat. Higher winter humidities are generally better for plants, people, and anything made of wood. Doctors say that a relative humidity of 15 percent, which often occurs in uninsulated houses, is detrimental to anyone, that a 50 percent level would reduce the number and severity of colds, and that levels as high as 70 percent would still be very good for people. However, problems with the building and its contents reduce the recommended maximum to 50 percent. Lack of humidity causes nasal and respiratory problems by drying the mucous membranes of the nose and throat. It also causes furniture and woodwork to dry up, shrink, and crack. Windows shrink and fit poorly, allowing more cold air to enter and reduce humidity levels still further. Low humidity encourages static buildup in carpets and fabrics causing shocks and sparks that not only startle people but can damage sensitive electronics.

WHERE DOES HUMIDITY GO?

Humidity is the invisible presence of water vapor in the air. Producing enough of it is not the problem; it comes naturally from a number of sources. Through breathing, perspiring, washing, cooking, and plants, an average family of four produces seven gallons of water vapor each day, and many homes add another seven gallons with a humidifier because the house is still too dry. That's a total of 14 gallons, or over 100 pounds of water evaporated within a house each day. What happens to it all? Why is it difficult to maintain even 30 percent humidity in severe cold weather?

Three things happen to the humidity. If window panes are cold enough, water vapor will condense out of the air onto the glass; when it is very cold the water will freeze there. Second, water vapor will actually migrate *through* porous building materials such as plaster, drywall, and unfinished wood, driven by its own vapor pressure toward areas of lower humidity. The third loss of humidity is transportation through cracks in the air-exchange process.

The three ways vapor is lost from heated buildings

1. Inside air, with its humidity, passing thru openings

2. Condensation, esp. on glass

3. Vapor, from its own pressure, passing thru porous materials

WINDOW CONDENSATION

Preventing condensation is a matter of keeping the inside surfaces of the container warm enough. In the case of windows, this means having enough layers of glazing so that the innermost surface temperature is above the dew point of the air. The recommended humidity levels of the last column of the accompanying table assume that the window has two layers of glass. Circulating warmed air over the glass will increase glass temperature and allow higher humidities but will waste a lot of heat. On the other hand, curtains and interior shutters lower the temperature of the glass and can lead to severe condensation unless special care is taken to seal shutters tightly against vapor. Therefore, include vapor barriers and a snug fit in the design of insulating curtains.

VAPOR WILL CONDENSE ON GLAZING AT THESE TEMPERATURES AND HUMIDITIES

Temperature (°F)	Condensation on Glazings (%)				Recommended Maximum Humidities
	Single	Double	Insulated	Triple	
30	32	50	57	70	40
20	24	42	48	65	35
10	18	35	42	60	30
0	12	30	37	55	25
−10	8	25	31	50	20
−20	5	20	27	45	15

It is reasonable to protect the window against temperatures about 20° lower than the winter average and then simply allow a little condensation whenever the weather is extremely cold. During such a severe cold spell, some moisture will condense out of the air and the humidity will stabilize at a lower level. If, however, you use a humidifier and find a lot of condensation on your windows, you should turn it down. Extreme condensation at windows will not only create damaging puddles of water on windowsills but is also a very good way to channel heat from the house to and out through the glass.

With snug double windows and an adequate vapor barrier in the walls, the humidity need seldom go below 30 percent and can usually be 40 percent or more. In a greenhouse, triple layers of glass or plastic would allow you to generate local humidities of 60–70 percent during the afternoon. Imagine the health benefits of spending a couple of hours a day in a tropical solarium during the middle of a cold northeastern winter! High humidities are terrific refreshers.

At the low humidity ranges, a more humid room is perceived as a warmer one. This is because higher humidities cause less evaporative cooling of the skin.

Humidity is lost when warm, moist air escapes from a house. When outside air enters a house, its water content is much lower than that of the air it replaces. To bring the new air up to comfortable humidity levels, we have to evaporate more water and add it to the air. This is equivalent to boiling water all winter long and requires a lot of heat. Therefore, whenever we reduce air loss from a house, we reduce the cost of humidification as well.

Infiltration is caused by a difference in air pressure between the inside and outside of the house and the opportunity for this pressure difference to equalize. Wind blowing against a building causes high pressures on the windward and low pressures on the leeward so that cold air, quite predictably, enters on the windward and warm air is lost on the leeward. This process is controlled through the stopping up of the openings through which air can pass: in other words, by improving the container, as discussed previously.

A less obvious cause of infiltration is the tendency of warmed air to rise. This warm air then escapes through openings at the upper portions of the house while cool air enters through lower openings. This process occurs whenever the air within the house is warmer than the outside, but the pressure difference at most openings is rather small and the effect can be neglected in modern low houses, *except in one particular case—the chimney.* Chimney flues are large openings and are *designed* to create substantial pressures. They intentionally and literally *draw* warm air out of the house and are the single greatest causes of infiltration in a house sheltered from severe winds.

The low interior air pressures created as furnaces and fireplaces consume interior air can be relieved through the provision of special ducts of outside air to locations of fuel combustion. The low air pressures at the base of the chimney, needed for proper draft, are thereby equalized in the immediate region and infiltration throughout the house is reduced. Older homes with admittedly little vapor protection and severe infiltration, in which *ducted air supplies* have been installed, have been found to maintain 25 percent humidity with ease when 5- to 10-percent levels were the previous norm.

Moisture will find its way through a solid wall unless there is a very good vapor barrier. The ability of a wall material to pass vapor is called its *permeability.* A material with a perm value of 1.0 used to be considered a good vapor barrier but higher temperatures and humidities create stronger vapor pressures so that perm values of 0.3 or less are now preferable. Layers of paint are better than nothing but not as good as plastic films and aluminum foil. Special care should be devoted to sealing small openings around electrical

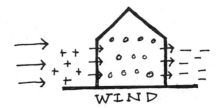

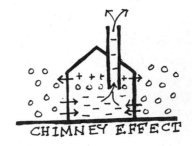

Infiltration is caused by a difference in air pressure.

VAPOR BARRIERS

½-inch Sheetrock	20
Plaster on lath	9
Plywood	2
Two coats of paint	0.6
4-mil polyethylene	0.1
Aluminum foil	0.05
Building paper	3.0
Siding—vinyl or aluminum	0.5

boxes and around window frames. Wet electrical boxes can be a fire hazard.

If it is difficult to visualize *vapor pressures* and to imagine large amounts of vapor passing through a small opening, think of what the air pressure inside a tire can do with a very small hole. When vapor locates a small opening and an opportunity to reach cold surfaces where it can condense, the shrinkage of vapor down to drops of water leaves the air itself drier. This dry air is a kind of vapor vacuum into which more vapor is drawn. In very little time there is a positive circulation of vapor in the direction of the point of condensation.

What happens when there is no vapor barrier at all? Old buildings seldom had vapor barriers, so what is all the fuss about? As long as a building has no insulation, vapor passes right through. The heat loss of such a building is usually enough to heat the entire thickness of the wall and permit vapor to pass the entire distance to the outdoors without condensing. Any vapor that might condense within the outer layers of wood would eventually be heated and evaporate. This is sometimes interrupted by impermeable paints at the outside siding, which trap moisture in the wood, weakening its bond with the paint and causing blistering.

By insulating such a wall we stop the heat loss that would keep the outside wall warm. Without a vapor barrier, vapor passing through will condense somewhere within the wall. Water then falls to the bottom to sit there and promote fungus dry-rot, which consumes a wooden structure. Some water stays in the insulation, where it causes degradation of thermal resistance. A good vapor barrier stops the passage of moisture on the warm side of the insulation, where it will not condense. *Anyone who has recently blown insulation into a wall should immediately consider some sort of vapor protection.* Blistering paint will be the first sign of trouble, then water stains around the sill. The wall is rotting away. Aluminum or vinyl siding conceals but does not correct this problem.

If you can't stop vapor from getting into the insulation, you can at least do it the courtesy to let it escape out the other side. The best way to achieve *cold side venting,* which should be a required element of the insulating contractor's job, is to drive small wedges between the clapboards or siding at about 4-foot

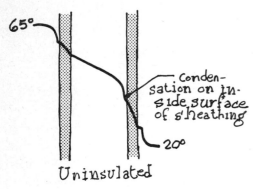

Uninsulated

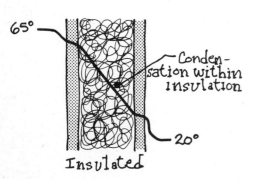

Insulated

Insulation changes the location of condensation.

intervals to allow air to enter and pass through the cavity on the cold side of the insulation. This will carry moisture safely away. Unfortunately it will also reduce the insulating value of the wall.

One of the selling points of aluminum and vinyl siding is that they tighten up the house. True enough, but they also put a vapor barrier on the outside of the wall, the worst possible place! Unless there is an excellent vapor barrier inside the wall, tight vinyl or aluminum is not a good idea. These need cold side venting most of all.

High levels of humidity, desirable as they may be, can be difficult to maintain. To summarize, the best solution, in concept, is to *develop a container for humidity*. Such a container must be impermeable to vapor passage and warm enough to prevent condensation. Walls are made impermeable and warm with vapor barriers and insulation. Windows are impermeable but must be warmed with additional layers of glass or properly designed curtains and shutters. The container is made complete with careful weather-stripping and caulking.

The remaining objection to maintaining humidity is what to do with high humidity in tight construction when it develops to excess. The main sources of high humidity are usually the bath and kitchen, each of which should have its own exhaust system for odor as well as humidity control. It is also possible to relieve high humidity by briefly opening a window to let in a little cold dry air.

If you still have a high humidity level and wish not to lose heat through an open window, you can build a simple dehumidifier. Take an old radiator and run cold water through it. As long as the radiator is colder than any of the window surfaces you should not have the worry of condensation on your windows. If this is part of a greenhouse system within the home, the condensation can be caught in a pan below and run back to water plants. Meanwhile you can be preheating hot water through the collected heat of vaporization at the radiator. You can use the process of condensation to collect energy instead of losing it.

VENTILATION

Air circulation has been found to be the single largest heat loss of a building, and you are urged to reduce air changes. Assuming we have the power to eliminate infiltration, how far can and should we reduce air changes and yet provide the fresh air that is needed for comfort and good health?

The quantity of air needed for good health is related to oxygen requirements and the control of odors. Ventilation rates are expressed in terms of cubic feet of fresh air per hour per person depending upon activity. A gymnasium obviously needs more ventilation than a house. But *the amount of air entering a building in excess of the ventilation requirement should be recognized as unnecessary heat loss.*

What, then, is a reasonable air-change rate for a home in terms of ventilation requirements? Although many homes have rates of 1, 2, and 3, we recommend a goal as low as ¼ air change. This can be reached, is being attained, in modern homes and is entirely comfortable if certain conditions are observed. The state of Minnesota now recommends for new homes a minimum air-change rate of 2 per day or 1/10 per hour. By comparison, our goal of ¼ is conservative.

To illustrate the process of translating ventilation requirements into air-change rates, let us use the following table to determine the air-change requirement of a small bedroom for two sleepers. A small room of 10 × 12 × 8 feet has a volume of 1,000 cubic feet. Since the oxygen requirement for two sleepers would be 100 cubic feet per hour, the air-change rate should be 1/10 to provide enough oxygen. The removal of odors would require an air change 5 times as fast, which would be ½ air change per hour. This is, however, a small room; many bedrooms and most living rooms will be larger in volume, requiring a slower rate of air exchange. When doors are left open between rooms, air is free to migrate about the house and the usable air volume is increased. Since odor control requires 5 times more air than the oxygen requirement, a design value of ¼ air change would allow the presence of odor as a sort of danger sign to increase ventilation. It is highly unlikely that anyone would remain in a stuffy room long enough to suffer from a dangerously low supply of oxygen.

VENTILATION REQUIREMENTS

	Oxygen (cu ft./hr.)	Odor (cu ft./hr.)
Sleeping	50	250
Seated	100	500
Working	300	1500

CONTROLLING ODOR

Studies of odor have revealed interesting results. When odors were separated into three categories—body odors, chemical odors, and cigarette smoke—it was found that body odors deteriorate quickly, even in an unventilated room in 5–10 minutes, while most household chemical odors survive 6–7 hours and cigarette odors for 17–48 hours. The same study discovered that the human tolerance to odor improves markedly as the air temperature decreases, so that a room at 60° would require much less odor ventilation than one at 70°. This occurs for two reasons: Our sense of smell is more easily stimulated by warm particles of odor, and the germs and bacteria that cause odor thrive in warmer environments.

A larger interior volume of space for oxygen supply allows

lower air-change rates. Large volumes also allow body and chemical odors to disperse and deteriorate on their own. A large-enough volume of air would take care of the odor problem without air exchange.

A large volume, combined with a greenhouse, could eliminate the need for ventilation altogether, because required oxygen can be produced by plants. It is estimated that *one square foot of leaf surface in sunlight can process one cubic foot of air per hour.* Plants do consume oxygen at night but this is only ¼ what they daily produce. If plants in a residential sunroom of 250 square feet of glass have 1,000 square feet of leaf surface, this leafage in 8 hours of sunlight would provide the oxygen needed for 3 people for a full 24-hour day. These plants would also absorb odors, pull dust and dirt out of the air, and provide beneficial humidity. Such a volume of space would be a self-sufficient capsule like a spaceship. This would almost eliminate the need for air exchange, which now accounts for so much of residential heat loss.

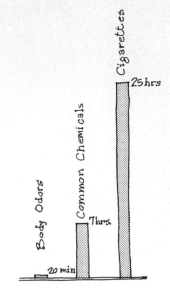

The life span of cigarette odor places a heavy load on ventilation requirements.

Our recommendations are to strive for ¼ air change in the house, provide this with vents that can be securely sealed, allow air to flow from room to room, and provide positive exhaust for kitchens and baths to remove odors at their source. The way to get down to this level of ventilation is to seal as many windows as possible for the winter with rope caulk or tape that can be removed in the summer. Leave only one operable window in each bedroom and carefully weather-strip it. The best solution for an old house is to install storm windows that fit inside the old windows and seal them tightly in place. Seal all other windows in the house with the exception of one in the kitchen and one in each bath. The entrance door should have a vestibule and all additional doors should be sealed for the winter. In new construction, an entrance complex should receive special design attention as a major element of the house. This entry room should open independently to workshops, basements, and the house proper. Such an entrance would relieve much unnecessary traffic through the warm center of the house.

These procedures are all aspects of a general approach which is, again, to create a controlled container. Such a container can be made economically with modern materials to be as tight as we wish and be provided with ventilation at the rates desired and under precise and adjustable control. If we can send men to the moon in such containers, we can certainly learn to make them for ourselves.

RECOMMENDATIONS

RADIANT HEATING

To review Chapter 2 a bit, heated materials give off energy by radiation, which is a form of heat exchange different from convection or conduction in that it doesn't require a medium of transfer. Radiant energy travels across empty space every day from the sun. Radiant heat travels only in straight lines until it strikes a solid opaque object, where it is absorbed or reflected. Two parallel surfaces of radiant heat, or one and a reflector, can exchange energy with little loss and can heat objects placed between without greatly heating the air. McDonald's keeps your Big Mac warm this way because it is an efficient way to do it.

THE RADIANT ENVIRONMENT

One way of estimating the benefits of radiant heating is to determine the *mean radiant temperature* or MRT of a room, which is one way of expressing radiant activity. Imagine you are in a sphere; how warm are its surfaces and how far away is the warmth? Average the temperatures, giving additional weight to those surfaces that are closer to you. The MRT changes for different positions of the same room.

Although the precise measurement of MRT is difficult and the equations complex, a rough estimate is sufficient to illustrate useful ideas. A system of radiant heating for floors or ceilings that produces surface temperatures of 80° and 90° can raise the MRT from a usual value of about 65° to nearer 75°. Portable electric-resistance heaters do the same thing. Sitting near a wood stove can raise your MRT to 80° or higher. Remember the pictures of King Henry VIII with furs on his back and his chest exposed. He was absorbing radiant heat from a fire in front of him and using furs to keep cold drafts off his back. Higher MRT allows you to reduce air temperatures and still maintain comfort, while the general heat losses for the building are reduced.

RAISING THE MRT

The benefits of higher MRT can be obtained without getting into elaborate heating systems. Simply moving furniture away from colder outside walls will improve the MRT. Anything that raises the apparent temperature of exterior walls will improve comfort. Closing curtains and shutters is the single most important way to do this. Placing fabrics, tapestries, and shelving systems against exterior walls will raise the apparent temperature of the walls by 5–10°.

These ideas become more important if you have a brick building (or a cold stone castle) that doesn't seem to have room for insulation. In such cases, even one inch of rigid-board insulation will greatly improve the MRT of the room. This first inch will more than double the resistance of the wall and slow the passage of heat enough to raise the interior wall temperature as much as 20°. The insulation isolates the interior space of the room from the cold mass of the actual wall. A wall surface in front of any amount of insulation will remain nearer the room air temperature. Placing a tapestry on a wall is a traditional example of this form of insulation. *If you can't insulate a wall, at least isolate it.*

RADIATORS

Now that we know more about radiant energies, let's talk about radiators. Some radiators do indeed radiate, especially cast-iron steam ones. How can we make them more efficient? The efficiency of radiant exchange of a heated surface is measured by its *emissivity*. Most materials have a high emissivity with the exception of those few that are reflective, such as polished metals. The way to get heat out of a radiator is to paint it—not with shiny aluminum paint, but with flat black or at least a deep color in flat latex. (Just be certain that the paint you use has a tolerance to heat.) Flat latex paint will also increase surface texture and area of the radiator to improve its convective exchange. A very old radiator with many layers of paint should be stripped to remove extra layers of paint, which may act as insulation. If you don't mind a black radiator, use stove black; you'll get the most heat out of it.

The next step toward better performance is to place a reflective metal surface behind the radiator to prevent radiant heat from going directly into the exterior wall and out of the building. This alone can give you 10 percent more heat. And finally, place a dark, absorbent surface on the opposite wall to absorb heat from the radiator. It will be like having two radiators and you'll know what it's like to be a Big Mac.

Carrying the idea further, the entire exterior should be lined with reflective materials over insulation. One way to obtain such a reflective exterior wall surface without having it shiny is to cover the wall with aluminum foil and finish with fabrics stretched from furring strips attached to ceiling and floor lines. Interior walls should be dark with highly absorbent and emissive surfaces. A person in such a room would receive heat directly from the radiator, perceive the warmth of the interior wall as a radiant panel, and feel the relative warmth of the suspended fabrics as yet a third generator of radiant heat.

For an interior wall to become a radiator it must be warmer than the objects in the room. It will usually be warmer than the room air itself, but not always. A wall struck by direct radiation or heated by internal heating coils will always be warmer than the air; such a wall then radiates this heat out to the objects in the room. Smaller radiant panels are now commercially available that look like paintings but plug into the electrical house current and are effective heaters, especially when near a seated person.

Another form of radiant wall obtains and distributes its heat primarily by convection of room air. This process is less efficient and requires larger surfaces but can be an important way to control the rising air temperatures that result from direct heat gain from southern windows. Large expanses of roughened stonework and textured sand-plaster walls can be used in this way to absorb surplus heat from the air during the day and return it when air temperatures fall in the evening. Such a wall will gain and lose heat primarily by convection but its generally warmer temperature will tend to raise the MRT of the room. Such a uniform distribution of relatively warm surfaces with reduced air temperatures is generally agreed to be a very comfortable and healthy condition.

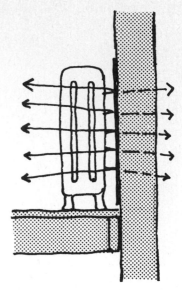

An aluminum reflector (e.g., foil) behind a radiator will reflect heat ordinarily lost through the wall back into the space.

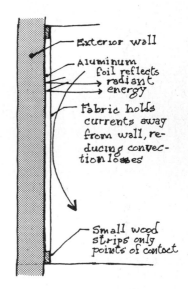

A wall-insulating system that uses no insulation

RADIANT WALLS

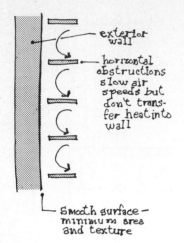

exterior wall

horizontal obstructions slow air speeds but don't transfer heat into wall

Smooth surface-minimum area and texture

Surface coefficients produce large air films, reducing air-to-mass heat transfer.

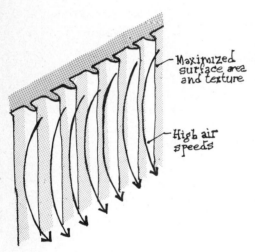

Maximized surface area and texture

High air speeds

High surface coefficients produce small air films, increasing air-to-mass heat transfer.

THERMAL MASS

The qualities of the film of air that forms the interface between the material of the wall and air of the room will determine the performance of radiant walls. The surface temperature of such a wall is determined by its *temperature difference* from the air it contacts, the *speed of the air* it contacts, and *surface texture* of the wall. The measure of the rate of heat exchange between wall and air is given by the wall's *surface coefficient,* which leads to a precise way to determine the thermal value of air films.

We have already discussed this phenomenon under several other names. Air films were mentioned as layers of still air on either side of the exterior wall. Landscaping was found to reduce wind speed and allow thicker air films. In general, smooth surfaces and streamlined air currents leave air films undisturbed. Textured walls, on the other hand, increase turbulence and give higher heat exchange.

The way to reduce heat transfer into an exterior wall is both to reduce air speeds and to decrease the surface texture. This is a paradox because the usual way to reduce air speed is to add texture. The answer to this problem is two exterior walls. The actual surface of the wall mass should be smooth, with an "apparent" surface forward of it. This forward surface should be textured to slow down air before it reaches the actual wall surface. A shelving system in front of a wall is one example of an apparent wall, which maintains room temperatures on the front surface of the books, reduces convection losses to the actual wall, and allows for a smooth plaster wall behind for minimal transfer of heat from the air into the actual wall material. Hung fabrics and tapestries are other traditional solutions.

On interior walls it is better to increase surface texture to improve their ability to absorb heat and thereby raise radiant surface temperatures. With concentric zoning, relatively massive interior walls of higher radiant energies compensate for exterior walls of lower temperatures, which results in less heat loss. *To raise the surface coefficient of an interior wall, increase texture while maintaining air motion.* This is best achieved through masonry surfaces and is highest with pronounced vertical grooves; for example, the fins of a convector. This sort of mass and surface is sometimes called a *heat sink* because it both collects and holds heat well.

A heavy masonry heat sink is very helpful when we wish to absorb excess afternoon heat, store it, and then release it during the evening. This natural system of heat storage is a major element of many simple solar heating systems. If your house has interior masonry with broad surfaces to absorb heat from the air, it should be worthwhile to increase the amount of south-facing window to allow more sunlight and heat into your house. If the sunlight can actually hit the masonry for several hours, so much the better; but it is not necessary. All the improvements we have just discussed help to prepare your house for solar energy, our purest form of radiant heating.

It should be noted that this process of adding windows and providing storage masses requires a certain amount of balancing. Admitting too much heat and exceeding your storage capacity or absorptive rate can create uncomfortably high interior temperatures, but this problem is unlikely if you add less than 100 square feet of window to a fairly large room. High temperatures in a small area can be alleviated by ducting the heat to other parts of the house. This is passive solar design, which is not the subject of this book. Read up on it and get expert advice before going ahead on a major project.

SUGGESTIONS FOR FURTHER READING

American Building: The Environmental Forces That Shape It, by James Marston Fitch. First published in 1948, this edition again pleads for a reintegration of natural forces as an essential element of design in a well-conceived but overdeveloped technical style.
Boston, Mass.: Houghton Mifflin Co., 1972. $15.00

Design with Climate, by Victor Olgyay. One of the earliest and still the finest discussion of the biological relationship between man and his environment. A bit light on generally useful theory and heavy on engineering application.
Princeton, N.J.: Princeton University Press, 1963. $19.50

Man, Climate and Architecture, by B. Givoni. An exhaustive study of man's physiological and architectural response to environment. Although heavy on the study of space cooling from his Israeli experience, this remains a gold-mine of research results.
London, Eng.: Elsevier Publishing Co., Ltd., 1969.

The Handbook of Fundamentals, published by the American Society of Heating, Refrigerating and Air Conditioning Engineers. This is the mechanical engineer's bible, from which he devises the systems that make modern architecture livable. A bit of a tome but it has most of the information needed to predict and provide comfort within unusual conditions of environmental stress.
Available from ASHRAE, 345 East 47th St., New York, N.Y. 10017, 1977. $40.00

10.
THE
MAKING
OF WARM

We have considered the whole house from top to bottom, complete with site and services. There is much here to think about; we are astonished ourselves at the variety of material. Nobody will use it all. In any given situation, an improvement may be inappropriate or, if plausible, too expensive for the benefits. This is where judgment is required. Some ideas are untried or not yet developed for general use. We have entered a new age and must experiment to perfect the unproven or prove it can't be done.

In all cases we have attempted to evaluate honestly the merits and demands of each improvement opportunity. We have also tried to indicate side-effects and interrelationships in simple numbers and plain English. All this is to prepare you to do your own thinking. Not every possible topic has been covered, but a framework is there and almost anything that comes along should fit somewhere on the Map of Household Energy.

A PROCESS OF ADAPTATION

As we see it, you should try to view your weatherization efforts as a long-term process of adaptation. Starting with your house as it is, you must reconcile the realities of climate and costs with your need for comfort and usable space. Weatherization should become one, but not the only, aspect of making life at home more livable—homemaking.

You should consider energy-conservation improvements together with the other things you wish to add, subtract, alter, or replace in the house. A ten-year plan should include at least enough weatherization projects to keep utility bills roughly the same even as the unit costs of fuel go up. All projects in the plan should be integrated to complement one another. Try each year to balance enjoyable projects with other, merely necessary ones. Do each project carefully and thoroughly so that it doesn't become a recurring problem and do it at a time when it won't be disrupted by future work. Whatever you do should be examined in a logical way for a maximum all-around benefit. This will be a hard job, surprisingly hard; we know because this is just the kind of thing for which architects are trained.

Part of the long-term adaptation process will include yourself—your mind and your body. There are many subjects of this nature in this book, including developing a tolerance for lower room temperatures, learning the art of woodburning, experimenting with living arrangements to minimize heat loss, and the whole business of "conservative" thinking generally. Knowing how energy works in your house should affect your attitudes toward home maintenance and the yearly process of weatherization that a house demands.

THE ANNUAL CYCLE

Home is created as we live in a place, experiencing the passage of time and the changes of the seasons. The natural cycles have given a pattern to our lives for thousands of years and much of our cultural heritage derives from observances connected to the seasons. When most of us were farmers and had to keep track of the passage of time, feast days were actually deadlines for the completion of certain tasks. The "holy-day" served as a celebration for a job well done.

All Hallows' Eve was the time to complete the harvest, before the spirits of the dead walked the earth and the mysterious frosts destroyed the crops. More recently, Thanksgiving was instituted as a time to celebrate the completion of preparations for winter. Candlemas was a pagan festival that marked the death of the year and the beginning of the quiet season of winter. Winter has long been a time to sit back, live off the year's harvest, reflect, and prepare for the coming year. May Day signaled the rebirth of life and activity and the time to swing back into motion. After intensive spring labors, the hot days of summer were the time to fatten the hog, relax a bit and enjoy ease and abundance. It was also a time to initiate projects and build against the next winter.

THE RHYTHM OF THE SEASONS

These seasonal rhythms fulfill a variety of human needs, the most important being a pattern of meaning and purpose, while still allowing for individual expression. When and how you go about harvesting is your choice, but a failure to do so will lead to hardship. Harvesting is hard work, a *chore;* but it is also a *ritual.* The difference between ritual and chore is important and needs emphasis, for both are repetitious activities performed on a regular basis. The main difference is in attitude: A ritual directs the awareness to new ideas and unexpected associations while a chore is simply menial and tedious. A chore can usually be turned into a ritual.

The common task of lighting a fire may be one of these chores-become rituals. Each year the Vestals of ancient Rome would

RITUAL ACTIVITY

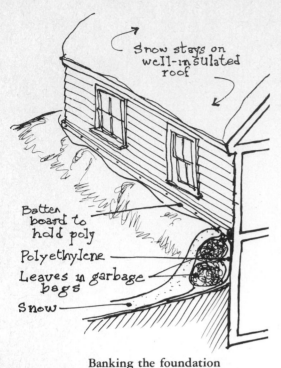

Banking the foundation

BANK THE HOUSE

PROTECT FOUNDATION
PLANTINGS

Foundation plant shelters

rekindle the sacred fire, from which all the hearths of Rome received new light and vigor. Campers still feel the value of fire and know that there is considerable art and skill in the making of a good one. There is always more to be learned in ritual activity. In this spirit we would like to discuss the annual maintenance of the home as a ritual activity that fits the changing of the seasons.

The Autumn Schedule

Autumn is a colorful and exciting season. In nature the end of summer is a time of vigorous activity; sap returns to the root, the squirrel stores its nuts, and the beaver completes its den. It is a good season to be outside working, as autumn breezes replace the summer heat and there is much to be done.

The first task is to harvest the garden before the frost. The falling leaves should be a reminder to finish cutting fallen timbers and to clear the paths into the woodlot. Most wood is gathered during the cold months with sleds, but winter wood needs a full year's cure, while fallen wood is usually dead and can be burned immediately.

Fallen leaves are raked up so as not to smother the lawn in the spring, but why throw them away? Seal them in plastic bags and use them to *bank the house.* A bag of fluffy leaves is like a pillow and makes good insulation. In the spring the leaves can be used again to mulch the garden. Bales of hay are also commonly used to bank the house. In severe climates a good job of banking will cover with snow and form an igloo around the lower parts of the house; it will maintain wall temperatures of 30° or more even in the most severe weather. This will greatly improve basement and first-floor temperatures.

Foundation plantings provide wind protection and can be good insulation but need protection themselves. It is a good idea to construct little wooden shelters to protect them from heavy snow loads and large downfalls from the roof. Groups of shelters can be constructed to contain snow between plants and form a solid wall of snow and plants to protect banked material behind from wind. Snow shelters should be put out before Thanksgiving at the same time as the storm windows.

Securing storm windows used to be strenuous work but is now a simple task if you have modern triple-track windows; it is just a matter of sliding down the storm glass. Yet you can walk down any street in mid-winter and find windows in summer position. Early November is the time to take a couple of weekends to caulk around windows and wash and secure storms. Get the entire family involved and turn it into a work party. This trip around the house is the time to look for other trouble spots, such as gutters and downspouts clogged with leaves, windblown roof flashing, or even little repair jobs left unfinished throughout the summer. Later in November you can wash the inside window, check the weather stripping, and put up your insulating curtains.

Finally, just in time for the Thanksgiving celebration, you can set up the wood stove, bring out the rugs, and rearrange the furniture toward central heat sources. Break up large inside spaces into smaller units with furniture and hangings to slow air motion. Cover wall surfaces with curtains, fabrics, and rugs to raise the mean radiant temperature. Clean the furnace and make sure it is in good operating condition. It will be a greater pleasure to sit down to Thanksgiving dinner knowing that you are buttoned up for winter. This leaves December for personal preparations for the holiday season and the rest of the winter for being relaxed and secure in your home.

Looking back over the fall schedule, we have progressed from working out-of-doors toward the inside of the house. We first added extra layers of insulation outside by banking the house and protecting shrubs, and inside by putting up curtains. Then we attended to our heating, controlled-air-motion, and room arrangements to create comfortable settings for winter.

The Spring Schedule

The spring schedule is pretty much the reverse of the fall. At a point in April the sun and breezes become too pleasant to keep outside and you feel the need to open the windows and air out the house. A little breeze flowing through the house will stir the dust that has settled during the winter and you will know it is time for *spring cleaning.* In one good family weekend, you can take down and store storm windows and snow shields. Haul the leaves over to the garden and till them in. Take down the curtains and beat the dirt out of the rugs. Dismantle the wood stove, clean and store the pipes, and give the house a thorough cleaning.

Summer comfort depends on ventilation. Remove fabrics from the path of air motion through the house. Rearrange the furniture to encourage the channeling of air through the rooms. Ventilation increases the accumulation of dust, so corners should be left open and easy to clean. You will want to spend more of your time outdoors anyway, so some of the furniture can go out onto the porch and patio.

As we see, the house should function very differently in summer and winter. During the winter we want to exaggerate the distinction between the warm interior and the harsh outdoors, while during the summer we try to smooth the transition between inside and out. Activities and room arrangements are oriented toward the outdoors in summer, with plenty of ventilation, while during the winter, air motion is discouraged and activities become focused within, toward sources of warmth. Air motion is discouraged by textured and fuzzy surfaces with multiple divisions of space in winter, while air motion is desirable in summer and encouraged by smooth clean surfaces with continuous, unobstructed paths through the house. A single year-round arrangement can never be as effective as an adaptable seasonal approach.

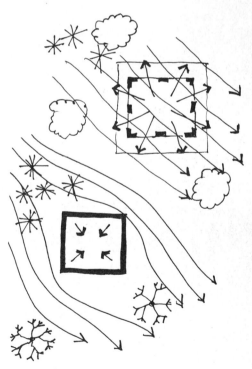

Summer—winter concepts

LEARNING THE PROCESS OF WOOD HEATING

We want to say more about wood heat at this point because it ties in with our theme of getting better results and greater efficiencies by taking care of things yourself. What might be done with wood heat if developed to the optimum? Starting with methods that are commonly known and advancing to the limits, we end with the speculation: What if the whole house became the wood stove?

A BRIEF HISTORY

Central heating was distinguished from earlier heating methods by several characteristics. Different fuels (first coal, then oil and natural gas) became available and were cheaper and easier to use than wood. The use of ducts and pipes for distribution made it possible to heat distant spaces of a building. Independent controls freed people from the need to tend the fire personally. These were great advantages over wood-stove heat and other methods . . . but we should look a little deeper.

Every method of doing things has a history of development and every "old-fashioned" process was once the newest. The fireplace was an advance over the open fire it replaced because the smoke was taken care of cleanly. Imagine the difference that made. Many improvements were made to the initial invention; the ultimate stage (so far) was the Rumford. What finally eliminated the fireplace as a serious method of heating was the enclosed metal stove devised by Ben Franklin. Perhaps it is local prejudice (for we live in the nineteenth-century town that was to stoves as Detroit is to cars), but stoves were very important and a major industry; everybody had to have one. Many types were developed and each did a better job than the last. Then the modern central-heating system, typified by a single furnace in the basement pushing heat throughout the building, superseded the independent stove as the thing you had to have. Now that is in question.

DISCOVERY AND REDISCOVERY

When a new method of doing things comes along and is accepted, the developments of the old method stop because it is no longer profitable or interesting to work on them. This does not necessarily mean that the old method couldn't still have been improved. It doesn't even mean that the old method is inferior to the new one in every way. It only means that most people have placed their attention elsewhere. Something may happen to change that attention again. Something *has* happened. All the characteristics of central heating that we listed before are now becoming disadvantages. The "new fuels" are now less cheap and less available. It is becoming too expensive to heat every space all the time.

Necessity is the mother of rediscovery. In this case, wood is being rediscovered as a fuel. Inventors are beginning to place the same kind of effort into wood-heat refinements that were previously devoted to central heating. We propose, as our contribution to this effort, to look at the relationship of wood heat to the well-managed house.

For a start we will make two claims and then describe the conditions that will make them true. The first claim is that nearly any centrally placed wood stove is inherently more efficient than an oil or gas furnace. Actually this should not be hard to believe since the heat is created and used in the same place so that there are no distribution losses. The second claim is somewhat more extravagant: that an intelligently managed Rumford fireplace in a well-built and well-managed home can rival the efficiency of a modern wood stove. It all depends on maintaining an efficient fire.

Firewood burns in three stages. First the water content evaporates with a hiss and a pop. This takes heat away from the fire at the rate of 1,000 Btu's per pound of water, of which wood is commonly 20 percent by weight. Next, fuel vapors are released and burn with long flames if the temperature is high enough. Finally, the carbon of the wood itself burns and turns into carbon dioxide at about 8,500 Btu's per pound of bone-dry wood.

In practice, wood is never bone dry, but green wood is very inefficient to burn and makes a very poor fire. A live tree is over 90 percent water and newly cut wood is sometimes burned with a moisture content as high as 70 percent. A pound of this is then good for only 2,500 Btu's, about one-quarter of which must go uselessly into boiling away the water. For this you need bigger, faster-burning fires than for dry wood. Luckily, the vaporization of water is accompanied by fuel vapor combustion or you wouldn't get any fire at all. What you do get is a hissing, popping, and steaming fire and large amounts of heat going up the chimney. Overall, *burning green wood is a sacrifice of half the burning efficiency of well-seasoned wood.*

An efficient wood fire is not the blazing pile of logs that looks so cheerful and sounds so exciting. It is rather moody and contemplative. It hardly flames at all; just quietly sits there and glows. Such a radiant bed of coals needs only a small amount of air motion to sustain its combustion, which is clean and even. To maintain such a bed of coals, you need a firebox of high heat capacity typified best by the broad back of a Rumford but achievable with a heavy cast-iron wood stove. As an illustration of the high heat and minimal air motion over a bed of coals, a small piece of dry wood placed on such coals will often turn to charcoal and then into glowing coal without going through a flame stage. A good heating fire will seldom have flames in excess of a couple of inches high. Correctly angled radiant surfaces can then deliver heat at efficiencies of 30 percent or more.

All fireplaces and wood stoves should have dampers. Wood stoves need them for safety reasons as well as for efficiency. Dampers should fit tight when closed and should be left in the closed position when not in use. Thermostatically closing dampers are now marketed to seal off the flue when the fire is out, since

THE PROCESS OF WOODBURNING

A fire needs heat, air, and fuel. High temperature in the firebox and intense radiant exchange between the logs produce high heat while using little fuel and air.

USE YOUR DAMPER

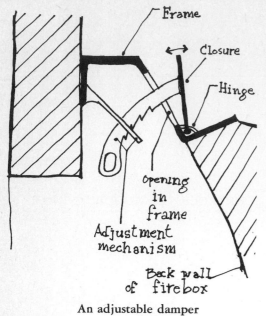

An adjustable damper

DUCTED AIR SUPPLY

AN AUTONOMOUS HOUSE

dampers left open encourage infiltration throughout the house.

A damper should have multiple positions. If necessary, additional notches should be filed into the control arm to provide additional adjustments. You will want to open the damper wide to get a draft started when beginning a fire. As the fire builds in intensity, you should be able to *adjust the damper to reduce air motion to just that needed to maintain a fire and completely exhaust smoke and gases.* As the temperature of the firebox builds, less air motion is needed, so you should have the capacity to make close adjustments to the damper. There is a strong relationship between wood-heat efficiencies and air motion, and the damper is the adjustable valve that controls the draw of a chimney over a slow and efficient radiant fire.

Wood-heating an Air-tight House

How do you provide ventilation for a fire in a tightly constructed house? In a house with only $\frac{1}{4}$ air change, as we've advocated, you might certainly have difficulty sustaining a fire. An open fire would not get enough air; the chimney would not be able to draw and the room would fill with smoke. A common recommendation to improve the draft of such a fireplace is to open a window a bit. This works, but it also sends a cold draft across the floor. It is not surprising that fireplaces have a bad reputation.

The better way to do this is to supply the fireplace itself, not the entire room, with outside air. Air should be escorted from the outside or basement and delivered directly to the firebox so that combustion uses outside air instead of valuable room air. We have already discussed the use of registers to allow cold window drafts to fall into the basement and then rise up through registers in front of the fireplace for this purpose. A similar method works for wood stoves and fireplaces on exterior walls.

Exterior air supply for the fire need not provide 100 percent of the fire's need, for it is good to use some room air, create air motion and pull in a little fresh air for the house when you are there and need it. A fireplace operated only when you are at home can do just that.

Now consider a tight house with an attached solar greenhouse, passive solar heating, and a Rumford fireplace with a ducted air-supply register mixing window downdrafts with a little exterior fresh air. During the day the house cruises along on solar heat and almost no air change because the fire was last fed in the morning and has burned down to small coals. When you come in for the evening, you put on more wood and open the damper a bit. Air will start to rise up the chimney and room air will be drawn over the fire, which will flare up and develop a strong draft up the chimney. This strong draft activates the air supply duct in front of the fire. It also draws a certain amount of stale air toward the living room, where it eventually works its way up the chimney.

This air lost throughout the house is made possible through a small increase in infiltration at each window and door. Meanwhile the fire is moving to a stable radiant level with reduced air requirements so that you can close the damper. Air motion through the house then continues at a reduced level as a means of convective heat distribution while the ducted air supply provides most of the air for the fire. We'll bet that such a heating system is far better than just 30 percent efficient.

In such a scheme, the building and the heating system merge and there is no way to think of them separately. The tight well-insulated building requires little heat, which is provided efficiently with precise dampering. Under favorable burning conditions, wood is a remarkably clean fuel and has few pollutants. The exhaust, in fact, is the same as you and I produce: just carbon dioxide and water vapor. The amount of oxygen required for a couple hours of efficient burning of well-seasoned wood can be produced by the attached greenhouse to make the cycle complete. The entire process could theoretically be maintained inside a closed space with the chimney sealed except while the fire is being built. Such a system would be 100 percent efficient. The house is alive; the fireplace is its heart and the greenhouse the lung.

SUGGESTIONS FOR FURTHER READING

Wood Heat, by John Vivian. A well-reasoned discussion that demystifies the science of wood heat. Expensive precision stoves are somewhat more efficient but down-home solutions can pull a close second. Text and drawings are a delight. An advocate of the Rumford fireplace.
Emmaus, Pa.: Rodale Press, Inc., 1976. $4.95

The Forgotten Art of Building a Good Fireplace, by Vrest Orton. Count Rumford lives on. His history is given and the secrets that made him legendary are revealed.
Dublin, N.H.: Yankee, 1969.

The Complete Book of Heating with Wood, by Larry Gay. A little book with a lot of wisdom. Ignores Rumford and degrades fireplaces generally while it supports wood stoves and Benjamin Franklin specifically.
Charlotte, Vt. (05445): Garden Way Publishing, 1974. $3.95

The Works of Benjamin Franklin, edited by Jared Sparks. Volume VI has a number of essays by the father of wood stoves that still hit the nail on the head, such as "On the Cause and Cure of Smoking Chimneys."
Chicago: Townsend MacCoun, 1882.

Fire on the Hearth, by J. H. Peirce. For a review of the diverse and peculiar varieties of parlor stoves of the nineteenth century, most of which are being re-invented today.
Springfield, Mass.: Pond-Ekberg, 1951.

11.
AND WHAT IT MIGHT LOOK LIKE

DENIS LAMOUREUX

Many new kinds of houses are being built around the country and they vary with the climate, the willingness of the client to venture with new ideas, and the talent and innovation of the designer. There are new problems and new solutions and we all have much to learn.

Most solar houses are now identified by the solar panels on the roof. This example, on the other hand, is solar-heated without them. This house, which is to be built in northern New York, is to be 75 percent solar-heated with southern glass and 25 percent heated with wood. It is provided with the correct roof angle for solar panels for hot water and eventually for photocells as they become economically available in a few more years.

The most surprising thing about this house is that it uses nothing more than what we have already discussed in the book to provide shelter and warmth, and it *costs less than a conventional house.* This house can be built for less than $30 per square foot because it doesn't have a furnace or system of ducts for heat distribution, it doesn't have mountains of insulation, it has a minimum of surface area exposed to the cold, and it doesn't have expensive solar collectors. It relies instead on clear thinking about essential needs, which leads to an efficient design. All aspects of this design have been discussed in earlier chapters, so let's put it all together and see what it might look like.

THE GENERAL FORM OF THE HOUSE

The first law of survival in the cold north regions is to merge into the land and avoid the brunt of the winter storms. Bitter cold and driving winds are most common on hilltops and overlooks, and

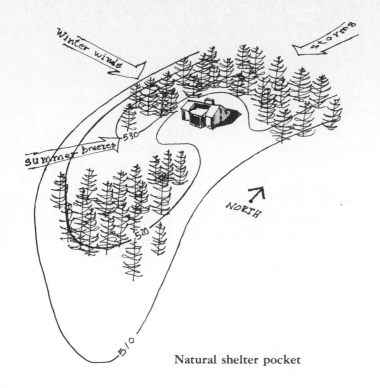

Natural shelter pocket

attractive as they may be in the summer, they are to be avoided as sites for year-round homes. When siting a house, spend a little time out on the land during the winter and determine those sites where you feel most comfortable, with a bit of a view, but also protected. Go out in a bitter storm with howling winds for a few hours; that place where you find protection from the elements is your *natural shelter pocket* and is the warmest place you could possibly place your house.

Into, not onto but *into,* this shelter pocket you should place a *compact* home that provides the spaces you need without seeming to disturb the natural patterns of the environment. If you settle into the ground a little, grade up the earth a little, and generally maintain a low profile, you are likely to avoid disrupting existing currents of air. *Minimum surface area exposed to the cold* from a compact form of house and *minimum wind exposure* from earth-berming and dense landscaping can reduce exposure by half and thereby double the value of the insulation you do use.

If you then add an *open southern exposure* with large expanses of glass and a reflecting field of snow you can easily gather the energy you need to heat the house. In northern regions, a vertical wall collecting sunlight off the snow as well as the sky is more effective than the precise roof angle at a perpendicular to the incoming rays of sunlight. The south face of the house is the place for the solar greenhouse.

A compact house

A SOLAR HOUSE IS JUST MASS UNDER GLASS

The difficulty of solar-heating a house is that one face of the building in 8 hours must absorb enough heat to make up for 24 hours of heat loss through six surfaces. Heat must enter the south window wall eighteen times as fast as it leaves the other walls.

THERMAL MASS

Bringing that amount of heat through a window is not much trouble, but finding a place to store it may be; this is where thermal mass and surface coefficients become important. Without enough mass to absorb the heat at a sufficiently rapid rate, the air of the house will rise to uncomfortable levels. The *amount of mass,* the *expanse of its surface area,* the *roughness of its texture,* and the *freedom of air circulation* through the house will determine the success of the transfer of surplus heat into storage.

WHERE TO PUT IT

When a little mass is placed outside the envelope (out on the roof) and connected with expensive copper pipes down to a compact storage mass in the basement (outside of the envelope), the system becomes complicated and expensive. But when, as in our example, the mass is within the house itself and involves direct heat transfers without the use of precious metals or mechanical equipment, the system becomes simple, cheap, and—surprisingly—more efficient. After all is said and done, a solar house is just *mass under glass.*

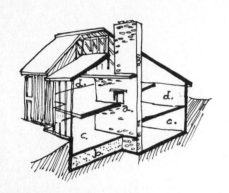

MASONRY THERMAL MASSES
a. Stone masonry b. Sand mass
c. Concrete walls d. Sand plaster walls

In our example house, energy collection occurs in the solar greenhouse, where most of the heat is absorbed by the sand mass under the concrete floor. Large clerestory windows under the roof, which light and heat the northern kitchen and dining areas, are an additional source of heat. A large masonry wall in the center of the house captures half of this heat and light and holds it through the day. Although most of the collected solar energy is stored in the floor and sand mass, the masonry wall is the visible symbol of it.

HEAT STORAGE IS WITHIN CENTRAL THERMAL MASSES

RADIANT CENTRAL WALL

The masonry wall of this house is 3 feet thick, 16 feet long and over 30 feet high; it isn't something to be easily ignored. Activity spaces and stairways of the house are arranged in relation to this wall as a large divider that allows areas to flow freely one into another in an open plan.

The masonry wall is a strong presence, and a fireplace in the living room and wood stove in the family room tie into it to reinforce its symbolism as the center of warmth. The spaces of the house exist as a relation between the radiant masonry wall and the enclosing outer wall. The furniture groupings of each area will change over the year to orient more toward the source of warmth in the winter or toward the source of view and ventilation at the windows in the summer.

BUFFER ZONES

This central open-plan layout is buffered by a series of accessory rooms on the east and by heavy landscaping, which already exists, on the west and north. The southern exposure is cleared to receive sunlight and the exposure will in fact be magnified through an opportunity to create an amphitheater-shaped front lawn, which, when covered with snow, will focus reflected sunlight into the house in winter.

The form of the house tends to surround and protect the greenhouse, while the bedrooms at the upper levels protect the clerestory windows. This reduces their exposure to wind and improves their capacity to concentrate heat. The form of the landscaping combined with the accessory rooms forms another of these protective surrounds for incoming energy. The *sun trap* of a man-made shelter pocket greets the sun at many levels and holds its heat with many layers of surrounding protection.

HEAT TRANSFER WITHIN THE ENCLOSURE IS BY CONVECTION

The house is divided at the masonry wall into five levels of activity placed at half levels from one another. Primary rooms of the house are to the south while service rooms are to the north. The service rooms are thereby made accessible to several primary rooms; the kitchen, for example, is at half levels to both the family and living room levels. The connections between these half levels are left open to maintain free air circulation vertically through the house.

On a daily cycle, radiant energy from the sun will enter the greenhouse and about half will be directly absorbed by the concrete floor. The other half will rise up over the living room balcony and pass into the body of the house. It will there be forced around the masonry wall and over into the dining room, by which time it will have cooled sufficiently to fall back down into the family room–greenhouse area to be reheated.

This process will continue until early afternoon, by which time the sand-plaster walls will have absorbed their limits and the house will begin to overheat. A small fan will then turn on to pull heated air from the uppermost portions of the house down a hollow duct in the masonry wall and through a system of aluminum pipes bedded into the sand mass. From there the air will be passed into the basement workshop from which it will be drawn up into the greenhouse and recirculated. Only a small amount of mechanical assistance will be necessary for two or three hours on a very good sunny day.

During the evening, curtains will be drawn over the greenhouse and clerestory windows to prevent evening heat losses. Evening heating will be provided by the radiant walls and floors, and especially by the large sand mass at the very base of the system. The same natural convection that was effective during the day will function at night.

The house is zoned vertically to take maximum advantage of convection currents and *thermal stratification*. The living room and bedrooms are at upper levels, while activity rooms and workrooms are down lower. The bedrooms at the top of the house are closed off during the day to prevent their overheating but will have

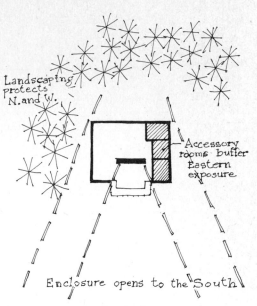

Planning the house

SOLAR GAIN AND STORAGE

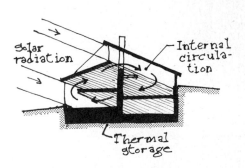

Solar collection and storage

HEAT RETRIEVAL

VERTICAL ZONING

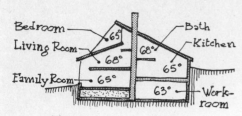

Temperature stratification

registers to allow heat to enter in the evening as desired. The living room will have supplementary heat from a Rumford fireplace; this, plus a wood stove in the family room, will carry the house through extended periods of reduced solar exposure.

Nearly a third of the wall surface is below ground level and only a 4-foot wall is exposed to the north. This short wall is maintained for light, view, and summer ventilation. The site is heavily wooded so that northern and western landscaping will divert winds smoothly over the house and permit as much as 2 feet of snow to settle on the roof and buffer it from severe cold.

BUILDING A SECURE ENCLOSURE

POST-AND-BEAM FRAMING

This house uses a post-and-beam framing system instead of studs. Its heavy columns of pine are placed on a metric grid to maintain easily remembered dimensions of 3 and 4 meters for all beams and joists. Timbers that have been left to season naturally for a winter are used without danger of twisting because the joints are rigidly mortised and tenoned. This frame is braced with steel cables and turnbuckles that will be further tensioned after a couple of years of additional timber seasoning to accommodate shrinkage which, in fact, tightens up all joints. A system using natural timber in this manner does add a few new intricacies into the construction process but is worth the effort to permit the use of materials purchased at 25 percent of the cost of factory-prepared western timber transported across the country.

MASONRY SERVICE CORE

The masonry wall is part of the structural grid and provides two points of support for framing members at each floor level. Its large size allows it to enclose a large fireplace, additional flues, the hollow duct for air circulation, a mechanical shaft to serve upper bathrooms and rooftop accessories, and a utility space at the base. All of this fits cleanly in one symbolic element.

This heavy masonry wall must not be allowed to settle at a different rate from the rest of the house and therefore requires special attention at the foundation. The foundation itself is a hollow of reinforced concrete with a 6-inch floor and 8-inch walls 8 feet high. The southern portion includes the sand-mass container with interior 6-inch concrete walls 4 feet high. These interior walls are reinforced and placed to receive and distribute evenly the weight of the central masonry wall. The sand-mass container is waterproofed to swimming pool specifications because the sand mass is to be saturated to a 10 percent water content for greater thermal storage capacity and improved conductivity. Into this sand mass is placed a system of corrugated aluminum pipe for air-to-sand heat exchange.

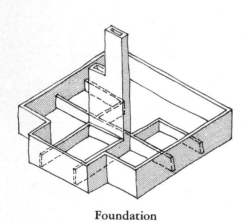

Foundation

AN INSULATED ENCLOSURE

The *house is totally enclosed* in an exterior layer of insulating foam. Two inches of foam-glass are placed under the foundation slab and along below-grade walls to isolate the building from the ground. This foam-glass is placed on a bed of well-drained gravel and is uninterrupted by footings or additional foundation elements. All loads from the house are applied by way of a flat slab onto which loads have been distributed and balanced. The entire house floats on insulation!

Two inches of Thermax insulation are used to sheath the walls outside a layer of diagonal firring, which is itself outside the timber frame. The 1 inch of firring space is very important when running electrical cable outside the internally exposed timber frame but within the vapor barrier provided by the aluminum facing of the Thermax. *This vapor barrier is the essential container of the house and must not be disturbed.* When placed in this manner, the vapor barrier is safely within the wall and may be carefully inspected, taped, and caulked just before application of interior finish. Any disruption left unrepaired will be a source of condensation, deterioration, and electrical hazard; this is now recognized as the greatest problem of existing solar homes in Canada. With exterior siding and a durable interior finish, a well-installed vapor barrier will ensure good life and high performance to a solar house.

Two inches of Thermax are placed on the roof over 2 inches of visible roof deck/ceiling. These 2 inches of insulation are sufficient for a shallow protected roof that is likely to be buffered by a blanket of snow. A steeper roof, a wind-blown location, or a more severe climate might be sufficient reason to justify additional insulation, but this usually is not cost-effective.

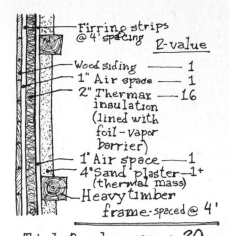

Typical wall section of house

The quality of the enclosure will be affected most by the detailing of the doors and windows. The simplest and best window is just a piece of insulating glass held firmly against the structural frame with a set of gaskets and wooden trim. Vents above and below the window should swing open to provide summer ventilation but must also fit tightly and be weather-stripped for the winter. Vents can be made sufficiently large to provide escape in the event of a fire.

WINDOWS

The doors to the house will now be the single largest source of heat loss. They should be placed in positions of stable air pressure (neither on the windy side of the house nor on the directly opposite leeward side, although, if necessary, the second case is the better of the two). The way to the door should be landscaped to divert winds. A closed vestibule that provides an air-lock maintains the enclosure of the house and extends the *way of the door* on into the house. The process of passage from the outdoors to the thermal center of the house should be made as gradual and extensive as your imagination allows.

THE DOORWAY

This example house will likely have about 10 percent the heat loss of most existing houses of similar size and probably less than half the heat loss of many modern solar houses. Our efforts taken to reduce heat losses to such an extent are handsomely rewarded through a reduced need to collect additional energy. This house

CONSERVATION REDUCES THE NEED FOR ENERGY COLLECTION

need collect only half the energy of many comparable solar houses and thereby places a reduced load on the air-to-thermal mass transfer system. Reduced amounts of incoming energy are in this example easily absorbed by extensive surfaces of distributed thermal mass, so that the system remains simple, efficient, and economical.

This discussion has been included as a summary of the previous chapters and as an overall demonstration of the compatibility of the various improvements to one another and to the requirements of comfortable and fashionable living. This is, however, only one of many such fine houses that are now being developed. When you evaluate *any* design for a solar house, see that it follows the general rules here developed and you will be assured of a quality home with many years of use and pleasure. As you prepare an existing home for solar energy, remember the general scheme of the book and you'll get your money's worth out of home improvements; first maintenance to acquire an enclosure, then weatherization to raise the thermal value of that enclosure, and only then, a system of solar collection to service that enclosure.

Comment by Tom Blandy

It has seemed fitting to include this project in a book otherwise about existing buildings because it so completely embodies everything that we have been talking about. Since it has been completely Denis's project, we decided he should get sole credit for the chapter.

There is one aspect about which I have to be a little skeptical, and that is cost. There have been passive solar houses built very economically in our area, but it has always been a rule with me not to make claims about construction costs, particularly about projects that are out of the ordinary, until one has a hard-and-fast agreement to construct it at a certain cost. There is too much variation, and too many things can happen to spoil the best intentions. But hopefully the project will go ahead; I for one would be delighted to see it.

THERMAL DIAGNOSIS

1. Description

Name: _____

Address: _____

Tel.: _____ Date: _____

Building type: 1-family   2-family   apt. bldg.

Age of building: _____

Type of construction: wood   masonry

Basement: yes   no

Heating fuel: _____ $/yr. _____

Hot-water fuel: _____ $/yr. _____

Yearly heating bill: _____

Remarks: _____

_____

_____

_____

_____

_____

No. of units _____

No. of occupied floors: _____

Snapshot

Plan of Building:

THERMAL DIAGNOSIS

2. Diagnosis

Name: _____

Address: _____

Elevations:

Window & Door Areas:

No.	×	Size	=	Area Without/With Storms
1.	×		=	
2.	×		=	
3.	×		=	
4.	×		=	
5.	×		=	
6.	×		=	

Without _____

With _____

Total _____

Wall Areas:

Perimeter × Height = Gross Wall

_____ × _____ = _____

Gross Wall − Windows/Doors = Net Wall

_____ − _____ = _____

Ceiling Areas:

Unheated Area:

Length × Width = Area

_____ × _____ = _____

_____ × _____ =

Total _____

Heated Area:

Area of ceiling below attic × Factor (p. 37) = Heated Area

_____ × _____ = _____

Floor Areas:

Area + Area + Area = Total

_____ + _____ + _____ = _____

Volume:

Area × Height × Factor (p. 37) = Volume

_____ × _____ × _____ = _____

_____ × _____ × _____ = _____

_____ × _____ × _____ = _____

Total _____

Infiltration:

Volume × Air changes/hour × 0.02 = _____

_____ × _____ × 0.02 = _____

THERMAL DIAGNOSIS

3. Program of Improvements

Name: _____

Address: _____

Diagnosis Summary:

$$\text{Heat-Loss Number (HLN)} = \frac{\text{Area} (\div 100) \times \text{Exposure Factor}}{\text{R-Value}}$$

Ceilings   +   Walls   +   Floors   +   Windows/Doors   + Infiltration =   Total HLN

_____(+)_____ + _____ + _____ + _____(+)_____(+)_____ + _____ = _____

Program of Improvements:

• Ceilings: _____
Additional R-Value: New HLN:
Old HLN: − New HLN: = Change of: Change: ÷ Total HLN: × 100 =   % change
Area (sq. ft.) × $ /sq. ft. = Cost of change: $
Total cost: $ ÷ Total savings/yr: $ = Payback: yrs.

• Walls: _____
Additional R-Value: New HLN:
Old HLN: − New HLN: = Change of: Change: ÷ Total HLN: ×100=   % change
Area (sq. ft.) × $ /sq. ft. = Cost of change: $
Total cost: $ ÷ Total savings/yr: $ = Payback: yrs.

• Floors: _____
Additional R-Value   New HLN:
Old HLN: − New HLN: = Change of: Change: ÷ Total HLN: × 100 =   % change
Area (sq. ft.) × $ /sq. ft. = Cost of change: $
Total cost: $ ÷ Total savings/yr: $ = Payback: yrs.

• Windows/Doors: _____
Additional R-Value: New HLN:
Old HLN: − New HLN: = Change of: Change: ÷ Total HLN: × 100 =   % change
Cost of change: $
Total cost: $ ÷ Total savings/yr: $ = Payback: yrs.

• Infiltration: _____
New HLN:
Old HLN: − New HLN: = Change of: Change: ÷ Total HLN: × 100 =   % change
Cost of change: $
Total cost: $ ÷ Total savings/yr: $ = Payback: yrs.

New Diagnosis Summary:

Old HLN − Total of changes = New HLN

_____ − _____ = _____

Change of ____%

Overall Payback:

$$\frac{\text{Total cost}}{\text{Total savings/yr.}} = \frac{\$ \rule{3cm}{0.4pt}}{\$} = \quad \text{yrs.}$$

THERMAL DIAGNOSIS

4. The House in Context

Name: _____

Address: _____

Evaluating the Site:

Exposure to cold	(1-40)	_____
Exposure to wind	(1-30)	_____
Exposure to sun	(1-30)	_____

Exposure Percentile Score = _____

Evaluating the House:

$$\text{Building Thermal Value} = \frac{\text{Surface Area of Heated Envelope } (\div 100)}{\text{Total Heat-Loss Number (HLN)}}$$

$$= \underline{\quad} = \underline{\quad} \quad \text{After Improvements: } \underline{\quad} = \underline{\quad}$$

Building Percentile Score (p. 44) = _____   *Score After Improvements* _____

Evaluating Services:

Heating Equipment

Furnace efficiency	(1-10)	_____
Distribution efficiency	(1-10)	_____
Temperature setting	(1-10)	_____
Temperature setback	(1-10)	_____
		_____
Woodburning	(1-40)	_____

Heating score (of 40) = _____ ÷2 = _____

Management

Space planning	(1-10)	_____
Window management	(1-10)	_____
Hot-water usage	(1-20)	_____
Electricity usage	(1-20)	_____

Utility score (of 60) = _____

Service Percentile Score = _____

THERMAL DIAGNOSIS

1. Description

Name: *J. Anyperson*

Address: *20 Cove Ave., Miller, MA*

Tel.: *248-3002*   Date: *11/2/79*

Building type: (1-family) 2-family   apt. bldg.

Age of building: *1948*

Type of construction: (wood) masonry

Basement: (yes) no

Heating fuel: *oil* $/yr. *600*

Hot-water fuel: *electricity* $/yr. *200*

Yearly heating bill: *$600*

Remarks: _____

No. of units _____

No. of occupied floors: *2*

Plan of Building:

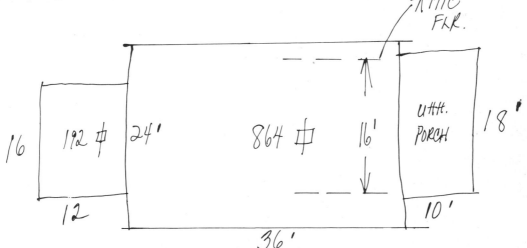

ATTIC FLR.

16   192 ☐   24'   864 ☐   16'   UHt. PORCH   18'

12   10'

36'

GROUND FLOOR

PERIMETER: 36+24+36+12+24+12 = 144'

THERMAL DIAGNOSIS

2. Diagnosis

Name: _J. Anyperson_

Address: _Miller, MA_

Elevations:

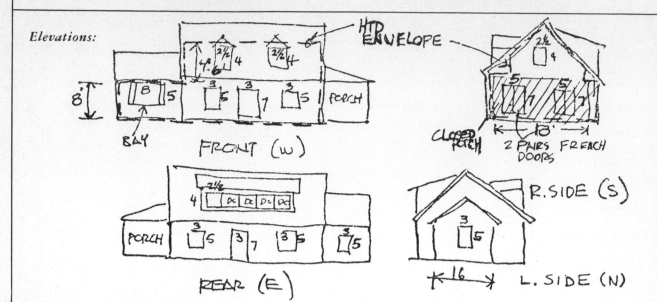

FRONT (W)

REAR (E)

R. SIDE (S)

L. SIDE (N)

Window & Door Areas:

No.	×	Size	=	Area Without/With Storms
1.	6	× 3×5	=	90
2.	8	× 2½×4 (dormer)	=	80
3.	1	× 8×5 (bay)	=	40
4.	2	× 3×7 (doors)	=	42
5.	2	× 5×7 (FR. doors)	=	70*
6.		×	=	

* Open onto porch:
Exposure Factor = .5

Without _190_
With _132_
Total _322_

Ceiling Areas:

Unheated Area:

Length	×	Width	=	Area
12	×	16	=	192
	×		=	

Total _192_

Heated Area:

Area of ceiling below attic × Factor (p. 37) = Heated Area

_864_ × _1.8_ = _1555_

Floor Areas:

Area	+	Area	+	Area	=	Total
192	+	864	+		=	1056

Wall Areas:

Perimeter	×	Height	=	Gross Wall
144	×	8	=	1152

Gross Wall	−	Windows/Doors	=	Net Wall
1152	−	322	=	830

Volume:

Area	×	Height	× Factor (p. 37)	=	Volume
(1st Floor) 1056	×	8	×	=	8448
(ATTIC) (36×16) 576	×	7	× .7	=	2822
	×		×	=	

Total _11,270_

Infiltration:

Volume × Air changes/hour × 0.02 = _451_

_11,270_ × _2_ × 0.02 = _451_

THERMAL DIAGNOSIS

3. Program of Improvements

Name: _J. Anyperson_

Address: _Miller, MA_

Diagnosis Summary:

$$\text{Heat-Loss Number (HLN)} = \frac{\text{Area} (\div 100) \times \text{Exposure Factor}}{\text{R-Value}}$$

(unheated) Ceilings (heated) + Walls + Floors + Windows/Doors + Infiltration = Total HLN

$$\frac{1.9 \times 1}{3} \quad \frac{15.6 \times .6}{4} \quad \frac{8.3 \times 1}{4} \quad \frac{10.6 \times .3}{3} \quad \frac{.7 \times .5}{1} \quad \frac{1.2 \times 1}{1} \quad \frac{1.3 \times 1}{2}$$

_.6_ (+) _2.3_ + _2.1_ + _1.1_ + _.4_ (+) _1.2_ (+) _.7_ + _4.5_ = _12.9_

Program of Improvements:

• Ceilings: _Add 6" fiberglass over wing. (Insulating attic is not feasible.)_
Additional R-Value: ✓ _6" × 3.2/inch = 19.2_   New HLN: _(1.9 × 1) ÷ (3 + 19) = .09_
Old HLN: _.6_ − New HLN: _.09_ = Change of: _.5_ Change: _.5_ ÷ Total HLN: _12.9_ × 100 = _4_ % change
Area (_200_ sq. ft.) × $_.30_/sq. ft. = Cost of change: $ _60_
Total cost: $ _60_ ÷ Total savings/yr: $ _12_ = Payback: _5_ yrs.

• Walls: _No change feasible._
Additional R-Value: New HLN:
Old HLN: − New HLN: = Change of: Change: ÷ Total HLN: × 100 =   % change
Area (sq. ft.) × $ /sq. ft. = Cost of change: $
Total cost: $ ÷ Total savings/yr: $ = Payback: yrs.

• Floors: _Insulate with 3½" fiberglass._
Additional R-Value _3½" × 3.2/inch = 11.2_   New HLN: _(10.6 × .3) ÷ (3 + 11) = .23_
Old HLN: _1.1_ − New HLN: _.23_ = Change of: _.9_ Change: _.9_ ÷ Total HLN: _12.9_ × 100 = _7_ % change
Area (_1060_ sq. ft.) × $_.15_/sq. ft. = Cost of change: $ _160_
Total cost: $ _160_ ÷ Total savings/yr: $ _60_ = Payback: _2.7_ yrs.

• Windows/Doors: _Add storms where none now (except French doors to porch)._
Additional R-Value: _+1 for addition of storms_   New HLN: _(1.2 × 1) ÷ (1 + 1) = .6_
Old HLN: _1.2_ − New HLN: _.6_ = Change of: _.6_ Change: _.6_ ÷ Total HLN: _12.9_ × 100 = _5_ % change
Cost of change: $ _300_
Total cost: $ _300_ ÷ Total savings/yr: $ _30_ = Payback: _10_ yrs.

• Infiltration: _Reduce by half._
New HLN: _4.5 ÷ 2 = 2.3_
Old HLN: _4.5_ − New HLN: _2.3_ = Change of: _2.2_ Change: _2.2_ ÷ Total HLN: _12.9_ × 100 = _17_ % change
Cost of change: $ _60_
Total cost: $ _60_ ÷ Total savings/yr: $ _84_ = Payback: _.7_ yrs.

New Diagnosis Summary:

Old HLN − Total of changes = New HLN

_12.9_ − _4.2_ = _8.7_

Change of _33_ %

Overall Payback:

$$\frac{\text{Total cost}}{\text{Total savings/yr.}} = \frac{\$ \ 580}{\$ \ 186} = 3.1 \text{ yrs.}$$

THERMAL DIAGNOSIS

4. The House in Context

Name: _J. Anyperson_

Address: _Miller, MA_

Evaluating the Site:

Exposure to cold	(1-40)	_10_
Exposure to wind	(1-30)	_15_
Exposure to sun	(1-30)	_5_

Exposure Percentile Score = _30_

Evaluating the House:

$$\text{Building Thermal Value} = \frac{\text{Surface Area of Heated Envelope } (\div 100)}{\text{Total Heat-Loss Number (HLN)}}$$

$$= \frac{39.5}{12.9} = \underline{3.1} \quad \text{After Improvements: } \frac{39.5}{8.7} = \underline{4.5}$$

Building Percentile Score (p. 44) = _25 %_   Score After Improvements _60 %_

Evaluating Services:

Heating Equipment

Furnace efficiency	(1-10)	_9_
Distribution efficiency	(1-10)	_4_
Temperature setting	(1-10)	_6_
Temperature setback	(1-10)	_2_
		_21_

Woodburning	(1-40)	_13_

Heating score (of 40) = _34_ ÷ 2 = _17_

Management

Space planning	(1-10)	_2_
Window management	(1-10)	_4_
Hot-water usage	(1-20)	_8_
Electricity usage	(1-20)	_12_

Utility score (of 60) = _26_

Service Percentile Score = _43 %_

INDEX